Studies in Economic Reform and Social Justice

THE PATH TO JUSTICE: *FOLLOWING IN THE FOOTSTEPS OF HENRY GEORGE*

Blackwell Publishing

The Series
Studies in Economic Reform and Social Justice

Laurence S. Moss, Series Editor

Robert V. Andelson, ed.
Land-Value Taxation Around the World

J. A. Giacalone and C. W. Cobb, eds.
The Path to Justice: Following in the Footsteps of Henry George

Studies in Economic Reform and Social Justice

The Path to Justice: *Following in the Footsteps of Henry George*

Edited by
Joseph A. Giacalone
and
Clifford W. Cobb

Foreword by
Joseph A. Giacalone

Series Editor
Laurence S. Moss

Blackwell Publishing

Blackwell Publishers, Inc.
350 Main Street
Malden, MA 02148 USA

Blackwell Publishers, Ltd.
108 Cowley Road
Oxford OX4 1JF
United Kingdom

Library of Congress Cataloging-in-Publication Data information is located at the Library of Congress.

Includes bibliographical references and index.
ISBN 0-631-230246 (case : alk. paper) — ISBN 0-631-230254 (pbk. : alk. paper)

ISBN 0-631-230246
ISBN 0-631-230254 (P)
ISSN 0002-9246

Contents

Foreword

THE HENRY GEORGE Program at St. John's University originated in 1981 with a grant from the Robert Schalkenbach Foundation that established the Henry George Chair in our College of Business Administration. Mr. Thomas Larkin, a member of the Foundation's Board of Directors and the St. John's University Board of Trustees, was instrumental in arranging the grant.

The Foundation's objective was to disseminate knowledge about the ideas of Henry George, the 19th-century economist and social reformer. George was appalled at the persistence of great poverty in the midst of the unparalleled economic progress brought about by industrialization. By utilizing the tools of economics, he sought to find an explanation for this phenomenon and a solution to it. His thinking was presented in the book *Progress and Poverty.* Originally published in 1879, it is one of the most widely sold books in history and has been translated into many languages. *Progress and Poverty* was followed by several other books, articles, and speeches that developed his ideas more extensively. Among these were *Protection or Free Trade, The Science of Political Economy,* and *Social Problems.*

According to George, the cause of poverty amidst abundance was due to monopoly in land ownership and land speculation. As a society grows, land values appreciate. The poor suffer because of higher rents and the withdrawal of land from productive use for speculative reasons. George characterized this return to land as an *unearned increment*, that is, the increased land values are not due to the productive efforts of the landowner but to the progress of society. Thus, he called for a tax on land values to the exclusion of all other taxes. The revenues from such a land-value tax, George believed, would be sufficient to fund all necessary municipal public services. Moreover, land held for speculation would be returned to productive use, thereby increasing employment opportunities for the working classes. In an effort to implement his theories, George ran for mayor of New York City, without success, in 1886 and 1896.

Each semester, an economist of national or international stature presents the Henry George Lecture. Over the years, the lecture series, which is open to the general public as well as the academic community, has featured seven current or subsequent winners of the Nobel Prize in Economic Science. These are James Buchanan, Wassily Leontieff, Gary Becker, Merton Miller, Lawrence Klein, Douglass North, and William Vickrey. The Lectures have addressed a variety of Georgist concerns such as land-value taxation, public finance, free markets and free trade, private property, and economic reform.

In addition to the lecture series, the Program has sponsored a number of related events. These have included faculty seminars, a scholarly paper competition, an occasional paper series, and alumni breakfasts with the speaker. The essays in this volume by Aslanbeigui and Wick, Martin, and Shapiro were winners of scholarly paper competitions. Since 1988, most of the lectures have been videotaped and are available in the Media Center of the University Library. This book provides the highlights of our Program.

On behalf of St. John's University, I would like to thank Drs. Nicolaus Tideman and C. Lowell Harris, current and past presidents of the Robert Schalkenbach Foundation, as well as the Foundation's past Executive Directors, Ted Gwartney and Dr. Oscar Johannsen. Their long-term support has been critical in sustaining the high quality of this endeavor. Also, Dr. Mason Gaffney of the Foundation's publication committee should be acknowledged for his efforts in making this volume a reality. My predecessor in the Chair, Dr. Northrup Buechner, deserves credit for putting the Program on solid ground and establishing its reputation in the academic community. Jerry D. Jean-Pierre, my former graduate research assistant, introduced me to the wonders of scanning and was instrumental in putting the articles in electronic form. Finally, I must commend co-editor Cliff Cobb who handled the bulk of the editorial responsibilities and did so in a highly focused and creative manner.

In each essay in this volume, the views expressed are those of the author and not necessarily those of any organization with which he or she is associated.

Joseph A. Giacalone, Ph.D.
Henry George Chair
St. John's University, NY

Introduction

OF THE MORE than thirty presentations in the Henry George lecture series and the winners of the Henry George Essay Prize sponsored by St. John's University (New York), thirteen were chosen for this volume. They were selected on the basis of their contribution to the Georgist intellectual tradition. The range of ideas within that tradition is sufficiently broad that it has yet to acquire a label that fully encompasses it. It contains strands of the prophetic elements in the Bible, the Natural Law tradition associated with Grotius, Pufendorf, Locke, and others, a blend of individualism and sociality similar to that of the Scottish Enlightenment, the Jeffersonian concept of democracy as rooted in a culture of small proprietors, and the forms of American frontier pietism that emphasized egalitarian social reform.

Since Henry George was no mere syncretist, he did not passively absorb ideas and patch them together. He was an original thinker in his own right. His most enduring intellectual contribution was his analysis of the role that location rents play in urban-industrial society and the damage caused by allowing that socially-created value to be collected for private benefit. From that core insight, he derived: 1) a theory of history that denied the inevitability of progress, 2) a doctrine of free trade more nuanced than most neo-liberal arguments of our own day,[1] 3) a sociological analysis based on the concept of "association in equality," 4) an analysis of the role of synergy in economics that contradicts the "no free lunch" dogma of modern theorists, and 5) a theory of rent-seeking, interest group behavior that partially explains the failure of public institutions (government agencies). Each of those ideas was a remarkable advance over the prevailing beliefs in the late 19th century. Some of them have not yet been developed more fully than George did.

There are many lines of inquiry that are in keeping with the concerns of Henry George. Not all of them fall within the confines of the discipline of economics. This book is divided into five categories that correspond with some of the elements present in George's own writing: history of thought, public policy implications, international trade, philosophy of justice (ethics), and religious foundations of a social philosophy.

In Section 1, the three essays by Mr. Johannsen, Prof. Yeager, and Prof. Aslanbegui and Ms. Wick deal with the history of ideas. Oscar B. Johannsen and Leland B. Yeager, in separate essays, discuss the relationship between Henry George and the Austrian School of economic thought. Johannsen analyzes similarities and differences between the two, yet emphasizes their contrasting views about property rights in land, the nature of the primary cause of poverty, and the business cycle. Yeager, by contrast, scarcely touches on the difference between George and the Austrians. Instead, he focuses on their commonalities in value theory, the derivation of money, planned and unplanned order, the critique of socialism, methodological individualism, and the importance of personal liberty. The essay by Nahid Aslanbeigui and Adele Wick analyzes the debate between George and Alfred Marshall, one of the key figures in the formulation of neo-classical economics. Rather than taking sides in the debate, Aslanbeigui and Wick simply try to clarify where the differences lay and why George and Marshall tended to talk past each other.

In Section 2, Profs. Gaffney, Vickrey, and Netzer discuss some of the public policy implications of adopting Henry George's proposal to appropriate the full annual value of locations, particularly urban sites, for public use. Mason Gaffney describes how public collection of ground rent or land value could revive dying cities and blighted neighborhoods. He explains how rent is created as a positive spillover of urban activities, how it is often dissipated through unwise policies, and how cities could achieve an urban renaissance if they would collect the economic surplus that is their due. Nobel Laureate William S. Vickrey discusses the optimal method by which cities should finance their public services: by charging each user the marginal cost and by collecting ground rent (land value charges) to cover the remaining, mostly fixed, costs. He uses postal service and public transit as examples. Dick Netzer asks "why, given the virtues of land value taxation, has there been so little success in persuading governments to adopt it?" He provides some possible answers to that question as well as an overview of the research that might make the case more persuasive: mostly research on implementation issues related to reform of property assessment and the taxation of land values.

In Section 3, Profs. Martin and Moss analyze the contribution made by Henry George and others to the long-standing debate over free trade. Thomas L. Martin discusses Henry George's personal engagement in tariff politics during the 1880s as well as the actual content of George's critique of protectionism. He then shows how George's analysis of how tariffs harmed labor anticipated the current Stolper-Samuelson theory of how protectionism leads to the overuse of a society's scarcest resources and underuse of the most abundant ones. Laurence S. Moss explains why, in a world of growing intolerance, free trade should be understood as a gospel of human harmony, to be preached anew in every generation, not merely a method of achieving narrow economic goals. He discusses the factors that motivated both Henry George and Paul Krugman to become advocates of this broader view of trade liberalization.

In Section 4, Profs. Tideman and Buchanan address philosophical issues related to the nature of a just society. Nicolaus Tideman considers the definition of justice put forward in various traditions in political philosophy: conservatism, majoritarianism, contractarianism, and egalitarianism. Finding all of them wanting in some way, he concludes that true justice, which leads to peace, can be found in the liberal philosophy of self-ownership in combination with an obligation to share equally all natural opportunities. Nobel Laureate James M. Buchanan raises an unusual and interesting question about justice, which implicitly challenges the principle of self-ownership relied on by Tideman: is it ethical for those with special skills to loaf? He concludes, contrary to accepted economic theory, that it is not, which implies that people do not entirely own themselves.

In Section 5, Profs. Andelson and Dawsey, and Rabbi Shapiro find in Henry George's thought echoes of the biblical prophets and a new basis for liberation theology. Robert V. Andelson's lecture is homiletic in tone and content. He considers how justice, individual rights, trusteeship, equality, and other political and legal concepts flow logically from the premise that God is the ultimate owner of the earth, which he sees as the spiritual principle that underlies Henry George's insights. James M. Dawsey shows how Henry George's thought is compatible with the tenets of liberation theology. Both regard social structures, particularly those associated with land ownership, as unjust, and both believe that oppressive structures can be changed. Aharon H. Shapiro presents the parallels between Mosaic reforms and the thought of Henry George, who himself admired Moses as a revolutionary leader, a political reformer, and a social reformer. He adds that George was particularly impressed by the virtues of the Sabbath, the Sabattical years and the Jubilee year, all forms of restoring justice and order in the world.

There is far more to Henry George than the "Single Tax," the idea for which he is best remembered. The public collection of land values is indeed the key to George's thought, for it provides an instrument that resolves enigmas such as how to achieve social equity and economic efficiency simultaneously—a possibility still ignored by most economists. George himself was less interested in particular policy instruments (community collection of land-rent or free trade) than he was in creating a civilization based on liberty and justice. Far more work needs to be done before scholars have begun to plumb the depths of his thought in this regard. By branching out in many directions, the essays in this volume go a long way toward revealing the breadth of understanding that made Henry George one of the wisest social thinkers in world history.

Note

1. Briefly, George hoped to persuade governments to capture land values as their primary source of revenue by showing the folly of using tariffs.

Clifford W. Cobb
Sacramento, California

Acknowledgements

The editors of this volume are indebted to the following for permission to reproduce some of the materials in this volume:

1. The AJES, Inc., for Nahid Aslanbeigui and Adele Wick, "Progress: Poverty or Prosperity? Joining the Debate Between George and Marshall on the Effects of Economic Growth on the Distribution of Income," *American Journal of Economics and Sociology* 49 (April 1990): 239–256; T. L. Martin, "Protection or Free Trade: An Analysis of the Ideas of Henry George on International Commerce and Wages," *American Journal of Economics and Sociology* 48 (October 1989): 489–501; Nicolaus Tideman, "Peace, Justice, and Economic Reform: The 1997 Henry George Lecture," *American Journal of Economics and Sociology* 56 (October 1997): 672–683; and Aharon H. Shapiro, "Moses—Henry George's Inspiration," *American Journal of Economics and Sociology* 47 (October 1988): 493–501.

2. Duke University Press, for Leland B. Yeager, "Henry George and Austrian Economics," *History of Political Economy* 16 (Summer): 157–174.

3. St. John's University, for Oscar Johannsen, "Henry George and the Austrian Economists," *Review of Business* 4 (Winter 1982): 7–9. Published with permission from Peter J. Tobin College of Business, St. John's University.

4. Office of Real Estate Research at the University of Illinois, for Mason Gaffney, "How to Revive a Dying City," *ORER Letter* 3 (Summer 1989): 1–7.

5. Lincoln Institute of Land Policy, for using parts of Dick Netzer, "The Relevance and Feasibility of Land Value Taxation in the Rich Countries," in idem, *Land Value Taxation: Can It and Will It Work?* Lincoln Institute, 1998.

6. The editors wish to acknowledge the kind editorial help of Professor Richard Arnott of Boston College who assisted in

the final editing of William S. Vickrey, "Site Value Taxes and the Optimal Pricing of Public Services."

The editors wish to acknowledge the award of several grants by the Robert Schalkenbach Foundation that aided in the final preparation of this manuscript.

SECTION 1

HISTORY OF THOUGHT

Henry George and Austrian Economics

By LELAND B. YEAGER*

HENRY GEORGE HAS been widely pigeonholed and dismissed as a single-taxer. Actually, he was a profound and original economist. He independently arrived at several of the most characteristic insights of the "Austrian" School, which is enjoying a revival nowadays. Yet George scorned the Austrians of his time, and their present-day successors show scant appreciation of his work. An apparent lapse in intellectual communication calls for repair.

Austrian Economics

THE AUSTRIAN SCHOOL traces to the work of Carl Menger, one of the leaders of the marginal-utility revolution of the 1870s, and his fellow-countrymen, Eugen von Böhm-Bawerk and Friedrich von Wieser. Notable contributors of a later generation include Ludwig von Mises, F. A. Hayek, and Ludwig Lachmann, each of whom worked first in Austria or Germany and later in the United States, and also the American Frank A. Fetter. In a still later generation, eminent Austrians—the word no longer carries any implications about nationality or mother tongue—include Murray Rothbard and Israel Kirzner. Some eminent young members of the school are Dominick Armentano, Gerald O'Driscoll, Mario Rizzo, Steven Littlechild, and Karen Vaughn; and apologies are in order for not extending the list further.[1]

What follows is an impression of the leading characteristics of Austrian economics.

*Ludwig von Mises Distinguished Professor Emeritus of Economics, Auburn University, Alabama. This article derives from a talk given at St. John's University, Jamaica, New York, on 29 March 1982. I am indebted to my hosts there, and particularly to Professor M. Northrup Buechner, for suggestions and encouragement.

(i) Austrians are concerned with the big picture—with how a whole economic system functions. They avoid tunnel vision; they do not focus too narrowly on the administration of the individual business firm and the individual household. They investigate how the specialized activities of millions of persons, who are making their decisions in a decentralized manner, can be coordinated. These diverse activities are interdependent; yet no particular agency takes charge of coordinating them, and none would be competent to do so. The relevant knowledge—about resources, technology, human wants, and market conditions—is inevitably fragmented among millions, even billions, of separate human minds.

(ii) Austrians take interest in how alternative sets of institutions can function. Von Mises in particular, and later Hayek, demonstrated the impossibility of economic calculation—scheduling of economic activities in accordance with accurate assessment of values and costs—under socialism. Centralized mobilization of knowledge and planning of activities is admittedly conceivable. In a Swiss Family Robinson setting, the head of the family could survey the available resources and technology and the capabilities and needs and wants of family members and could sensibly decide on and monitor production and consumption in some detail. In a large, modern economy, however, sensible central direction is not possible. Austrians are alert to possibilities of unplanned order and to what Hayek (1967) has called "the results of human action but not of human design." They investigate how the market and prices function as a vast communications system and computer, transmitting information and incentives and so putting to use scattered knowledge that would otherwise necessarily go to waste.

(iii) Not only do Austrians appreciate the implications of incomplete, imperfect, and scattered knowledge; they also appreciate the implications of change, uncertainty, and unpredictability in human affairs. They take these facts of reality seriously not only in confronting supposed theoretical and econometric models of the economy but also in assessing alternative sets of institutions and lines of policy.

(iv) In connection with the implications of fragmented knowledge, change, and unpredictability, Austrians pay attention to disequilibrium, process, and entrepreneurship. While not totally scornful of elaborate analysis of the properties of imaginary equilibrium states and of comparative-static analysis, they recognize how incomplete a contribution such analyses can make to the understanding of how economic systems function. They do not suppose, for example, that cost curves and demand curves are somehow "given" to business decisionmakers. On the contrary, one of the services of the competitive process is to press for discovery of ways to get the cost curves down—if one adopts such terminology at all. Austrians tend to accept the concept of X-efficiency[2] and to appreciate the role of competition in promoting it. Far from being an ideal state of affairs with which the real world is to be compared—unfavorably—competition is seen as a process. Entrepreneurs play key roles in that process; they are men and women alert to opportunities of advantageously undertaking new activities or adopting new methods.

(v) As already implied, Austrians have certain methodological predilections. They are unhappy with the tacit view of economic activity as the resultant of interplay among objective conditions and impersonal forces. They are unhappy with theorizing in terms of aggregates and averages (real GNP, the price level, and the like). They take pains to trace their analyses back to the perceptions, decisions, and actions of individual persons: methodological individualism is a key aspect of their approach. Austrians recognize introspection as one legitimate source of the facts underpinning economic theory. They emphasize subjectivism: not only do personal tastes help determine the course of economic activity, but even the objective facts of resources and technology operate only as they are filtered through the perceptions and evaluations of individuals. Insofar as Austrians recognize macroeconomics as a legitimate topic at all, they are concerned to provide it with microeconomic underpinnings.

(vi) Although Austrians like to think of their economics as value-free and although some of them, at least, emphasize that it is not logically linked with any particular policy position, Austrian insights into positive economics, coupled with plausible value judgments of a humanitarian and individualistic nature, undeniably do tend toward a particular policy postion—noninterventionistic, laissez-faire, libertarian. More about this later.

George's Independence

I SHALL TRY to show Henry George's affinities with the Austrians by citing passages from his writings. The demonstration proceeds from partial agreement on theoretical points to agreement on major questions. First, however, we should note George's misunderstanding of and even scorn for the Austrians of his time, suggesting that his Austrian-like insights were original with him.[3] George did not understand the marginal revolution in value theory that was getting under way in the last decades of his life. He regretted that "'the classical school' of political economy" seemed to have been abandoned:

> What has succeeded is usually denominated the Austrian school, for no other reason that I can discover than that "far kine have long horns." If it has any principles, I have been utterly unable to find them. The inquirer is usually referred to the incomprehensible works of Professor Alfred Marshall of Cambridge, England . . . ; to the ponderous works of Eugen V. Böhm-Bawerk, Professor of Political Economy, first in Innsbruck and then at Vienna . . . or to a lot of German works written by men he never heard of and whose names he cannot even pronounce.
>
> This pseudo-science gets its name from a foreign language, and uses for its terms words adapted from the German—words that have no place and no meaning in an English work. It is, indeed, admirably calculated to serve the purpose of those powerful interests dominant in the colleges . . . that must fear a simple and understandable political economy, and who vaguely wish to have the poor boys who are subjected to it by their professors rendered incapable of thought on economic subjects.[4]

Later, as quoted below, George complains about the "grotesque confusions" of the Austrian School.

The Austrians, for their part, have not adequately appreciated George. Böhm-Bawerk criticized the natural-fructification theory of interest presented in *Progress and Poverty*, apparently unaware of the advance (discussed below) that George achieved in *The*

Science of Political Economy.[5] Among present-day Austrians, Murray Rothbard shows the greatest acquaintance with George's writings, or some of them. (For example, he recognizes George as a free-trader and applauds his "excellent discussion" of the distinction between patents and copyrights.) Yet Rothbard is mostly concerned with what he considers the unsatisfactory moral and economic arguments used in favor of the single tax.[6] With the Austrians as with other present-day economists, George's reputation does seem to suffer from his being pigeonholed as a propagandist for dubious reforms.

Value Theory: Subjectivism, Productivity, and Time

GEORGE HELD A kind of labor-in-exchange or exertion-saved theory of value, following Adam Smith, but not a Marxian labor-cost theory (*SPE*:212–56, 503). Still, he had some Austrian-like subjectivist insights:

> . . . the value of a thing in any time and place is the largest amount of exertion that any one will render in exchange for it; or to make the estimate from the other side, . . . it is the smallest amount of exertion for which any one will part with it in exchange.
>
> Value is thus an expression which, when used in its proper economic sense of value in exchange, has no direct relation to any intrinsic quality of external things, but only to man's desires. Its essential element is subjective, not objective; that is to say, lying in the mind or will of man, and not lying in the nature of things external to the human will or mind. There is no material test for value. Whether a thing is valuable or not valuable, or what may be the degree of its value, we cannot really tell by its size or shape or color or smell, or any other material quality, except so far as such investigations may enable us to infer how other men may regard them. . . .
>
> Now this fact that the perception of value springs from a feeling of man, and has not at bottom any relation to the external world—a fact that has been much ignored in the teachings and expositions of accepted economists—is what lies at the bottom of the grotesque confusions which, under the name of the Austrian school of political economy, have within recent years so easily captured the teachings of

> pretty much all the universities and colleges in the English-speaking world. (*SPE*:251–52)

George goes on to say that the Austrians have drawn wrong inferences from

> . . . the truth that value is not a quality of things but an affectation of the human mind toward things. . . .
>
> What is subjective is in itself incommunicable. A feeling so long as it remains merely a feeling can be known only to and can be measured only by him who feels it. It must come out in some way into the objective through action before any one else can appreciate or in any way measure it. . . .
>
> [W]hat value determines is not how much a thing is desired, but how much any one is willing to give for it; not desire in itself, but . . . the desire to possess, accompanied by the ability and willingness to give in return.
>
> Thus it is that there is no measure of value among men save competition or the higgling of the market, a matter that might be worth the consideration of those amiable reformers who so lightly propose to abolish competition.
>
> It is never the amount of labor that has been exerted in bringing a thing into being that determines its value, but always the amount of labor that will be rendered in exchange for it. (*SPE*:252–53)

Actually, George and the Austrians were not as far apart as he thought when alleging "grotesque confusions." Admittedly, though, some present-day Austrians do invite misunderstanding by insisting that value in general, as well as the interest rate in particular, is *entirely* a subjective phenomenon, instead of being determined—as of course it is—by interaction between objective reality and subjective perceptions and appraisals.

The valid subjective element in George's doctrine also appears in his recognition that wealth can be produced not only (1) by physically shaping things and (2) by growing things but also (3) by *exchanging* things:

> [T]his third mode of production consists in the utilization of a power or principle or tendency manifested only in man, and belonging to him by virtue of his peculiar gift of reason. . . .

> [I]t is by and through his disposition and power to exchange, in which man essentially differs from all other animals, that human advance goes on. . . . [I]n itself exchange brings about a perceptible increase in the sum of wealth. . . . Each of the two parties to an exchange aims to get, and as a rule does get, something that is more valuable to him than what he gives—that is to say, that represents to him a greater power of labor to satisfy desire. Thus there is in the transaction an actual increase in the sum of wealth, an actual production of wealth. . . . Each party to the exchange gets in return for what costs it comparatively little labor what would cost it a great deal of labor to get by either of the other modes of production. Each gains by the act. . . . [T]he joint wealth of both parties, the sum of the wealth of the world, is by the exchange itself increased. [*SPE*:331–32]

George had some glimmerings of the marginalist and Austrian idea of *imputation*: the values and remunerations of the factors of production are imputed to them according to what they contribute to producing outputs valued by consumers. Labor, George explained, does not transmit value to whatever it is applied to. Instead, labor derives its wages from its productive contribution and from the value that consumers attribute to the output produced. This insight refuted the wages-fund doctrine (*P&P*, pp. 23, 50–70). Even labor employed on a project of long duration is effectively deriving its wages from the project's growth in value as it comes gradually closer to completion.

Some authorities credit George with contributing to the development of the marginal-productivity theory of functional income distribution.[7] Even John Bates Clark recognized his contribution:

> It was the claim advanced by Mr. Henry George, that wages are fixed by the product which a man can create by tilling rentless land, that first led me to seek a method by which the product of labor everywhere may be disentangled from the product of coöperating agents and separately identified; and it was this quest which led to the attainment of the law that is here presented, according to which the wages of all labor tend, under perfectly free competition, to equal the product that is separately attributable to the labor. The product of the "final unit" of labor is the same as that of every unit, separately considered; and if normal tendencies could work in perfection, it would be true not only of

each unit, but of the working force as a whole, that its product and its pay are identical. (1899:viii)

George did not see how his marginal-productivity theory of the wages of labor applied in a similar way to all factor remunerations (Collier in Andelson 1979:228). Neither did the early Austrians; it was left to Wicksteed to make that contribution in 1894.

Regarding land rent, George was avowedly a follower of Ricardo (*P&P*:165–72). His conceptions of capital and its productivity were incomplete. He had a fructification theory of interest, centering around a supposed "reproductive or vital force of nature," illustrated by the growth of crops, the reproduction of animals, and the maturing of wine in storage (*P&P*, esp. pp. 179–82).

He did share insights with the Austrians, however, on the vital role of time in the productive process. He devotes a whole chapter of *Science of Political Economy* to this topic:

> [I]f I go to a builder and say to him, "In what time and at what price will you build me such and such a house?" he would, after thinking, name a time, and a price based on it. This specification of time would be essential. . . . This I would soon find if, not quarreling with the price, I ask him largely to lessen the time. . . . I might get the builder somewhat to lessen the time . . . ; but only by greatly increasing the price, until finally a point would be reached where he would not consent to build the house in less time no matter at what price. He would say [that the house just could not be built any faster]. . . .
>
> The importance . . . of this principle that all production of wealth requires time as well as labor we shall see later on; but the principle that time is a necessary element in all production we must take into account from the very first. (*SPE*:369–70)

The implication, which practically cries out to be made explicit, is that output is not even ultimately attributable to labor (and land) alone; the tying up of wealth over time is also necessary. Since this service is both productive and scarce—since it is demanded and is limited in supply—one can hardly expect it to be free. In short, George was on the right track in capital and interest theory; but his achievement was incomplete.

Money

GEORGE AND THE Austrians shared insights even on such relatively specific topics as money and the analogy that money and language bear to each other. They were not simply agreeing with everyone else that both are useful social institutions. They recognized both, in Hayek's words, as "results of human action but not of human design." (That insight may be familiar nowadays, but it was not so when George and Menger and even when Hayek were developing it.) Instead of being deliberately invented and instituted, money evolved spontaneously. George explains that it evolved from the most readily exchangeable commodities, which individuals employed in indirect barter because doing so afforded them economies in conducting their transactions. The medium of exchange naturally drifted into being also used as the measure of value or unit of account.

George anticipated the analogy more recently developed by Hayek and others:

> While the use of money is almost as universal as the use of languages, and it everywhere follows general laws as does the use of languages, yet as we find language differing in time and place, so do we find money differing. In fact, as we see, money is in one of its functions a kind of language—the language of value. (*SPE*:494)

George anticipated, in at least a rudimentary way, the cash-balance approach to monetary theory later developed independently by von Mises (1981 [1912]) and others. The demand for cash balances is accounted for by the services that they render to their holders (George presents examples in *SPE*:484–87). The development of credit promotes economies in the holding and transfer of the actual medium of exchange. "Money's most important use today is as a measure of value."[8]

Knowledge, Coordination, and Unplanned Order

SO FAR THIS study has reviewed points on which George shared or anticipated Austrian insights only incompletely. Now it turns to some major points of agreement.

He and the Austrians agree that a central task of economics is to explain how specialized human activities may be coordinated without deliberate direction. First he distinguishes two kinds of cooperation, each of which increases productive power. One kind is the combination of effort, illustrated by men joining forces to remove a rock or lift a log too heavy for any one to move alone. The other is the separation of effort—the division of labor, specialization. Next George distinguishes two ways of arranging cooperation itself. The first is conscious direction by a controlling will, illustrated (ideally) by the deployment of an army.

The second way, achieving "spontaneous or unconscious coöperation," draws George's chief attention. One example, reminiscent of Bastiat's essay "Natural and artificial social order" (1964:1–19), is

> [t]he providing of a great city with all the manifold things which are constantly needed by its inhabitants. . . . This kind of coöperation is far wider, far finer, far more strongly and delicately organized, than the kind of coöperation involved in the movements of an army, yet it is brought about not by subordination to the direction of one conscious will, which knows the general result at which it aims; but by the correlation of actions originating in many independent wills, each aiming at its own small purpose without care for or thought of the general result. (*SPE*:383)

As further examples of the two kinds of coordination, George offered, respectively, the sailing (arrangement of sails and so forth) and the construction and equipping of a large ship. He elaborated on the latter example in rather poetic passages:

> Consider the timbers, the planks, the spars; the iron and steel of various kinds and forms; the copper, the brass, the bolts, screws, spikes, chains; the ropes, of steel and hemp and cotton; the canvas of various textures; the blocks and winches and windlasses; the pumps, the boats, the sextants, the chronometers, the spy-glasses and patent logs, the barometers and thermometers, charts, nautical almanacs, rockets and colored lights; food, clothing, tools, medicines and furniture, and all the various things, which it would be tiresome fully to specify, that go to the construction and furnishing of a first-class sailing ship of modern type, to say nothing of the still greater complexity of the first-class

> steamer. Directed coöperation never did, and I do not think in the nature of things it ever could, make and assemble such a variety of products, involving as many of them do the use of costly machinery and consummate skill, and the existence of subsidiary products and processes. (*SPE*:389)

When he receives an order for such a ship, the builder does not send men out with detailed instructions for doing all the necessary work—cutting various woods, mining and refining various metals, planting hemp and cotton and breeding silkworms:

> Nor does he attempt to direct the manifold operations by which these raw materials are to be brought into the required forms and combinations, and assembled in the place where the ship is to be built. Such a task would transcend the wisdom and power of a Solomon. What he does is to avail himself of the resources of a high civilization, for without that he would be helpless, and to make use for his purpose of the unconscious coöperation by which without his direction, or any general direction, the efforts of many men, working in many different places and in occupations which cover almost the whole field of a minutely diversified industry, each animated solely by the effort to obtain the satisfaction of his personal desires in what to him is the easiest way, have brought together the materials and productions needed for the putting together of such a ship. (*SPE*:389–90)

Deploying insights later also achieved by F. A. Hayek (1945), George goes on to speak of the mobilization of knowledge that is inevitably dispersed and that simply could not be centralized and put to use by a single mind or a single organization:

> So far from any lifetime sufficing to acquire, or any single brain being able to hold, the varied knowledge that goes to the building and equipping of a modern sailing-ship, already becoming antiquated by the still more complex steamer, I doubt if the best-informed man on such subjects, even though he took a twelvemonth to study up, could give even the names of the various separate divisions of labor involved.
>
> A modern ship, like a modern railway, is a product of modern civilization . . . ; of that conscious coöperation which does not come by personal direction . . . but grows . . . by the relation of the efforts of individuals, each seeking the satisfaction of individual desires. A mere master of men, though he might command the services of millions,

> could not make such a ship unless in a civilization prepared for it. (*SPE*:390–91)

The cooperation required for sailing a ship is relatively simple. The kind required for building one is beyond the power of conscious direction to order or improve. "The only thing that conscious direction can do to aid it is to let it alone; to give it freedom to grow, leaving men free to seek the gratification of their own desires in ways that to them seem best" (*SPE*:391).

George has more to say on the spontaneous mobilization of dispersed knowledge. Physical force can be aggregated, but not intelligence:

> Two men cannot see twice as far as one man, nor a hundred thousand determine one hundred thousand times as well. . . . No one ever said, "In a multitude of generals there is victory." On the contrary, the adage is, "One poor general is better than two good ones." (*SPE*:392)

In spontaneous cooperation, however,

> what is utilized in production is not merely the sum of the physical power of the units, but the sum of their intelligence.
>
> . . . while in the second kind of coöperation the sum of intelligence utilized is that of the whole of the coöperating units, in the first kind of coöperation it is only that of a very small part.
>
> In other words it is only in independent action that the full powers of the man may be utilized. The subordination of one human will to another human will, while it may in certain ways secure unity of action, must always where intelligence is needed, involve loss of productive power. (*SPE*:392–93)

George understands the roles of exchange, markets, prices, and money in accomplishing spontaneous coordination; and he is skeptical (*SPE*:445–46) that government regulation of prices and wages and interest rates can achieve its intended purposes:

> Exchange is the great agency by which . . . the spontaneous or unconscious coöperation of men in the production of wealth is brought about and economic units are welded into that social organism which is the Greater Leviathan. To this economic body, this Greater Leviathan, into which it builds the economic units, it is what the nerves or perhaps the ganglions are to the individual body. Or, to make use of another illus-

> tration, it is to our material desires and powers of satisfying them what the switchboard of a telegraph or telephone or other electric system is to that system, a means by which exertion of one kind in one place may be transmitted into satisfaction of another kind in another place, and thus the efforts of individual units be conjoined and correlated so as to yield satisfactions in most useful place and form, and to an amount exceeding what otherwise would be possible .(*SPE*:399–400)

Socialism

GEORGE REJECTS SOCIALISM, understood as collective or state management of all means of production (*SPE*:198), on the grounds that it would restrict the scope of spontaneous coordination. Attempting conscious coordination of work requiring spontaneous coordination

> is like asking the carpenter who can build a chicken-house to build a chicken also.
>
> This is the fatal defect of all forms of socialism—the reason of the fact, which all observation shows, that any attempt to carry conscious regulation and direction beyond the narrow sphere of social life in which it is necessary, inevitably works injury, hindering even what it is intended to help.
>
> And the rationale of this great fact may ... be perceived when we consider that the originating element in all production is thought or intelligence, the spiritual not the material. This spiritual element, this intelligence or thought power as it appears in man, cannot be combined or fused as can material force. (*SPE*:391–92)

The last sentences quoted remind us of the emphasis of present-day Austrians on the creative role of entrepreneurship. They also remind us of Julian Simon's emphasis, in a recent book, on *The Ultimate Resource*—human intelligence and ingenuity.

To develop his points further, George asks us to imagine that "the very wisest and best of men were selected" to direct a socialist economy. Consider

> the task that would be put upon them in the ordering of the when, where, how and by whom that would be involved in the intelligent direction and supervision of the almost infinitely complex and constantly changing relations and adjustments involved in such division of labor

> as goes on in a civilized community. The task transcends the power of human intelligence at its very highest. It is evidently as much beyond the ability of conscious direction as the correlation of the processes that maintain the human body in health and vigor is beyond it. [The human body functions without being consciously directed by the mind.] . . .
>
> And so it is the spontaneous, unconscious coöperation of individuals which, going on in the industrial body, . . . conjoins individual efforts in the production of wealth, to the enormous increase in productive power, and distributes the product among the units of which it is composed. It is the nature and laws of such coöperation that it is the primary province of political economy to ascertain. (*SPE*:394–96)

These passages remind us again of Hayek's conception of the chief task of economics and of his and von Mises's analyses of why accurate economic calculation would be impossible under full-fledged socialism.[9]

Methodology

GEORGE'S VIEWS ON methodology are remarkably similar to those of Carl Menger and of the modern Austrians.[10] George and Menger agree that the economist's job is not merely to catalogue economic phenomena but to search for cause-and-effect relations among them, to formulate laws expressing dependable coexistences and sequences, and to discover uniformities underlying superficial diversities.

Perhaps the leading methological tenet of both men is that these elementary uniformities cannot be found solely in panoramic study of the economic system as a whole. They must be sought by penetrating to the level where decisions are actually made, the level of the individual person, family, firm, and agency. This approach, recommended by today's Austrians as *methodological individualism*, recognizes the legitimacy and necessity of appealing to purpose and motive. The relevant facts include not only the objective characteristics of resources and activities and products but also the characteristics attributed to them by fallible human beings, as well as human preferences and intentions. Again the subjectivism of George and the Austrians comes to the fore. Both recognize that economics does, after all, concern human action (and these two words form the title of von Mises' magnum opus).

George asserts a basic principle that people seek to satisfy their desires with the least possible exertion, and Menger expresses similar ideas. This is not an assumption that people behave like the economic man of the familiar caricature or that they act only on selfish motives.[11]

George and Menger, as well as von Mises and other later Austrians, help clarify the nature of so-called armchair theorizing. Economists can discover basic facts by observation of their own and other people's decisionmaking. They even have the advantage of being able to observe the basic elements of their theoretical generalizations (human individuals and their strivings) directly, while the natural scientists must postulate or infer their basic but not directly observable elements from whatever phenomena they can observe directly. Much as geometers deduce many theorems from a few axioms, so economists deduce a powerful body of theory from a relatively few empirical generalizations, ones so crushingly obvious that their failure to hold true is almost inconceivable in the world as we know it. The axioms underpinning economic theory include ones like George's least-exertion principle and the fact that labor continued beyond some point becomes irksome (as well as others that could be added to George's list, such as the fact of scarcity itself and the principle of eventually diminishing marginal returns). (The banality of empirical observations is not related inversely to the scope and importance of their implications in economics; indeed, one might argue that a direct relation is the more plausible.) Armchair theorizing need not be the mere sterile juggling of arbitrary assumptions; it can have a sound empirical basis.

George considers how economists can disentangle the complex intermingling of many causes and many effects that occurs in the real world. He explains the method of "mental or imaginative experiment," the method of testing "the working of known principles by mentally separating, combining or eliminating conditions" (*SPE*:100; *PFT*:27–29).

George and Menger share a skeptical attitude toward the "organic" conception of society. Both recognize how an economic system seems to have a life and purpose and orderliness of its own, as if it had been shaped and were operating by deliberate design. Yet they do not join the holists and institutionalists in supposing that this apparent organic unity requires concentrating research on the system's overall institutional arrangements and supposed evolutionary trends. Instead of taking the coherence and order of the market economy for granted, they regard these as among the chief phenomena crying out for explanation. Both employ methodological individualism in developing their explanations.

George and Menger offer the same two examples of how features of the system as a whole can arise, without being deliberately contrived, from the efforts of individuals to gratify their separate desires: (1) money evolves from the most marketable of commodities under barter; (2) new communities grow and their economic activities evolve into the appearance of a rational pattern, even though settlers move in and take up particular occupations only with a view to satisfying their separate desires.

George and Menger—to summarize—conceive of economic theory as a body of deductions from a few compellingly strong empirical generalizations. They employ methodological individualism because they realize that economists' "inside" understanding of human purposes and decisions is a leading source of empirical axioms. (Not sharing George's and Menger's understanding of how empirical content can enter into armchair theory, many economists of our own day apparently regard theoretical and empirical work as two distinct fields, with adverse consequences for both.)

Social Philosophy

A FINAL AFFINITY between George and the modern Austrians concerns social or political philosophy. Austrian economists tend to be libertarians (although several of them insist that there is no *necessary* connection). Many libertarians—to look at the relation the other way around—tend to regard Austrianism as their own "house brand" of economics. This is unfortunate.[12]

Anyway, the ideological affinity between George and the Austrians remains a fact. As C. Lowell Harriss says:

> George could probably have considered himself a libertarian had the term been current in his day. . . . And such twentieth-century libertarian champions as Albert Jay Nock and Frank Chodorov professed themselves outright Georgists. It was Nock, in fact, who acclaimed George "the philosopher of freedom," "the exponent of individualism against Statism," "the very best friend the capitalist ever had," and the "architect of a society based on voluntary cooperation rather than on enforced cooperation."[13]

George rejected socialism not only out of concern for economic efficiency but also (anticipating Hayek 1944) out of concern for human freedom:

> The proposal which socialism makes is that the collectivity or state shall assume the management of all means of production, including land, capital and man himself; do away with all competition, and convert mankind into two classes, the directors, taking their orders from government and acting by governmental authority, and the workers, for whom everything shall be provided, including the directors themselves. . . . It is more destitute of any central and guiding principle than any philosophy I know of. . . . It has no system of individual rights whereby it can define the extent to which the individual is entitled to liberty or to which the state may go in restraining it. (*SPE*:198)

George, like many libertarian Austrians, champions the concept of natural rights or the rights of man.[14] He emphatically includes property rights. He was no redistributionist.

In a chapter entitled "The rights of man" he asserts:

> some facts [are] so obvious as to be beyond the necessity of argument. And one of these facts, attested by universal consciousness, is that there are rights as between man and man which existed before the formation of government, and which continue to exist in spite of the abuse of government; that there is a higher law than any human law—to wit, the law of the Creator, impressed upon and revealed through nature, which is before and above human laws, and upon conformity to which all human laws must depend for their validity. To deny this is to assert that there is no standard whatever by which the rightfulness or wrongfulness of laws and institutions can be measured; to assert that there can

> be no actions in themselves right and none in themselves wrong; to assert that an edict which commanded mothers to kill their children should receive the same respect as a law prohibiting infanticide.
>
> These natural rights, this higher law, form the only true and sure basis for social organization [*SP*:92].

He denies any "real antagonism between the rights of men and the rights of property—since the right of property is but the expression of a fundamental right of man." He challenges those who imagine any conflict between human and property rights "to name any denial of the rights of men which is not or does not involve a denial of the rights of property; or any denial of the rights of property which is not or does not involve a denial of the rights of men." (*PPh*:209–10)

> This is not an accidental, but a necessary connection. The right of life and liberty—that is to say, the right of the man to himself—is not really one right and the right of property another right. They are two aspects of the same perception—the right of property being but another side, a differently stated expression, of the right of man to himself. The right of life and liberty, the right of the individual to himself, presupposes and involves the right of property, which is the exclusive right of the individual to the things his exertion has produced.
>
> This is the reason why we who really believe in the law of liberty, we who see in freedom the great solvent for all social evils, are the stanchest and most unflinching supporters of the rights of property, and would guard it as scrupulously in the case of the millionaire as in the case of the day-laborer. (*PPh*:210–11)

> I have been an active, consistent and absolute free trader, and an opponent of all schemes that would limit the freedom of the individual. I have been a stancher denier of the assumption of the right of society to the possessions of each member, and a clearer and more resolute upholder of the rights of property than has Mr. Spencer. I have opposed every proposition to help the poor at the expense of the rich. I have always insisted that no man should be taxed because of his wealth, and that no matter how many millions a man might rightfully get, society should leave to him every penny of them.[15]

> This, and this alone, I contend for—that he who makes should have; that he who saves should enjoy. I ask in behalf of the poor nothing whatever that properly belongs to the rich. Instead of weakening and

confusing the idea of property, I would surround it with stronger sanctions. Instead of lessening the incentive to the production of wealth, I would make it more powerful by making the reward more certain. Whatever any man has added to the general stock of wealth, or has received of the free will of him who did produce it, let that be his as against all the world—his to use or to give, to do with it whatever he may please, so long as such use does not interfere with the equal freedom of others. For my part, I would put no limit on acquisition. No matter how many millions any man can get by methods which do not involve the robbery of others—they are his: let him have them. I would not even ask him for charity, or have it dinned into his ears that it is his duty to help the poor. That is his own affair. Let him do as he pleases with his own, without restriction and without suggestion. If he gets without taking from others, and uses without hurting others, what he does with his wealth is his own business and his own responsibility. (*SP*:86–87)

Schumpeter's Assessment

In conclusion I remind the reader, but without quoting the whole passage verbatim, of Joseph Schumpeter's assessment of Henry George. "He was a self-taught economist, but he *was* an economist." He acquired most of the economics taught in the universities of his time. He was at home in scientific economics up to and including Mill's *Principles*, although he did fail to understand Marshall and Böhm-Bawerk. Barring his single tax and the phraseology connected with it, he was an orthodox economist, conservative in method. Whatever else might be said about his panacea, it was not nonsense; and as a competent economist, "he was careful to frame his 'remedy' in such a manner as to cause the minimum injury to the efficiency of the private-enterprise economy." What George said about the economic benefits to be expected if it were possible (as Schumpeter doubted) to remove other taxes was even "obvious wisdom" (Schumpeter 1954:865).

The present article lends support, I hope, to this assessment.

Notes

1. Since this article chiefly concerns Henry George, I am assuming that the reader has enough acquaintance with contemporary Austrian economics to make detailed citations unnecessary. In addition to the specifi-

cally cited works of Menger, Böhm-Bawerk, von Mises, Hayek, and Rothbard, he might well consult, for orientation, books written or edited by Dolan, Moss, O'Driscoll, and Spadaro; see the bibliography.

2. See, in particular, Leibenstein 1976. (Leibenstein himself, however, is not usually considered an Austrian.)

3. One referee hypothesizes that George and some of the Austrians, including von Mises, were deriving inspiration in common from French liberals such as Bastiat and Dunoyer. Investigating that hypothesis must be left for another occasion—or for another researcher.

4. *SPE*, p. 208. Citations are made to George's works by abbreviated titles. Theabbreviations, in the same order as the titles in the bibliography, are *PPh*, *P&P*, *PFT*, *SPE*, and *SP*.

Referring in particular to the confusion over the meaning of wealth, George complains that "the 'economic revolution' which has in the meanwhile displaced from their chairs the professors of the then orthodox political economy in order to give place to so-called 'Austrians' or similar professors of 'economics,' ha[s] only made confusion worse confounded" (*SPE*:121).

5. Böhm-Bawerk 1959, 1: 336–39, 366, 474.

6. Rothbard 1962, I:148–49, 152, 410, 442; 2: 512–13, 813–14, 888, 915, 930, 933, 944–45; Rothbard 1970, viii, 37, 57, 91–100, 200, 201, 204, 209, 210; Rothbard 1973, 33–35.

7. Charles Collier:223–26, and Aaron Fuller:298–300, both in Andelson 1979.

8. The quotation is taken from a subheading in *SPE*, p. 504. The insight expressed there brings to mind present-day proposals for achieving monetary reform and macroeconomic stability by defining a stable measure of value distinct from the medium of exchange, with the choice and the supply of the latter being left to unregulated private enterprise. Describing such proposals, however, would carry us too far from our present topic.

9. For other comments by George on socialism, though earlier and less insightful ones, see his *PFT*:320–34. Although an emphatic opponent of socialism, George did advocate not only public schools but also government ownership of what he conceived to be natural monopolies. In these he included railroads, the telegraph and telephone, and urban systems of water, gas, heat, and electricity *SP*:198 and nearby pages.

10. George's remarks on the topic occur mostly in *SPE*, with a chapter in *PFT* and scattered observations in *P&P*. Menger 1950 develops views of 1883. An earlier discussion, with more detailed citations, appears in Yeager 1954.

11. See *SPE*, esp. pp. 91, 99. In this respect George anticipated Wicksteed 1933, esp. ch. 5.

12. Economics is a tool for understanding and possibly reshaping the world—for trying to make one's deepest values prevail, whatever they may be. Everyone, therefore, has an interest in getting his economics straight. The truths of economics, as of any other field of objective research, once discovered, will be the same for everyone. There is no one truth for libertarians, another for collectivists, and so on. Of course, both George and the Austrians have much to contribute toward getting economics straight; and the capacity to contribute is not confined to any particular school. What is unfortunate is a belief in different house brands of truth. Ludwig von Mises (1949) was duly emphatic in attacking this notion, which he called "polylogism."

13. Hariss in Andelson 1979:367 (citations omitted here). Harriss goes on to cite passages from *P&P*:434–36, that make George look like a supply-sider also, passages on the great release of productive energies to be expected if laborer and capitalist alike were allowed, through the abolition of taxes (other than the single tax), to capture the full reward of what they produce.

14. Besides the passages cited below, see Andelson in Andelson 1979:386–87.

15. *PPh*:70–71. Herbert Spencer is the person referred to in the book's title and in the passage quoted.

Henry George and the Austrian Economists

By OSCAR B. JOHANNSEN*

ALTHOUGH, UNFORTUNATELY, HENRY GEORGE did not appreciate the Austrian School of Economics, there is much in common between his thinking and that of the Austrians.

Professor Yeager has pointed out "how similar Henry George's views on economic research methods are to the views of his Austrian contemporary, Carl Menger," noting among other similarities, the parallelism of their methodological tenets.[1]

The Austrian School, of whom besides Carl Menger, the founder, the most prominent members have been Eugene von Böhm-Bawerk, Ludwig von Mises, and Friedrich A. Hayek, is known for its individualistic approach to economics. Mises goes so far as to state that "economics is not about goods and services, it is about the actions of living men."[2]

Murray N. Rothbard, the best known of the American economists who espouse the Austrian School's approach, emphasizes that "only an individual has a mind; only an individual can feel, see, sense, and perceive; only an individual can adopt values or make choices; only an individual can *act*."[3]

While the individualism of Henry George may not be quite as apparent as the Austrians', his life's work was directed toward creating conditions which would enable the individual to lead the kind of life he wished, qualified only by his not interfering with the right of another individual to live as he wished. And George was only too aware that it was people who created the institutions which he believed were not only the cause of poverty amidst plenty, but were also largely responsible for inhibiting the freedom of the individual.

*Former President, Henry George School of Social Science, New York; former Executive Director, Robert Schalkenbach Foundation, New York.

While George rejected the Austrian theory of value, and argued for what amounts to a labor-saving theory, nonetheless his concept of value did in some measure coincide with the Austrians'. He said value's "essential element is subjective, not objective; that is to say, lying in the mind or will of man, and not lying in the nature of things external to the human will or mind."[4]

Since the very basis of the Austrian concept of value is subjective, it is apparent that George's understanding of value paralleled theirs. However, he either did not understand or did not appreciate the importance of marginal utility, a concept of which Menger was one of the original propounders.

Both George and the Austrians are free market economists. They believe in the free and unhampered marketplace, with governmental interference reduced to a minimum.

Point of Divergence

BUT ONE FUNDAMENTAL difference exists which is of major significance: The treatment of land as property. Any other differences, such as value and the degree of governmental activity, fade into insignificance by comparison.

As regards property, Menger said "The entire sum of goods at an economizing individual's command for the satisfaction of his needs, we call his *property*."[5]

Rothbard states that "each individual, as a natural fact, is the owner of *himself,* the ruler of his own person. The 'human' rights of the person that are defended in the purely free-market society are, in effect, each man's *property right* in his own being, and from *this* property right stems his right to the material goods that he has produced."[6]

Henry George essentially arrives at the same basis of property. He asks, "[W]hat constitutes the rightful basis of property? . . . Is it not, primarily, the right of a man to himself, to the use of his own powers, to the enjoyment of the fruits of his own exertions? . . . As a man belongs to himself, so his labor when put in concrete form belongs to him."[7]

Although both George and Rothbard base property rights on the fact that each individual owns himself, Rothbard does not infer from this fundamental principle the same deduction that George does.

Rothbard broadens his concept of property to include land. He says, "[I]f a free society means a world in which no one aggresses against the person or property of others, then this implies a society in which every man has the absolute right of property in his own self and in the previously unowned natural resources which he finds, transforms by his own labor and then gives to or exchanges with others."[8]

Just why, because an individual owns himself and thus that anything he produces means that he also owns "previously unowned natural resources," that is, owns land, is not clear. Rothbard sets up as the criteria for the ownership of land that it is "a prime condition of free-market property rights, namely, that new, unowned land be first owned by its first user, and that from then on, it becomes the full private property of the first user or those who receive or buy the land from him. This is the free-market method; any other method of allocating new, unused land to ownership employs statist coercion."[9]

Thus, private property in land, according to Rothbard's standard, originates in the "first user, first owner" concept. Assuming this is correct, how great an area of land is concerned? What are the boundaries—a square foot, a square mile, a million square miles? If boundaries are set, who sets them? Rothbard is opposed to any governmental agency delimiting the boundaries, as this would constitute "statist coercion." But, certainly some boundaries must be set, and if that is the case, someone has to do it. Who does it? Who in the free market does it?

Of course, the Biblical student might wryly point out that Adam was the first user of the earth, as he must have expended his labor on it. Thus, he owned it, as there was no one else before him, not even Eve. As he owned it, he could give it to anyone he wished. Since all the peoples of the world are his heirs, and since presumably he willed the land to his heirs, then all the people of the earth own it. This is the concept which, in effect, is implied in George's thought.

Since, according to George, property rights are based on human labor, then private property in land could not be justified as no human created the land. He said, "This right of ownership that springs from labor excludes the possibility of any other right of ownership. If a man be rightfully entitled to the produce of his labor, then no one can be rightfully entitled to the ownership of anything which is not the produce of his labor, or the labor of someone else from whom the right has passed to him. If production give to the producer the right to exclusive possession and enjoyment, there can rightfully be no exclusive possession and enjoyment of anything not the production of labor, and the recognition of private property in land is a wrong."[10]

Though George believed that private property in land is wrong, it did not mean that he opposed the private possession of land. On the contrary, he urged it. He recognized that unless an individual (after taking into account the rights of others) was assured that the entire product of his labor was his own property, he would not produce, or at least would only produce as little as possible. For George, in effect, the question was a simple one. Since all men have equal rights to the land, and since it is impossible for two men to occupy the same place at the same time, some means must be adopted to allot the land with justice to all. In his view, in a sophisticated society, this could be accomplished by society renting out the land to the highest bidder, thereby collecting what is known as economic rent. In other words, since all could bid, all had an equal opportunity to have access to whatever land they wished.

Because he recognized that his suggestion was a revolutionary one, and because governments exist throughout the world, George advocated an expedient. This was to leave land in the hands of the present owners and utilize the governmental apparatus to do what it is already doing in most nations. In America, local governments were already taxing real estate. He suggested, then, that all that needed to be done would be to tax only the value of the land, so as to obtain the economic rent, and to remove all taxes from improvements and production. This remedy has come to be known as the *single tax*.

Most of the Austrian economists are not opposed to government. On the contrary. For example, Mises said, "[S]tate or government is the social apparatus of compulsion and coercion. It has the monopoly of violent action . . . The state is essentially an institution for the preservation of peaceful interhuman relations."[11] However, Rothbard's view of government is such that, even if he believed that the government's collection of economic rent would result in better conditions (which he does not), he would still be opposed since he is against all governmental activity.

Cause of Poverty

BECAUSE THE AUSTRIANS and George view private property in land differently, it is not surprising that their views of the causes of involuntary poverty and unemployment, as well as of the business cycle, also differ.

The Austrians, on the whole, believe unemployment is caused by governmental interferences which cause wage-rates to exceed labor's marginal productivity. Either by government lease or indirectly by means of the monopolistic power of unions which is granted by government, wage-rates are kept above the point at which all who wished to work could work. So, just as when the price of a commodity is kept above the point which would "clear the market," a surplus of the commodity results, so artificially maintaining wage-rates above what would be the market rates causes a surplus of labor, i.e., unemployment.

In Mises' view, the rises and falls of the expansion and deflation of the business cycle are caused by governmental interference in the monetary system. By means of its central bank, the government fosters the artificial expansion of money and credit. This easy money policy results in lower interest rates, which make it appear profitable to erect plants and produce goods which are really not desired. The depression which follows is the curative by which the excesses are removed from the marketplace.

George, on the other hand, posited that involuntary poverty and unemployment are due to the hindrances placed on access to land. Private property in land leads to speculation, with the speculators holding land out of use for ever higher prices. This means, in effect, that land is not readily available to labor and capital, so that unemployment results. This is easily seen in an agricultural society for, if farmers do not have land on which to work, they become unemployed. In highly developed industrial societies, while the relationship of man to the land persists, it is not as obvious. Thus, few recognize the relationship between the system of land tenure practiced and unemployment.

In George's eyes, the principal cause of the business cycle is speculative increases in land values. In boom times, speculation in land becomes so intense that prices rise to heights that make land too expensive for businessmen to hire or buy. Production then slows and with it labor becomes unemployed. In deflation, the speculative increases in land values drop until finally a point is reached where businessmen find it once again profitable to produce. Business then goes back to work, hiring labor and investing in capital, so the cycle starts again.

Though there are differences between George and the Austrians, there is probably a greater degree of parallelism between his views and theirs than with any other school of economic thought. While the difference in the treatment of the land is important, both George and the Austrians are alike in their emphasis on the individual as the motivating force.

They both believe in allowing the individual the greatest degree of freedom of action possible to produce. They both tried to be as scientific in their work as possible, and yet underneath it all, an ethical base appears. Though as economists, the Austrians tried to erect an amoral science, yet as private citizens they advocated the free market, the freedom of the individual and justice to all, as did Henry George.

Notes

1. Yeager, Leland B., "The Methodology of Henry George and Carl Menger," *American Journal of Economics and Sociology*, April, 1954, pp. 233-238.

2. Mises, Ludwig von, "Human Action," Yale University Press, New Haven, 1949, p. 354.

3. Rothbard, Murray N., "Individualism and the Philosophy of the Social Sciences," Cato Institute, San Francisco, 1979, p. 57.

4. George, Henry, "The Science of Political Economy," Robert Schalkenbach Foundation, New York, 1981, p. 251.

5. Menger, Carl, "Principles of Economics," The Free Press, Glencove, Ill., 1959, p. 76.

6. Rothbard, Murray N., "Power and Market," Institute for Human Studies, Inc., Menlo Park, Calif., 1970, p. 176.
7. George, Henry, "Progress and Poverty," Robert Schalkenbach Foundation, New York, 1979, p. 334.
8. Rothbard, "Power and Market," p. 1.
9. Ibid., p. 98.
10. George, "Progress and Poverty," p. 336.
11. Mises, "Human Action," p. 149.

Progress: Poverty or Prosperity?

Joining the Debate Between George and Marshall on the Effects of Economic Growth on the Distribution of Income

By NAHID ASLANBEIGUI* and ADELE WICK**

Two Late-19th-Century Authors

HENRY GEORGE AND Alfred Marshall were among the most influential authors of the late 19th century. George's best-selling *Progress and Poverty* fueled many policy debates of the time; and Marshall's *Principles of Economics,* the standard textbook for decades, laid the foundation for modern economics. Each recognized the other's influence. In 1883, at the height of George's fame in the British Isles, Marshall acknowledged George's "singular and almost unexampled power of catching the ear of the people" (Marshall and George [1884] 1969:221); and over a decade later, when Marshall's *Principles* had begun to establish its academic preeminence, George described this text as "the latest and largest, and scholastically the most highly indorsed, economic work yet published in English" (George *SPE*:125).

Not only were George and Marshall important figures in intellectual history, but they had an important common ground in their deep concern with poverty. Both considered poverty mentally and morally debasing in large part because of its general association with relentlessly hard manual labor. The commonality of their views is best seen by simple juxtaposition. Said George:

> The poverty to which in advancing civilization great masses of men are condemned . . . is a degrading and embruting slavery, that cramps

*Professor of Economics, Monmouth University, New Jersey.

**Formerly a graduate student in economics, University of Chicago. Currently residing in New Hampshire.

> the higher nature, dulls the finer feelings, and drives men by its pain to acts which the brutes would refuse (George *P&P*:356–357).

In a similar vein, Marshall stated:

> We scarcely realize how subtle, all pervading and powerful may be the effect of the work of man's body in dwarfing the growth of the man. . . . [T]he poor labourer may live and die without even realizing what a joy there is in knowledge, or what delight in art; he may never have conceived how glorious a thing it is to be able to think and to feel about things and with many men (Marshall, in Pigou 1925:105–06).

Indeed, the "destruction of the poor is their poverty" and the study of the causes of poverty is the study of "the causes of the degradation of a large part of mankind" (Marshall 1920:3).

George and Marshall also shared the optimistic belief that "progress" could eliminate poverty from society. Neither carefully—nor casually, for that matter—defined this term,[1] but it is tellingly equivalent to growth in national income in George's work. Marshall therefore uses the same terminology in his three lectures on George's issues, and we employ it here instead of the modern term because of the importance of the historical coupling of "progress" and "poverty."

Unlike some modern critics of economic growth who emphasize the concomitants of debasing materialism, degradation of the environment, dehumanization of the masses by technology, and destruction of important elements in the "quality" of life, both George and Marshall were keen advocates of economic progress and regarded it as necessary but not sufficient for the good life. For George, as we shall see, sufficiency conditions involved redistributing land rents, while Marshall required educating the population and inculcating habits of thrift and restraint in breeding. Without such public distribution of rents, George owned that industrialization worsened the plight of the poor because of the deleterious effects of the division of labor on the laborers' independence and well-roundedness. Marshall deplored the unhealthy living conditions of the urban poor as a temporary cost of growth before the effects of his training programs became apparent.

However, George and Marshall both asserted that because poverty is the major source of moral degradation, a society rich enough to eliminate material poverty could achieve in spiritual wealth as well. In such a society, wages for crude labor would become so high that the hours anyone expended in such work would be minimal. To George,

> The hard toil of routine labor would disappear. Wages would be too high and opportunities too great to compel any man to stint and starve the higher qualities of his nature, and in every avocation the brain would aid the hand. Work, even of the coarser kinds, would become a lightsome thing, and the tendency of modern production to subdivision would not involve monotony or the contraction of ability in the worker; but would be relieved by short hours, by change, by the alternation of intellectual with manual occupations (George *P&P*:468).

Similarly, in Marshall's ideal world, manual work would be limited by high wages and improved technology; and people would no longer ". . . carry on mere physical work to such an extent as to dull their higher energies . . . The active vigour of the people would continuously increase; and in each successive generation it would be more completely true that every man was by occupation a gentleman" (Marshall, in Pigou 1925:114–15).

Here the similarity ends, however; for George and Marshall stated profoundly different analyses of the theoretical and actual relationships between progress and poverty. To George, actual progress was not uplifting the poor, but rather increasing their want; while to Marshall, progress had temporarily worsened the plight of the poor but was now dramatically improving their lot along with that of the rest of the society. As a result, the interaction between George and Marshall unhappily belied the belief that men with the time and energy for reflection would be noble and co-operative in bent.

Consider first the following indirect exchanges. Far from cowed by the British endorsement of Marshall's *magnum opus,* George called the work utterly incoherent and incomprehensible (George, *SPE*:126, 208). Although Marshall found George's *topic* of sufficient importance to deliver "Three Lectures on Progress and Poverty"[2] in 1883, he intended "to avoid talking very much about George but to discuss his subject" (Marshall, 1883 (1969):184, fn. 1), because "trying to refute George . . . was like throwing oneself against a door that is not fastened. There was no resistance anywhere" (Marshall, in Hebert 1979:57). George was neither an economist nor a "scientific thinker." Rather, he was "by nature a poet" and "a successful rhetorician" who did not understand the economic doctrines he had attacked with such vituperation (Marshall [1883] 1969:186 and 185, fn. 1).

George and Marshall's only direct exchange, during the former's public lecture at Oxford (see *infra*), was even less gentlemanly. Perhaps because of the rigors of his intensive travel and his many sleepless nights, perhaps because of the "patronizing phrases [Marshall] chose to direct towards him, George answered [even the don's more serious] questions all too captiously" (Barker 1955:404). Also Marshall's opening remarks set a remarkably rowdy tone for the entire question-and-answer period that followed the speech.

George and Marshall wrote for wide but disparate audiences. George's readership was basically nonacademic; his purpose, the increasingly messianic one of persuading the public to adopt his policy recommendations. Marshall spoke almost exclusively to the economics profession, modestly hoping to "put in one brick just where it should be in the slowly rising economic edifice" (Marshall [1883] 1969:185, fn. 1).

In any event, because they communicated so successfully to their own audiences, but never, it seems, to each other, it is our purpose to join their debate on the important topic of progress and poverty after a century has stilled their tempers and tongues. Trying to keep our own voices silent, we place side by side for perhaps the first time George's and Marshall's strikingly disparate analyses of the relationship of progress and poverty, followed by the politics they advocated to help progress eliminate poverty. Because these recommendations differ as much as their causal explanations, we set up a rebuttal drawn from both their writings and their direct confrontation and conclude the paper with summary remarks.

Causes of Poverty

GEORGE AND MARSHALL identify profoundly different relationships between progress and poverty. To George, progress has worsened the distribution of income and created more poverty; while to Marshall, progress temporarily debased the poor, but is now dramatically improving their condition.

Henry George

George approaches the problem of progress and poverty as essentially a question of relative power and relative income. When land is privately owned, as population grows landowners will increase their share of income in spite of labor's increased average productivity and regardless of what happens to the quality of land at the margin. George therefore rejects the Malthusian population dynamic that ineluctably drives wages to subsistence levels and employs Ricardian rent theory as a condition that is sufficient but not necessary for his results (George *P&P*:235–36).

George begins with the premise that land[3] is crucial to man's existence.

> [L]and is the habitation of man, the storehouse upon which he must draw for all his needs, the material to which his labor must be applied for all his desires; for even the products of the sea cannot be taken, the light of the sun enjoyed, or any of the forces of nature utilized, without the use of land or its products . . . Take away from man all that belongs to land, and he is but a disembodied spirit (George *P&P*:295–96).

Because land is so economically and existentially important to labor, land-owners have immense power, the power to command large shares of income in a growing economy. Moreover, as we shall see, they maintain this "monopoly" power, because in any bargaining game, landlords can wait, while workers cannot.

Rejecting Malthus' theory of population growth without any replacement of his own, George simply assumes the population, and therefore the supply of labor, continues to grow. He then asserts that this growth increases, rather than decreases, the average productivity of labor—even without any technological advances and *a fortiori* with them: because "with every additional pair of hands which increasing population brings, there is a more than proportionate addition to the productive power of labor," population growth "seldom can, and probably never does, reduce the [average] production of wealth" (George *P&P*:232, 234).

All of the benefits from this growth in average output, however, "attach" themselves to the land, increasing the income only of the landlords.

> [T]he increased power which comes with increased population . . . brings out a superior power in labor, which is localized on land—which attaches not to labor generally, but only to labor exerted on particular land; and which thus inheres in the land as much as any qualities of soil, climate, mineral deposit, or natural situation, and passes, as they do, with the possession of land. (George *P&P*:235)

When the land is more valuable, landlords can and do force workers to pay higher rent for its use. All increased benefits from growth are therefore "intercepted," and labor and capital[4] become relatively worse off (George *P&P*:283).

> [T]hus all the advantages gained by the march of progress go to the owners of land, and wages do not increase. Wages cannot increase; for the greater the earnings of labor the greater the price that labor must pay out of its earnings for the opportunity to make any earnings at all. The mere laborer has thus no more interest in the general advance of productive power than the Cuban slave has in the advance in the price of sugar. (George *P&P*:283)

Land speculation can, however, make workers lose absolute, as well as relative, ground as society progresses. During an economic upswing, some speculators deliberately withdraw land from production, holding it only for the anticipated appreciation in its price. They therefore accelerate the increase in rent[5] both by increasing the demand for land and by reducing the amount in use, pushing production prematurely out to inferior margins. Hence,

> the condition of the free laborer [may] be positively, as well as relatively, changed for the worse by the increase in the productive power of his labor. For begotten of the continuous advance of rents, arises a speculative tendency which discounts the effect of future improvements by a still further advance of rent, and thus tends, where this has

> not occurred from the normal advance of rent, to drive wages down to the slave point—the point at which the laborer can just live. (George *P&P*:283)

Thus can landlords over time "command all the fruits of labor save enough to enable labor to exist," conveying the impression that the world operates according to Malthusian principles because Malthusian predictions are confirmed (George, *P&P*, 294). In truth, however, poverty is created not by overpopulation but by "the causes which prevent social organization from taking its natural development and labor from securing its full return" (George *P&P*:122).[6]

Alfred Marshall

Marshall sharply disagrees with George that private land ownership causes poverty in a growing economy. Nothing intrinsic to that process forces people into pauperism. In a free market economy, with its ability to harness individual energy and to sustain incentives, progress improves the plight of all, "though unfortunately at a very slow rate" for the lowest stratum of society (Marshall [1883] 1969:188).

In general, the highest wages are found in countries with the highest national incomes. Marshall agrees with Ricardo that there are eventual diminishing returns to land; indeed, "the diminishing productiveness of the free soil has a greater influence in lowering wages than the payment of rent fees." But he argues that increasing returns from technological advances, internal and external economies created by expansion of industries, and other benefits from the "closeness" of population have a tendency to offset this check to prosperity "[s]o long as the population is not excessively thick" (Marshall [1883] 1969:188 and 196).

"Alas! there is one great hindrance" to progress. One of the first applications of increased knowledge

> is, as it ought to be, to save from disease and want multitudes who . . . would have sunk under their influence. As a result, population is increasing rapidly . . . and there is kept up a constant supply of unskilled labourers, who have nothing but their hands to offer for hire, and who offer these without stint or reserve. Thus competition for food

dogs the heels of progress, and perpetually hinders it. (Marshall, in Pigou:116–17).

The problem is not growth in the population *per se*, but growth of the unskilled. Marshall's explanation relies on supply and demand analysis in a competitive framework.[7] He concludes that workers are paid low wages not because they are exploited by landowners, but because there are too many of them and/or their marginal productivity is low.

The supply of unskilled workers is growing too fast not only because medical advances are saving the sickly, but also because the market system has replaced traditional arrangements and their "preventive check" to population growth. When "civilization is settled and simple in form, custom quietly does the work that is done by cruel struggle for existence among wild animals and among savage nations." In such a society, neither the "physically or morally infirm, nor anyone else without a definite position in the village which would enable him to bring up a family," can marry. As a result, "children brought into the world find places ready made for them" (Marshall [1883] 1969:188). However, the process of industrialization has replaced the personal relationships of stable village life with the impersonal market nexus and the mobility of modern life; and population growth has accelerated as a result.

Two external shocks and two inappropriate government policies in Britain exacerbated these inevitable difficulties of transition from pre-industrial to industrial life. Not only did bad harvests and an expensive war cut back on available resources, but the Corn Laws prevented foreign trade from acting as a buffer for domestic grain shortages and the Poor Laws provided an "artificial stimulus" to population growth. Indeed, the well-intentioned but ill-conceived poor laws were responsible, in Marshall's estimation, for "probably half of all the lives of extreme misery and want in the country" (Marshall [1883] 1969:189).[8]

Factors on the demand side interacted with this "keenest of competition" among working men to depress wages of the unskilled even further. "The employers, many of them but recently working men, were often harsh and ignorant," and their resources were "straitened" by the war (Marshall [1883] 1969:189). Additionally,

> [t]he truth that every father owes to his children the duty of providing them with a lot in life, happier and better than his own, has not yet been grasped. Men who have been brought up, to use their own phrase, "anyhow" are contented that their children should be brought up "anyhow" (Marshall, in Pigou:117).

These children become workers whose low marginal productivity keeps the demand for them low.

Remedies for Poverty

HAVING IDENTIFIED THE primary causes of poverty, George and Marshall advocate with ardor and energy special remedies for this gripping problem. Their policy recommendations have as little in common as their causal analyses.

Henry George

George's solution is to eliminate private ownership of land. He argues not for land nationalization, but for the appropriation of all rent by a land tax that exempts the income from its increased value due to improvements. All other taxes can be eliminated, because this single tax can produce sufficient revenue to finance all appropriate government spending. Much current spending will no longer be necessary when people become more cooperative (see *infra*).

George believes that his reform has numerous advantages. It "accords with all that is politically, socially, or morally desirable" (George *P&P*:545). Equal right to land is necessary, George argues, to fulfill the political equality of the Declaration of Independence: "Political liberty, when the equal right to land is denied, becomes, as population increases and invention goes on, merely the liberty to compete for employment at starvation wages" (George *P&P*:545).

By eradicating "the monopolization of the opportunities which nature freely offers to all," the single tax will promote the "fundamental law of justice" and remove the "great cause of unnatural inequality in the distribution of wealth and power" (George *P&P*:545).

> The tax upon land values is . . . the most just and equal of all taxes. It falls only upon those who receive from society a peculiar and valuable benefit, and upon them in proportion to the benefit they receive. It is the taking by the community, for the use of the community, of that value which is the creation of the community. (George *P&P*:421)

Compensation for the social appropriation of rent would be morally wrong. Private land has always been stolen from the community, and even if everyone at one time overtly agreed to its privatization, each generation thereafter would be born with rights to this land (George *P&P*:339).

In addition to providing society with political liberty and justice, a single tax on land promotes economic efficiency. It eliminates taxes on labor and capital that raise prices and reduce incentives and output. Because it "expresses nothing but the advantage of expropriation," rent is "in every respect fitted for taxation" (George *P&P*:412–13).

> Hence the community can take it all without in any way lessening the incentive to improvement or in the slightest degree lessening the production of wealth. Taxes may be imposed upon the value of land until all rent is taken by the State, without reducing the wages of labor or the reward of capital one iota; without increasing the price of a single commodity, or making production in any way more difficult. (George *P&P*:413)

George realizes that landowners will bear the burden of this fiscal reform. But "a moment's reflection," he argues, will show that the costs are not significant. "[T]his measure would make no one poorer but such as could be made a great deal poorer without being really hurt," and the richest landlord "would still have all he could by any possibility enjoy, and a much better state of society in which to enjoy it." Moreover, although they may experience a relative loss, total production will increase so much that these landlords may gain more from their interests as capitalists and workers than they will lose as rentiers" (George *P&P*:452 and 448).

Nor should farmers, the small landowners, be alarmed. They gain from the single tax because taxes on land improvements would be eliminated. "The land of the working farmer is improved land, and usually the value of the improvements and of the stock used in cultivating it bears a very high proportion to the value of the bare land" (George *SPE*:222). The farmers will also benefit from the elimination of all other taxes.

> Let the working farmer consider how the weight of indirect taxation falls upon him without his having power to shift it off upon any one else; how it adds to the price of nearly everything he has to buy, without adding to the price of what he has to sell; how it compels him to contribute to the support of government in far greater proportion to what he possesses than it does those who are much richer, and he will see that by the substitution of direct for indirect taxation, he would be largely the gainer. (George *SPE*:222)

Finally, because the single tax eliminates land speculation, the population will be diffused

> where it is too dense and . . . concentrate[d] . . . where it is too sparse. . . . The people of the cities would thus get more of the pure air and sunshine of the country, the people of the country [will no longer be] cut off by the sparseness of population from the conveniences and amusements, the educational facilities, and the social and intellectual opportunities that come with the closer contact of man with man. (George *P&P*:451)

Liberty, justice, and the natural law become one; justice and expediency are one. Equality of opportunity, fully understood to include access to Nature's bounty, promotes growth in production as well as in humanity by reducing the amount of time and energy spent in squabbling. As society approaches the ideal of a Jeffersonian democracy, the government need no longer be a "directing and repressive power"; it can provide fewer jails and more public baths, music and dancing halls, technical schools, shooting galleries, and the like (George *P&P*:545, 367, and 456).

In brief and in sum, this "simple, yet sovereign remedy"

> will raise wages, increase the earnings of capital, extirpate pauperism, abolish poverty, give remunerative employment to whoever wishes it,

> afford free scope to human powers, lessen crime, elevate morals, and taste, and intelligence, purify government and any civilization to yet nobler heights. (George *P&P*:405–06)

Truly, for George the single tax is *the many in the one, the one in the many!*

Alfred Marshall

Marshall recoils from anything so sweeping and radical. In his view, *natura non facit saltum*. Instead, Marshall believes in educating the poor so that competitive forces gradually raise their wages above poverty levels. Education[9] of the masses will create "direct" as well as "indirect" benefits. The direct benefits come from eliminating much of "that wasteful negligence which allows genius that happens to be born of lowly parentage to expend itself in lowly work." "All that is spent during many years in opening the means of higher education to the masses would be well paid for if it called out one more Newton or Darwin, Shakespeare or Beethoven." Education also

> confers great indirect benefits even on the ordinary workman. It stimulates his mental activity; it fosters in him a habit of wise inquisitiveness; it makes him more intelligent, more ready, more trustworthy in his ordinary work; it raises the tone of his life in working hours and out of working hours; it is thus an important means toward the production of material wealth; at the same time that, regarded as an end in itself, it is inferior to none of those which the production of material wealth can be made to subserve. (Marshall 1920:212, 216, and 211)

Another benefit of education is that it reduces income inequality by raising incomes at the bottom and lowering them at the top. Other things equal, education reduces the supply of unskilled workers, thus raising their wages. Moreover, "the remedy for the too large fortunes of employers" is to educate the children of working men so that they may gain "every advantage to climb up to become employers, to compete with employers and force down employers' earnings, and distribute a large share of an increased total production amongst the working classes" (Marshall [1883] 1969:198).

Marshall has no doubt that the benefits of education far exceed the costs. Education is therefore a good investment from a material as well as a moral perspective. However, ignorance and the long-run and social nature of the benefits preclude parents and employers from making this investment. Even though "most parents are willing enough to do for their children what their own parents did for them; and perhaps even to go beyond it if they find themselves among neighbours who happen to have a rather higher standard," they have not yet acquired the habit of "discounting the future at a low rate of interest" (Marshall 1920:216 and 217). Moreover, "[t]o get as much out of people and put as little as you can into their bodies and into their minds may be penny wise from the point of view of the individual [employer], but it is pound foolish for the nation at large" (Marshall [1883] 1969:197).

Accordingly, "the State should give, at a nominal price, a good general and technical education to all, and a first-rate education to even the poorest child who shows a special fitness for it" (Marshall [1883] 1969:209). Although Marshall boldly asserts that "[t]o this end public money must flow freely," he makes no specific tax policy recommendations. Not all the revenue will, however, come from the State. The financial burden will be shared in vague proportion among parents, the state, and wealthy people imbued with principles of economic chivalry so strong that they voluntarily contribute to this cause (Marshall 1920:718, 719).[10]

Although Marshall's commanding solution to the problem of poverty is education, he also exhorts individuals to behave responsibly, with thrift and self control. They should postpone marriage and have fewer children so that excessive breeding does not offset education in its effect on the supply of unskilled workers. Moreover, he urges the rich to grasp the social possibilities of "economic chivalry" or charitable contributions (Marshall 1920:719).

Once a state of high education and prosperity is attained, it is maintained by the heightened sense of parental duty and absence of the degrading effects of keen poverty. Diminished competition from a smaller labor supply as well as enhanced education thereby unite to eliminate poverty.

> A century ago we took off the last shackles from that fierce monster—competition. That was necessary for our own freedom. Without it there have been free aristocracies, but there has never been, and cannot ever be, a free nation. The unshackled monster was terrible to deal with; but we are learning fast how to manage him. The education of working men's children in schools, and the education of working men in managing their own affairs, is progressing at an enormous rate. . . . Let us then take courage. It may be too late to get rid of poverty in our generation; let us resolve that our children, or at any rate our children's children, shall be free from it. (Marshall [1883] 1969:197)

Reactions of Henry George and Alfred Marshall

HENRY GEORGE AND Alfred Marshall's interaction was quite limited. Their only direct encounter occurred on the Ides of March in 1884 when an exhausted George addressed an Oxford audience that included Marshall, then a political economy lecturer just beginning to build his reputation. When George's "simple and inspirational" speech was cut short to answer questions (Newton 1971:321),[11] Marshall was the first to rise. Abandoning completely his customarily calm and co-operative stance, he excoriated George for using his admittedly "magnificent talents" of oratory "to instill poison" into the minds of the people. He had repeatedly challenged "any person to show him one single economic doctrine in Mr. George's book that was both new and true. But no one had come forward." George had not understood "in any single case . . . the authors whom he had undertaken to criticize" nor could he have been expected to, lacking, as he did, any "special training" (Marshall and George [1884] 1969:221).

With equal phlegm, George responded that Mr. Marshall was correct that the book "contained nothing that was both new and true" because "the book was based upon the truth; and the truth could not be a new thing; it always had existed and it must be everlasting" (George, Jr. 1900:436). "Mr. Marshall," added George, "said he had already refuted [George's] doctrines. Well, he was a good deal like their English General, he did not know when he was beaten" (Marshall and George [1884] 1969:221).[12]

In this part of the paper, we dispassionately construct Marshall's and George's reaction to each other by using not only this direct encounter stripped of its phlegm, but also Marshall's indirect response in his three lectures on George's topic, and various of his and George's other writings that address the arguments without the argumentativeness.

Alfred Marshall

Marshall emphasizes that the system of land ownership in England "suits [the English people] on the whole fairly well." This system

> is the only one in which whatever farming skill there is in the country can be turned to the best account. It is chiefly owing to this cause . . . that England has been the pioneer of agricultural progress of the world. Almost every grand improvement in modes of cultivation, in agricultural machinery, and in breeding of cattle has been made in England . . . . (Marshall [1883] 1969:204, 202)

The English laborer is now better off "as far as material enjoyments go" than the foreign peasants under other land tenure systems, and in fifty more years the economies of large farms would make them better off "in almost every respect" provided that "all the changes of the last fifty years continue in the same direction" (Marshall [1883] 1969:204).

Moreover, ownership of land involves more sentimental than material incentives.

> A man who buys land gets a much smaller net income from it than he could get in other ways; he pays this extra price chiefly for the social position that it gives. If he makes himself unpopular he deprives himself of that very thing for which he has paid so high a price. He has every inducement to befriend his poorer neighbours. Allowing for some exceptional cases, it is . . . indisputable that he exerts himself more to do good to others than the rich man in any other country of the world does. (Marshall [1883] 1969:202)[13]

People in England are *not*, therefore, in the "power of landlords," Marshall argues. Indeed, the monopoly power that George decries arises not from *private* ownership *per se*, but from *single* ownership of all the land. He challenges George "to prove in an island owned by many, who were not acting in combination but in competition, it would be possible for the landlord to screw the people down to the verge of subsistence." In such an island, the landlords "could only get as much as competition allowed them," which does not "amount to much more than a shilling a pound" (Marshall and George [1884] 1969:221, 223–24).

Moreover, rent appropriation would not raise enough revenue to eliminate all other taxes. Marshall debunks the notion of revenue sufficiency by showing that current public spending figures in Great Britain are significantly greater than the total rent from unimproved land. Taxes on capital and labor would have to finance the difference, so George's tax could not remain a single tax (Marshall [1883] 1969:207–08).

In addition to its practical defects, Marshall considers George's single-tax remedy unfair. It will not promote justice because ancient wrongs cannot be corrected by incorrect policies. Even if one concedes that

> the original landholders had no good right to their title-deeds, are not an immense number of the present landholders the descendants of working men and others who have bought the title-deeds with the sweat of their brow? (Marshall [1883] 1969:201)

Although Marshall considers much speculation "anti-social" and even an "evil manipulation of the sources from which ordinary investors derive their guidance," he calls for more economic studies before policy recommendations are advanced. "Hasty attempts to control speculation by simple enactments have invariably proved either futile or mischievous" (Marshall 1920:719).

George is not only wrong to blame the landlords, but even more at fault to do so at the expense of discounting the role of thrift. "Mr. George said, 'if you want to get rich, take land,' and he was far from saying that if [the poor] wanted to get well off they should work well and be thrifty." George is unjustified to allocate only one chapter in *Progress and Poverty* to thrift, and that solely with the intention of showing "working men how they could not benefit their position by thrift and industry" (Marshall and George [1884] 1969:221, 222).

Henry George

Denying Marshall's assertions about improvements in the lives of the common laborers in England, George invites his audience to

> go anywhere almost through this country and see with their own eyes human beings who had gained nothing whatever by the advance of civilization. Go up into the north and see the cotters . . . living on poorer and poorer than their fathers had been, crowded down and driven off good land on to poor land. Their crops had been diminishing, and they could not keep their cattle; the women were used as beasts of burden to do work that horses ought to do. If they went into their great cities they would see men and women living in dens in which no decent man would keep a dog. (Marshall and George [1884] 1969:218–219)

Marshall's theory, George argues, fails to address the important issue of disparities in power. Monopoly power can result not just from single ownership, as Marshall believes, but also from class ownership. With support from Adam Smith, George argues that landlords operate "almost under a tacit combination." By virtue of their ownership, landlords

> could hold out for the highest price for the land and they could wait; the man who must eat could not wait, and the man who could not wait must give way in the bargain to the man who could. (Marshall and George [1884] 1969:223)

The apparatus of supply and demand, George asserts, may provide insights into how *relative* wages are determined, but it is altogether inappropriate for the determination of average wages.[14] Marshall therefore errs in his analysis of how education affects the working classes. "To educate men who must be condemned to poverty, is but to make them restive" (George *P&P*:10). Education adds "but to the capacity for suffering. If the slave must continue to be a slave, it is cruelty to educate him" (George *SPE*:147). As long as rents are expropriated as private income, education succeeds only in raising the relative wage of the educated worker; average wages continue to fall (George *P&P*:308). The same holds true for thrift. Thrift cannot improve the conditions of the working class as long as land remains privately owned.

> Let one man save and he would get ahead of his fellows, but let the whole class save, let them reduce the expenses of living, and by an inevitable law so long as land is private property, wages must fall proportionately. If the working classes of England were today to agree to live on rice like a Chinaman, how long would it be before wages would come down to a rice-eating level? They stood merely on the verge of starvation, and the only thing that kept wages above a certain point was that below that point men, with the habits of Englishmen, could not live. (Marshall and George [1884] 1969:222)

Nor will charity improve the lot of the poor.

> . . . [T]here were but few men who, looking round them and seeing the misery and vice and degradation that existed, could rest content without doing something; their charitable societies, with the enormous sums that were spent in efforts to alleviate the conditions of the poor proved that . . . But what was accomplished? . . . Something more was needed than charity, and that something was justice . . . and that was the highest call that could be made to any man. (Marshall and George [1884] 1969:219)

Not only does George make a frontal attack on the applicability of supply and demand to problems of excessively low average wages, but he also fires some salvos at the relevance of Marshall's theory of competitive labor markets to the problem of poverty. Competition for *land* and not for *wages* forces the wages down to subsistence. The problem is not "overpopulation" or excess supply of unskilled workers. In fact, George believes, "in a natural state of things they would never have an overwhelming population" (Marshall and George [1884] 1969:224, 225).

Conclusion

GEORGE AND MARSHALL both believe that aided by a proper set of policies, progress can eliminate poverty. With a tax that appropriates rent from the unimproved value of land, George sweeps away all other taxes, all unearned and undeserved private income, poverty, greed, and only one aspect of private land ownership—its entitlement to residual income. With more public education and a higher sense of duty, Marshall's tamed competition gradually eliminates poverty and its attendant evils.

Marshall had such respect for special training that he insisted on the separation of Economics from the other Cambridge Triposes. But although George once remarked that the only title he cared for was "Professor," he also believed that "[f]or the study of political economy you need no special knowledge, no extensive library, no costly laboratory. You do not even need text-books nor teachers" and advised his eldest son to work at a newspaper rather than go to Harvard (George, Jr. 1900:275, 278, and 365).

George thought that he had the Truth—a Land Theory of History and a Labor Theory of Ownership, if you will; while Marshall thought he had an accurate engine of analysis to track down the Truth—and delayed publishing it in hopes of finding it.

And so George found Marshall incomprehensible and incoherent, while Marshall found George to have said nothing new and true—nor new and false, for that matter (Hebert 1979:57).

Notes

1. Nor did they explicitly define "poverty." As with many of his other terms, George seems to shift between relative and absolute concepts. Marshall also discusses both absolute and relative poverty, emphasizing the former. His relative concept is more inter-generational in spirit.

2. The New York Public Library has a bound copy of the three lectures entitled: "Wealth and Want" (see Newton 1971:317, fn. 41). We have chosen Stigler and Coase's title because it coincides with Marshall's own selection: "'Progress and Poverty,' the title of the course of three lectures that I am about to deliver, is taken from a book by Mr. George, which is the last outcome of the feeling that we ought not to be content with our progress as long as there is so much suffering in the world . . ." (Marshall 1883 (1969):184).

3. George's definition of land is an expansive one. It includes "the whole material universe outside of man himself . . . The term land embraces, in short, all natural materials, forces, and opportunities, including such natural resources as raw materials, land surface, air, water, and minerals" (George *P&P*:38). We shall honor this definition throughout the paper.

4. George pays little attention to the theory of capital because "[i]n truth, the primary division of wealth in distribution is dual, not tripartite. Capital is but a form of labor, and its distinction from labor is in reality but a subdivision, just as the division of labor into skilled and unskilled would

be." Wages and interest thus always move in the same direction: interest falls as wages fall, and vice versa. Because labor is the only "active" factor of production and can produce wealth on land without capital, "the law of rent and the law of wages must correlate each other and form a perfect whole without reference to the law of capital." "Profit," to George, is a nonsensical term. It is really a combination of wages, the reward to capitalists' labor; and interest, which springs from "the power of increase which the reproductive forces of nature, and the in effect analogous capacity for exchange, give to capital" (George *P&P*:203, 164, 188).

5. George divides rent into a "*necessary* or real" component determined by its use and an "*unnecessary* or fictitious" element determined by speculation (George Jr. 1900:223).

6. Speculative advances in land values also provide George with a theory of "periodical industrial depressions" to which all countries with the institution of private land ownership "seem increasingly liable." As speculation, not current productivity, raises rent, the returns to labor and capital must fall. Once they hit subsistence or maintenance levels, production declines sharply, and depression ensues (George *P&P*:264–265). Land prices and real values gradually come back in line, and the economy begins to recover; but this very recovery sets the stage for the next cycle. George therefore predicts wild swings of activity in most economies over time, and asserts that land speculation, which raises prices but reduces output, is their primary cause.

7. Indeed, Marshall uses the apparatus of supply and demand to determine prices of all factors of production—not just wages of unskilled workers, but also wages of the skilled, rent, and interest; he also uses it to show how wages and interest can move in opposite directions according to their relative scarcity and productivity.

8. In Marshall's view, the poor laws discriminated "against the industrious and in favour of the dissolute." He held: "The industrious were so much worse provided for than those who went to the parish, that in time independent labourers almost ceased to exist. Wages were lowered all round and eked out by parish aid. He got on best who was the best adept at the arts of imposition. . . . Mischief was done, not by the amount of relief given, but by its being given in the wrong way and to the wrong persons, so as to cause the survival of the worst in place of the best" (Marshall 1883 (1969):189).

9. Education for Marshall implies much more than teaching children how to read and write:

> The schoolmaster must . . . educate character, faculties and activities; so that the children even of those parents who are not thoughtful themselves, may have a better chance of being trained up to become thoughtful parents of the next generation. (Marshall 1920:718)

10. Marshall was, however, more explicit about these financial matters in the *Economics of Industry*, co-authored with his wife, Mary Paley Marshall. They proposed having the government pay for education by borrowing at the current interest rate (then three percent). With such an attractive rate, this expenditure was a good investment: "About a tenth of the total income of the country is paid to Government in Imperial and Local taxes; so that with the present rate of taxes Government will gain about a tenth of whatever increases in the national wealth comes from an improved system of education. And it is probable that this tenth would be sufficient to repay with interest any outlay that Government may make on that general and technical education" (Marshall and Marshall 1879:113).

11. Perhaps George's fatigue explains cutting the lecture short, the "captious" tone of many of his responses, telling Marshall "his head was small and his mind was tired, and he could not remember so many questions when they were put together," and professing not even to remember his own book (George in Marshall 1883 (1969), 221, 222).

12. The antagonists' lack of sympathy and understanding, their captiousness and condescension were due more, we believe, to basic differences in personality and background than to the peculiar setup of the Oxford encounter. On the one hand, George was self-trained and messianic, a true son, says Barker, of his city of birth, Philadelphia, "during the age we name for Andrew Jackson. . . . [In this] bustling city . . . an idealist's mind turns naturally to events of state and society . . . [to] Jefferson's ideas and the historic statement of great principles" (Barker 1955, 3–4). On the other hand, Marshall had impeccable formal training, and was careful and qualifying—the very model of a modern academic economist. He was a difficult public speaker, generally eschewed controversy, and used his magnificent talents in mathematics as a private language to check the internal consistency of his theories.

13. Marshall does mention the desirability—in *new* countries—of long-term government leases of land, a policy resembling George's rent appropriation (Marshall 1883 (1969):205). But Marshall does not develop this idea in his more formal writings as he does most of the other concepts in the three lectures; and it seems to be made more in response to other land reform schemes than as a proposal standing on its own merits. We relegate it to the footnotes rather than incorporating its mention into the main body of the text.

14. George argues: "When it is said, as is commonly said, that the general rate of wages is determined by supply and demand, the words are meaningless. For supply and demand are but relative terms. The supply of labor can only mean labor offered in exchange for labor or the produce of labor, and the demand for labor can only mean labor in the produce of labor offered in exchange for labor. Supply is thus demand, and demand

supply, and, in the whole community, one must be coextensive with the other" (George *P&P*:208–09).

SECTION 2

PUBLIC POLICY IMPLICATIONS

The Role of Ground Rent in Urban Decay and Revival

How to Revitalize a Failing City

By MASON GAFFNEY*

Introduction

YOU MAY THINK me an outlander but my parents were New Yorkers and never forgot it. One grandfather even went to St. John's, although not this St. John's—it's what they once called Fordham in the Bronx, now one of those dying cities we need to revive. He was to become a priest and lead the celibate life. As you see, he was not equal to the calling. His official obit tactfully says, "After leaving college he enlisted in the U.S. Navy," but Aunt Fan wrote privately, "Papa left Fordham before finishing and went to California where he taught school. Fordham required mostly brawn, he said." Violence here is not new.

He married late, so late a young man like me has a grandfather who served in the Big War. That is not remarkable except that means the Civil War. Ours is a family of long generations. My other grandfather, the Yankee Presbyterian, lived in Brooklyn Heights when that was a suburb for stockbrokers, and that goes way back too.

Now these old timers, to whom the past was only yesterday, spoke always of New York City as the center of civilization. It was a livable, optimistic place—a great, growing, vibrant, trend setting, prospering, cultural city. A little crooked, sure, and great-grandfather was probably no saint at paving streets for Tammany Hall. But it had a present and a future, a life and a soul, not like the dead-end hopeless despair of today's Bronx.

*Professor of Economics, University of California at Riverside.

Henry George

BUT WE'RE HERE to talk of the future. I'd like to see those good times and better ones come again, preferably without the graft. And we're here to review the ideas of another commuter between New York and California, Henry George, and how his ideas might be used to revive dead cities. Henry George was a journalist who taught himself economics. He had a flowing pen and a brilliant mind, and his book, *Progress and Poverty*, became and remains the all-time best seller in economics.

People remember him today not for the volume of his sales, but for the enduring quality of his ideas and proposals. The reform program he worked out combines the *magic of incentive* with the *magic of justice*. It comprises a plan not just to revitalize cities but to reunify society.

George's fans have boosted him for the Hall of Fame. It is ironic he never made it. Not that he would have cared, a stone face was not his style. The irony is that the Hall of Fame is now decaying and abandoned in the Bronx, a setting also decaying and abandoned for failure to use George's formula for keeping cities healthy and robust. The Hall of Fame in the Bronx exemplifies a malignant propensity to pour the national treasure into dead monuments while their living matrices starve, rot, and crumble. For further evidence, tour the purlieus of your state Capitol, contrasting the vulgar ostentation on the marbled side of the street with the squalid reality on the living side.

Dead and Dying Cities

WHAT ARE THESE moribund cities? Some extreme cases are East St. Louis, Camden, Benton Harbor (Michigan), Ford Heights (Illinois), along with Robbins, Harvey, Gary, and Newark.

But more commonly and generally, large parts of once vibrant cities are half dead, seriously blighted and trending downwards. One of these is the South Bronx, which New Yorkers know well enough to avoid knowing any better. In Milwaukee, it is the near north side, called locally the "inner core," a galloping blight whose area I have seen triple in the last 20 years while Milwaukee's population dropped 20 percent. In Chicago, it is South State Street, only a few blocks from the Madison Street crossing which for generations was the most valuable corner in the nation. In Tampa, it is Ybor City.

Note that blight is not restricted to stagnant or declining regions and cities. In booming Los Angeles, there is Watts. In nearby Riverside, California, one of the fastest growing cities in the nation, the central business district (CBD) is surrounded by blight which, among other things, frustrates years of subsidies aimed at reviving the moribund CBD itself.

But let us sound deeper to gauge the full mass of this iceberg. These extreme cases are not just anomalies. They are more than ghettoes and embarrassments; they are symptoms of systemic malfunction. They could be portents and symbols for the rest of the economy. Blight may be defined as a failure to maintain, to replace, and to renew the capital inherited from the past. Many studies of American industry indicate that it has this problem, compared with vigorous foreign competitors. In learning to cure blight, we may learn to restore the greatness and pride in this whole troubled nation.

Cities that Have Revived

THERE IS GOOD news too; some cities have risen from the grave. Indeed, all land development is resurrection in some sense; all land has been used before by someone for something from the beginning. Trace the history of any city lot, and you'll usually find there were several antecedent improvements, layered like the ruins of ancient Troy. It is a matter of making renewal happen faster and more widely, while we are still here to benefit.

Germany and Japan recovered from World War II with breathtaking speed. Atlanta even recovered from General Sherman too, although in its own courtly time. Chicago burned almost completely in 1871 leaving 90,000 people homeless, but recovered without breaking stride. San Francisco and Anchorage recovered from devastating earthquakes. Washington, D.C. recovered from the 14th Street riots and arson. The basics were right; the locations remained good. The disasters may even have helped by forcing the demolition of obsolescent capital and releasing land for rebuilding. "Instant urban renewal" is more than street jive; it can be true perception.

But some other revivals, less dramatic and publicized, are more impressive and relevant to us because they are revivals from normal decay and obsolescence, pushed along by good public policy, which we can analyze and replicate. There is Southfield, Michigan, bordering on Detroit and thriving and flourishing as fast as its parent central city is dying. There is Rosslyn, Virginia, just across the Potomac from D.C., a forest of high-rises that rose up while Washington was burning and derelict during the 1960s. There is Sacramento, California, whose once-depressing center has found new life. There is Pittsburgh, of grimy repute, recently named the most livable U.S. city. There are Hong Kong, Singapore, and Taipei, once best known as rather fetid ports of call, now three of the "Four Tigers" of Southeast Asia.

In all those modern success stories of economic and social revitalization, we find the hand of Henry George at work, if we seek out the local politics and policies. In Taipei, we learn they are guided by the philosophy of Dr. Sun Yat-Sen, and if we read Dr. Sun, we find he was an enthusiastic Georgist convert. In Pittsburgh, we find a "graded tax plan," applied, framed, and supported by something called The Henry George Foundation. Throughout Pennsylvania today, we now see several smaller cities emulating Pittsburgh's partial application of George's policies: Harrisburg, Scranton, McKeesport, New Castle, Washington, and Duquesne. *Fortune* reviewed their progress favorably in a 1983 article. Recently, steel-depressed Aliquippa signed on too, as did Clairton. These once declining cities bear close watching today as they bounce back.

Then there are cities of explosive growth after slow periods. These include Sydney and Johannesburg, both notable for their use of Georgist policies. Whatever their social faults, these two cities have burgeoned to become the economic capitals of their respective continents, an economic achievement hard to dismiss. There are several other good examples, like Nairobi in East Africa and Brisbane and Auckland in the Antipodes. Many cities of western Canada, including Edmonton, Saskatoon, Victoria, New

Westminster, and Vancouver, grew up with partial use of Georgist policies in the early 20th century. Less explicit application of Georgist policies was made informally (through assessment discrimination) by Seattle, Portland, San Diego, Houston, San Francisco, and many other growing western cities during the same period.

It is good to know degeneration and failure are not our predestined fate. We may choose them, but we may also choose renewal and success. It's a matter of attitude and know-how.

Why Cities Should Be Revived

SOME CITIES AND towns may and should be abandoned. Camps and towns around played-out mines are obvious examples. Some small farm towns and hamlets become redundant when roads let customers range farther and patronize the larger or better towns. Salvage what you can and move on.

Some would apply the same logic to all cities. Dead cities aren't lost, they say, but are just rebuilt elsewhere. They were cash cows that have been milked dry, meaning their depreciation allowances are reinvested on new frontiers and the people and vitality moved with the capital. That's a clever and important half-truth; but remember a half-truth is also half wrong. The basic original site stays put; land can't move. A lot of costly social capital, public and private, can't move either.

We have little room left for throwaway cities in this finite world. New natural sites aren't that common. There is only one water level route west along the Mohawk, only one Hudson Valley with only one mouth, and here New York City has stood for 350 years. We can't really afford to kiss off the Bronx and build a duplicate environment elsewhere. We can't rebuild the natural setting at all, and the sunken social capital is too costly: shipping, docks, rails, the New York Thruway, airports, streets, expressways, subways, water lines, power lines, sewer lines, gas lines, phone lines, churches, schools, bridges, tunnels, museums, Halls of Fame, universities . . . .

Of course, we can replace the Bronx out at the east end of the Long Island Expressway, but that means not only duplicating the micro-infrastructure but adding the Expressway and corresponding trunk lines for all the utilities, and paying the price or commuting in time, fuel, pollution, auto and tire purchases, repairs, paint jobs, insurance, gridlock, and traffic casualties. And then ultimately, when we tire of the new suburbs, where do we go next?

Look at the Earth from a lunarcraft photo. There is only so much, and we already have a big portion of the best temperate zone. This is our Promised Land. "Don't blow it," God keeps telling Israel in the Bible. "Don't think I'm giving you another Promised Land if you can't handle this one." It seems a reasonable attitude. Nor are other nations disposed to give up their crowded slices of this small, scarce Earth for us.

Furthermore, these blighted areas have high potential market values. Picture a topographic map of a city where the contour lines represent points, not of equal elevation but equal market value per square foot (psf). On this kind of topo map, the peaks, the Everests and McKinleys, are in the city retail centers where just one square foot rises to $2,000 (that's about $90 million per acre, and an acre is about 91 yards on a football gridiron). Land just a few miles or blocks away from such dizzying altitudes can hardly be worthless. Harlem is near Park Avenue; Watts is near Beverly Hills; South State Street is very near the Sears Tower. Newark is 15 minutes by train from Manhattan. Newark office rents are $25 psf per year. That is less, of course, than in Manhattan, but in Riverside, California we are throwing up offices to get rent of $12 psf per year while Newark stagnates.

The capital you invest that earns $25 psf is more productive, obviously, than that yielding $12 psf. I don't mean the capital in the floor atop the high-rise, because that is likely to cost $25 psf (in annualized terms) to build and operate. I mean the capital in the middle and bottom floors, which costs less to build but rents for as much and yields a surplus. To get more such middles and bottoms, and the corresponding surpluses, renew more land in those neglected areas of high potential like Newark. *Not* to renew those lands is to waste those potential surpluses. Each year's loss is lost forever, for the services of land perish with the passage of time.

Shall we treat the Bronx as a residence of last resort for people who can't afford anything decent? That's hardly necessary. To many people, cities are the Big Apple—desirable locations of positive values and strong magnetism. Rich foreigners come from around the world and pay top dollar to locate in Manhattan, not because they have to, but because they want to. So it is too with San Francisco, Miami Beach, Beverly Hills, Newport Beach, Cambridge, and Georgetown. If they want open country, there is plenty left in North Dakota, Texas, and Nevada—but they want cities.

Urban revival works best when a healthy piece remains on which to anchor new development. In the worst scenario, no such place remains, but even Camden has Campbell Soup. Newark has a great airport, a new Hartz Mountain Industrial Park, and the Prudential. Life is persistent and resilient. Vital seedlings keep sprouting; they only want sunshine, water, care, and cultivation.

The Urban Surplus

ONE OF THE reasons we remember Henry George was his pioneering work on cities, how they work and what good they do. Previous economists showed limited or no understanding of location value and its causes. Even Heinrich von Thunen, father of location theory, approached cities in an arid, antiseptic way that left out most of the sperm and egg, enzyme and ferment that today we call urban linkages and synergy. George was a mensch, like Holly Whyte or Jane Jacobs, seeing cities in intensely human, interactive terms.

George saw cities as foci of communication, cooperation, socialization, and exchange, which he considered the basis of civilization. He saw cities as the new frontier, an endless series of new frontiers, because the city as a whole enjoys increasing returns. The presence of people with good mutual access associating on equal terms expedites cooperation and specialization through the market. Multivariate interactions in cities are synergistic. Indeed, while each part—each parcel of land—is developed in the stage of decreasing returns, the composite city is generally in a stage of increasing returns, thanks to synergy. The whole is greater than the sum of its parts; and increases to the whole yield more than the sum of increases to the parts.

This synergistic surplus, says George, lodges in urban land rents. Thus he explained an outstanding phenomenon of his times, which other economists were overlooking completely: the unparalleled rise of urban rents and land prices, and the wealth and power of the owners.

To the investor in a building, it looks like this. The first $10,000 he spends yields him 30 percent or $3,000; but he pays ten percent interest or $1,000, leaving him a surplus of $2,000. To acquire the superior location that confers that surplus, he'll pay up to $2,000 annually, which means he'll pay up to $20,000 for title to the land (at ten percent, $20,000 will cost him $2,000/year).

Of course, the next $10,000 he spends may yield him more than ten percent, say 20 percent, conferring more surplus and adding more value to the land. But the idea is the same. He'll add to the building until the last unit of $10,000 yields him just ten percent, enough to pay interest and no more. (You have just taken a flying tour through the theory of diminishing marginal productivity.)

To understand ground rents and land prices is to understand cities; not to understand is to remain mired forever in confusion and fallacy, to be gulled and misled and bamboozled, which is, indeed and alas, the common lot of mankind. Let it not be yours.

These ground rents are annual, they continue forever, and they generally tend to rise. To buy title to land, therefore, people pay prices that look very high relative to current cash flow. In Riverside, California, a city of low density and 208,000 people, land prices go up to $18 per square foot. In San Francisco, a city of high density and 800,000 people, prices go up over $1,000 per square foot. In Manhattan, they go over $2,000. In Tokyo, probably the top of the line, one sale is reported at $25,000 per square foot.[1] An official agency has appraised the top value at $20,000 per square foot, although this may be puffed up. But $25,000 per square foot is high enough; urban land prices take your breath away.

Land prices vary extremely from city to city and block to block. The actual cost of building a square foot of floor space is fairly constant from place to place, but demand varies with location. A small rise of floor space rentals translates into a large percentage rise of ground rent and land price, because rent gets everything above what is required to operate and amortize the building.

Thus in Riverside at a small neighborhood mall, a floor space rental of $12 per square foot just pays for the building with only a little left over to pay for land, resulting in land prices of perhaps $5 to $8 per square foot. In Manhattan, rentals are triple or quadruple those in Riverside with all the surplus going to ground rent, resulting in land prices up to $2,000 per square foot, which are about 300 times higher than Riverside.

This is due to several factors. One is "leverage." Say the annualized costs of constructing and operating a building are $11 per square foot, whether in Riverside or Manhattan. That leaves $1 per square foot for ground rent in Riverside ($12–$11), and $37 per square foot in Manhattan ($48–$11). This factor alone makes Manhattan land worth 37 times Riverside land.

A second factor is intensity. At the higher level of floor rents in Manhattan, it pays to pack more floor space per acre, with high-rise buildings. Also, in Manhattan there is little need to provide workers and customers with parking space, while in Riverside six square feet of free parking are often required for each square foot of floor space.

Other factors are the greater pooling of demand in the bigger metropolis, which steadies its flow and gives more assurance of its continuation and predictability. The commercial vacancy rate in Riverside is pushing 30 percent.

In bigger cities at key locations, land prices are not just high per square foot; they are higher per capita than in small cities. Surprisingly, they are even higher relative to building values in spite of the high rise buildings. Remember each added floor until the top one adds more ground rent, because floor space rentals are more than enough to cover the added cost.

Urban land is also highly concentrated in ownership, meaning a handful of people and corporations own most of it. It is heavily favored by absentees of great wealth who want to diversify their holdings and acquire stable, secure wealth they can manage by remote control, so today a growing share of income property is held by aliens. Aliens even hold a good deal of residential property in selected communities of international jet-set ambiance and repute, places like Palm Beach, La Jolla, Greenwich, Belvedere, or Beverly Hills.

In comparing cities and neighborhoods, land prices are much more differentiated than other measures economists commonly cite. The median income in Upper East Side Manhattan is about eight times higher than that north of Central Park. But the price of land per square foot is probably 40 times higher. Margaret Reid presents many more contrasts of the same kind (Reid 1962); so does Harold Brodsky in his studies of Washington, D.C. (Brodsky:239).[2]

Sharing the Surplus

URBAN RENTS ARE a social surplus, not a payment in reward for anyone's making or supplying land. So others than the landowner have a claim. A good deal of American politics deals with how to assert that claim and share that surplus.

It seems a pleasant enough problem, cutting up a big pie. The ancient Chinese knew better: "It is easier to face a common enemy than share a surplus," Confucius said. The common ways of sharing this surplus are clumsy, divisive, and destructive. They bear some responsibility for dead cities. With too much quarreling and gouging over spoils, there are no more spoils to dispute. Macauley wrote nostalgically in *Lays of Ancient Rome*: "Then lands were fairly portioned; then spoils were fairly sold. The Romans were like brothers, in the brave days of old." The same might be said of New Englanders in the early 17th century, whose traditions we still honor in word and name. But we have come a long way from brotherhood. Let us see how spoils are shared now, and then how we might do better.

Looting and Graft

Looting is sharing by direct action. We had a bellyful of that in 1967, and its destructiveness needs no homily. Graft and patronage, the basis of ethnic-populist political machines, are more tempered kinds of looting which destroy incentives more quietly and insidiously. Featherbedding, stealing, parasitic behavior of all kinds, all cut into the surplus. The problem is they are blindly indiscriminate; they cut into productive incentives, too. But the more the surplus the more the temptation—the easier is the self-righteousness that rationalizes looting and graft.

Rent Control

Rent control shares the surplus with tenants. It is a tempting route and several cities follow it, including New York. Why not? Renters are the majority. Many landlords are rich and remote; they work through layers of faceless minions so you probably don't even know their names. The managers are tough and tight so you have a lot of abuse and negligence to avenge. Supply is inelastic, at least in the short run, so the owners can't cut and run. Poetic justice is served. But there are several spots on this policy.

- **Limited number of beneficiaries.** The original tenants carve out an equity in the landlord's estate, but the benefits spread no wider. Tenants may, and many do, sublet to others, becoming landlords themselves. Rent control is at best a zero-sum game among the few, not a social reform.
- **Lower incentive to maintain supply.** It becomes unattractive to build new rental units. At first, these are allowed higher rents but are vulnerable to future caps. So rent control is worse than a zero-sum game; it becomes negative-sum.

  What rent control confiscates is not just land-income, but building-income too. Land is fixed, but buildings need maintaining and replacing which they will not get if there is no return. Too, land can be reallocated to uncontrolled uses; we all know about condominiumization. The new wrinkle in Santa Monica is to buy a rent-controlled apartment building cheap and convert it to a single-family residence for the new owner.
- **Wasted space.** Tenants lose much incentive to economize on space, because it is underpriced to them. In the extreme, some tenants move away, but retain the apartment to use a few weeks of the year.
- **New class society.** Old renters become a privileged class vis-à-vis new ones in new units, which are temporarily uncontrolled or controlled at a higher level. With the lower new

supply and wasted space, uncontrolled rents are forced up above the free market level.

- **Owner/tenant clashes**. An owner's main goal under rent control is to evict and repossess. The resulting nastiness and intimidation have become routine, and the war stories legendary. In Tokyo, outright extortion and violence are frequent
- **Aborted incentive to maintain and improve**. Landlords lose all economic motive to serve and to maintain, let alone to improve. Tenants retaining precarious tenures have at most very limited motivation even to maintain, let alone improve property.
- **Dogged obstructionism**. A sitting tenant cannot gain by site renewal, but only faces eviction. Tenants therefore fight it every way they can. A class is created of dogged self-righteous obstructionists with a vested interest in the status quo, however obsolescent, however decayed, however inappropriate to the site.
- **Undertaxation**. The equity that tenants carve out of the landlord's estate has no market value, because it is inalienable (at least legally). Assessed values therefore drop, and tax yields drop correspondingly. The new privileged class not only gets preferential low rents, but also avoids contributing any share to support public services. The resulting higher tax burdens are dumped on others; the worsened public services are suffered by all.

Rent control is usually conceived of in terms of urban land, but the principle applies to other resources as well. I have personal familiarity with the perverse effects of capping the price of both water and energy.

I'm a small farmer with shares in a canal company, and the shares give me the right to receive water far below the market price but no right to sell my water. So my fellow shareholders and I do the only thing the law allows: we waste water and collectively create that chronic artificial crisis called the southern California water shortage. I'd be better off to have the state tax the water, raise the rates, and use the money to raise the salaries of—well, how about University of California professors?

The Federal Power Commission (now FERC) has long done the same thing with gas and earlier with oil, capping the field prices. Their Chief Economist, David Schwartz, opened my eyes to the moving spirit behind the policy when he joined a conference I sponsored in Vancouver. Our subject was how British Columbia (B.C.) might best collect rents from gas flowing from provincially owned wells. Dave Schwartz is a likable gentleman, selflessly dedicated to the public weal, but he grew impatient and finally blurted, "Lets not *collect* rent; let's cap the price and *eliminate* rent." That one foolish remark suddenly flashed more light onto 20 years of FPC regulation than tomes of NBER studies. They actually had so little understanding as *to believe* and act on that notion. By doing so they contrived to create, among other problems, the great gasoline shortage of the 1970s.

The rationale with housing, water, and energy all three is that these basics are too important to leave to the market and must be price-controlled. The result is to create systems of regulation much worse than anything a market could accomplish. Around 1973, there was also a great coffee crisis, a dearth of raisins, and even a crisis in toilet paper. These were too unimportant to regulate so their prices rose, demand fell, supply rose, and the crises quickly disappeared without a trace or a memory. Rent control ensures that we will not ever overcome the housing crisis so simply or at all.

"French Equity" (Equity in Kind)

Under the Code Napoleon, every French testator must divide his real estate equally among all children. There is no substituting money for land; the Code requires equity in kind, and nothing else will do. The resulting fine subdivision is called *morcellement,* and the Code demands it with no regard for efficiency. It goes further. Each heir must get an equal share of land of each quality: meadowlands, pastureland, woodland, etc. The even finer subdivision is called *parcellement,* which was once carried (like most human error) to absurd lengths.

Today, we approach "French Equity" indirectly and expensively. First, we distribute the land haphazardly, but *then* seek to make every parcel as good as every other. We do so by extending public utilities and roads to every parcel on the same terms, regardless of location and differential costs of service. A familiar example is the U.S. Postal Service, and it has given its name to this kind of pricing, called by economists "postage stamp pricing." Here are some quick examples.

- **B.C. Ferry Service.** This socialized system has two main lines to its Big Apple that make money: Vancouver-Victoria and Vancouver-Nanaimo. But the whole system hardly breaks even because there are some dozen lesser lines serving small islands and peninsulas. The worst of these costs $12 for every dollar of revenue. The losses are made up from the profits of the trunk lines. The generic name for that is *cross-subsidy.*
- **B.C. Hydro.** This socialized power system serves the entire province, an area so vast it exceeds those of California, Oregon, and Washington combined. Its rates are uniform throughout. Half of the people live in Vancouver at high density and are cheap to serve. A few live up north on the Yukon border where (I surmise) it costs several hundred dollars to earn one dollar of revenue. That is *cross-subsidy.*
- **Water and sewer service in Milwaukee County, Wisconsin.** Here the city investments have been captured, controlled, and milked by suburban interests, with a lot of help from the state legislature. Capacity in the city plants is taken up to serve the suburbs, and capital is poured into long interceptors (trunk lines) linking suburban land developments to city plants. That is *cross-subsidy* and has been called worse things.
- **College and university campuses.** The legislative ethic demands something for every electoral district. Not every assemblyman requires a college campus, for there are other prizes too, but the horse trading process seems to spawn too many. Just now we have eight UC Campuses, most of them with excess land, a few with excess floor space. Faced with rising enrollment, the preferred solution in Sacramento is not the lower-cost option of intensifying, improving, and staffing existing campuses, but the higher cost option of creating new ones. Each will enrich some influential land speculator and

tantalize a hundred others who are busy lobbying for the new spoils.

- **Water supply in California.** To summarize a complex tale, the low real cost of serving older settled areas is passed on to new settlements through an accounting device called "melding," a nice name for shutting your eyes and stirring all the accounts in the same pot. Melding passes through several levels: a state wholesaler serves the Metropolitan district, which serves local districts that serve cities. But the net result I have calculated is this: at the end of the line in Riverside, it costs society $1,800 to serve the marginal acre-foot (a unit of water) which sells for $20. That is *cross-subsidy*. It is worth fortunes to people developing land at the end of the line; the cost is spread over everyone else so they won't notice. Professors are supposed to keep quiet about it, but some of us never learn the rules.
- **Postal service.** How we love to dump on the postal service for raising rates and to moralize about the inefficiency of government. But do the harassed clerks really deserve the entire onus? Manhattan has 64,000 residents per square mile, plus the daytime population; Montana has 5.4 per square mile. It obviously costs a lot more to collect and deliver the mail in Montana. The main reason postal rates rise is because the whole U.S. urban population is spreading out more like Montana and less like Manhattan (which once had over 100,000 per square mile). Henry Schechter calls it the "cost-push of urban sprawl."

What's Wrong with "French Equity"?

There are two big problems with cross-subsidy as an approach to equity. First, it is not equitable; second, it is wasteful and inefficient.

The kind of equity achieved by regional cross-subsidies is not interpersonal, but inter-regional. It is something like Washington's programs of "foreign aid," which tax poor people in rich countries to aid rich people in poor countries. Some of the main beneficiaries are among the richest people and corporations in the country and world.

Here are a few who hold speculative land and enjoy subsidies on the growing fringes of southern California. Largest is probably The Irvine Company, owned by Donald Bren, among the 20 richest Americans on *Forbes'* latest list. This company holds some 70,000 acres in Orange County, including and surrounding Newport Beach, Irvine, and Corona del Mar. Others include Robert Campeau, who recently acquired Federated Department Stores; Chevron; Edward J. De Bartolo, also high on *Forbes'* list; Kaiser Development Bedford Properties; Connecticut General Life; Mobil; Lusk Realty; Bell Canada; Southern Pacific; Union Pacific; Cadillac Fairview (Olympia and York); Bank of Montreal; the Hunt oil family; and Newhall Land. The list goes on, but you see the point. Equity is not served by milking middle class neighborhoods to enrich owners like these. "Public works for private gain" is bad enough, but worse when the profiteers are already the richest.

How about efficiency? Subsidy creates waste in the amount of the subsidy, almost by definition. *Spread City,* by the New York Regional Plan Association, estimated that the social cost of creating one new lot at the metropolitan fringe is four times (4x) the value of the lot (and that is probably an underestimate, for the truth is so awful many readers would block it out or blame the messenger for the bad news). Why do people develop lots worth only one quarter of their cost? Because other people are paying the other three-quarters.

This process does transfer ground rent from areas of overcharge to areas of undercharge. But in the process, it simply destroys much of the ground rent, a process known to economists as "dissipation of rent." To spread the surplus, we lose much of it.

Being neither equitable nor efficient, has "French Equity" any kind of merit? Once it passed for a way to make jobs, in the salad days of J. M. Keynes, when he actually urged waste as a route to full employment. Those ideas are now dormant, but we still don't have the feel of it. If we had to fire a few teachers or policemen each time some city council yields to a major campaign donor and extends utilities to his raw acres, we would better sense the true cost of these "public works for private profit."

Sharing Surpluses Constructively

IT IS IN fact possible to mobilize the social rent surplus and put it to good use without waste. It is possible to create a just society of people unified and bound together in mutual satisfaction with the terms of their association, without contempt for their own government.

People do care about justice, always have and always will. They have funny ways of showing it sometimes: just now we're absorbing the "me generation," but this too shall pass. The problem is the older sharing-caring generations did some fuzzy thinking and foisted on us some clumsy, wasteful, and counter-productive ways to share and care, including substantial exploitation of the new generation they now brand as selfish. The "me generation" reacts against the stupidity and hypocrisy, not the noble impulse itself.

Rent will be shared, one way or another. Chicago economists preach that economists should only care about getting resources allocated efficiently to maximize the national product. "Entitlements" they say are arbitrary and don't much matter, just so they are clear and definite and everyone knows exactly what he owns and can trade it freely. In practice, that means leave them as they are today, whatever their origins. But life doesn't work that way. Eager supplicants swarm around rent like flies around fresh pie.

The key to renewing cities is shifting from *ob*structive ways of sharing rent, like rent control, and the *de*structive ways, like looting and cross-subsidy, to *con*structive ways.

George's Constructive Program

THIS BRINGS US to Henry George, for whom these lectures are named. He showed us how equity and efficiency go hand in hand: how to combine the *magic of justice* with the *magic of incentive.*

First, by George, equity need not be in kind, that's clumsy. Use the monetary mechanism, that's what it's for. If you and your brother and two cousins inherit a house sized for one family, you don't crowd all four families in; you sell and divide the money. Or one buys out the others. There is equity in money as well as real estate. Money is often better; you can reinvest it anywhere. It puts your house on a magic carpet to follow you around. Money is wonderful! (Just take care not to blow it.)

Second, by George, use the tax mechanism. Don't divide land into unusable morsels; don't shackle the market with rent controls; don't dissipate rent in cross-subsidies. But turn land over to the highest bidder, and tax ground rents to support government.

Taxing ground rent produces a range of social dividends. First, it overcomes the traditional trade-off between equity and efficiency by achieving both simultaneously. Second, it promotes renewal by permitting a reduction of taxes on buildings. Third, it encourages construction by reducing the liquidity constraints on developers of new buildings. Fourth, it produces synergistic effects (i.e., increases productivity) through positive spillover effects in the surrounding region. Fifth, it promotes better stewardship and more efficient land use by encouraging owner-occupancy. Sixth, it stimulates capital formation. Seventh, it encourages economy and discourages corruption in government.

Those are strong claims. Can economic policy do everything? No, but those are the things it can do, as I will explain more fully below. The basic impulse, however—the striving for justice and brotherhood and the sense of personal ethics—those come from within, from family, community, schools, and religion. So too does the sense of workmanship, the striving for excellence and competence, without which no system works.

The Primary Effect: Reconciles Efficiency and Equity

We've always heard that taxes destroy incentives. Economist Colin Clark said years back that the country would fall when taxes exceeded 25 percent of income. Arthur Laffer said tax yields would actually fall if rates rise, and rise if rates fall.

The news in Henry George is we can tax all the rent out of land and not one square foot will walk away. Nor will God switch off the Creation. Man creates capital by saving; some Other Force created land and sustains and serves it every day the sun rises, undeterred by taxes.

Nor will Georgist taxes leave owners sulking on their land, but the contrary. *Fortune* headlines them as "Higher Taxes that Promote Development" (Breckenfeld 1983). The tax is a fixed charge based on land's market value, derived in turn from its opportunity cost. The owner will use it harder and improve it more to meet the fixed tax. If he doesn't care to do that—if he has more than he can use—he will sell, releasing surplus land to meet the demands of others, of whom there are many with urgent needs and many more with enterprise wanting more space. Taxes stifle enterprise only if they increase with enterprise. Land taxes increase only with opportunity cost, which is independent of the enterprise of the individual owner. The only incentive this tax impairs is the incentive to withhold land from use.[3]

George's land tax promotes equity toward the landless in at least four ways: (1) it relieves them of taxes, to the extent that landowners pay more, (2) it supplies them with more goods and services as land is used better, (3) it offers them jobs producing those same goods and services, and incomes with which to buy these, and (4) it offers them a better chance to acquire land themselves, as surpluses are released to the market.

This is supply side economics with a real kick. It works through tax transformation rather than tax reduction—the total tax take may be raised or lowered as a separate issue. If desired, we can raise taxes and stimulate supply together; there is no hard choice to make between them.

So George's simple program not only reconciles efficiency and equity, it squares taxes and incentives. What more can a reasonable person demand of economic policy than to resolve these ancient basic standoffs that have confused and divided us, blocked understanding, and deadlocked constructive action for generations? It is an achievement on a par with resolving Evolution and Creation, except George's program is something we can do something about. We can use and implement it as quickly as we are willing to unclog the cerebral arteries and follow through with action.

Many people, it is true, are morbidly fascinated by deadlocks and standoffs and cling to them as old friends and comforters. They actually prefer irreconcilable disputes as cherished parlor games. It may ease the conscience to think justice must be sacrificed for efficiency, and schools starved and libraries closed to free up incentives, so nothing really can ever be done.

We all feel compassion by nature, but to survive and stay whole in this world of beggars and bandits, we learn to harden our hearts and cork it in. We learn to screen out evidence of suffering and injustice and rationalize what we cannot deny. This mindset, while understandable, is unaffordable in a period of dangerous national decline and growing division between haves and have-nots. Corking in feelings is hard on a person, too. There is relief and satisfaction in venting compassion via support of constructive public policies.

The Double Effect: Permits Untaxing of Building

The counterpart of sharing rent through taxation is to untax things people do and make, like buildings. This doubles the incentive effect. If the land tax is the stick, untaxing buildings is the corresponding carrot, and George's program is to make both of them larger.

Every lot with an old building is pressed between that building, the "Defender," and a potential replacement, the "Challenger." The trouble with taxing buildings is that it stacks the fight; it rigs the score against the Challenger. Say the lot-cum-Defender is worth \$100K and the Challenger would cost \$500K to build. Challenger cash flow must exceed Defender cash flow by enough to pay off the \$500K *plus* added taxes based on it. If the tax rate is high, that will stifle new investment as thoroughly as a communist coup.

The Georgist tax by contrast is impartial between Defender and Challenger, and lets the market decide. In Milwaukee in 1965, after a long detailed study, I found switching to the George program would let 30 percent of the city be renewed forthwith, simply by untaxing Challengers vis-à-vis Defenders. (The sad news is the mayor went the other way, so Milwaukee has lost 20 percent of its people and more of its wealth and is a sick city today.)

The Triple Effect: Enhances Flow of Credit

Most buildings when new have to surmount a liquidity crisis. Almost every one is built on credit with a small equity and takes a while to yield cash. During this critical period, builders need all the help they can get.

The property tax on buildings is a maximum during this crisis. The timing is such as to maximize the damage for any given tax yield over time. Now, of course, a building uses public services and something must be taxed to pay, but new buildings in older cities nearly always pay for more than they receive, while old ones receive more than they pay for. Think of building taxes as a kind of forced loan from the builder to the treasury, to be recovered down the line when buildings are older. But what could be more counterproductive than forcing a loan from a person passing through a credit crisis already?

The Georgist tax works the other way. It spares the builder when he needs it, and rises slowly under him over time as the site ripens to its next best use.

The Quadruple Effect: Produces Regional Spillovers

Urban blight is cumulative and self-reinforcing; blighted buildings cast a pall on land around them, discourage upkeep, and stifle renewal. Whatever slows renewal of one site therefore slows the neighborhood, which reflects back blight to the first—a vicious downward spiral.

Conversely, new buildings help stimulate renewal around them. There are exceptions, I know. Some new buildings, especially banks and corporate headquarters, sterilize a block with blank walls. I will not defend that, but the exception is not the rule; the abuse is not the precept. The rule is new buildings draw tenants from old ones and weaken other Defenders, so other owners have to renew, too. When they do, where better but next to the newest, hottest building? So renewal is cumulative, just like blight, only upwards in a benign spiral.

This competition for sites raises the tax base—not from buildings but from land prices derived from ground rents. Using the higher base, the city can improve public services, if needed, but without taxing any building, without scaring away any generators of fiscal surpluses. In this scenario, buildings raise the tax base indirectly by raising the value of land around them.

The Quintuple Effect: Reunites Ownership and Occupancy

Riverside, California built itself a lovely downtown pedestrian mall, back when that was in vogue, and has been sorry ever since. Nothing worked out, retailers deserted, and half the stores are empty. Recently I asked the developer of Tyler Mall, a success, why he thought downtown failed. I got the answer in two words: "absentee ownership." I should have known; I've preached it for years.

An agricultural adviser in Fresno once told an impressionable boy, "The best dressing for soil is the owner's shadow, applied daily." In town they say, "Who's keeping the store?" Absentees aren't the only negligent owners, nor are they all bad. Torpid owners are the problem, and they come in many forms. Basically to make a city go, you want to be rid of owners who see real estate mainly as a cash cow for their retirement and replace them with owners who see it as a vehicle for their enterprise, who apply their shadows daily. Those shadows will also follow them into local civic clubs and enterprising downtown and neighborhood associations for making joint improvements.

This is a surprisingly delicate area. Walter Goldschmidt was persecuted and maligned for his classic *Small Business and the Community,* 1946 (republished in his *As You Sow,* 1947). His sponsor, the Bureau of Agricultural Economics, fared even worse; it was terminated with extreme prejudice. But he documents the points abundantly by contrasting Arvin, Dinuba and Wasco, California.

It is the surplus in land use that attracts outside buyers. Absentees are redundant parties in production, but often top bidders for pure ownership; that is the legal privilege of receiving ground rents plus unearned increments that accrue over time. Georgist taxation spares the rewards of enterprise and cuts most directly into those "runs of free income" (as Veblen called them in *Absentee Ownership*), which attract absentee owners. For that reason, it slowly makes the market transfer ownership from absentees to occupants and managers on the spot, with all the good community effects that must follow. In a period of rising concern over alien takeovers of U.S. real estate, these points merit focused attention.

The Sextuple Effect: Increases Capital Formation

Untaxing buildings obviously draws in outside capital, which is good but is not capital formation to the whole economy. In Keynesian models, however, reducing taxes on new capital raises the rate of return after taxes ("marginal efficiency of capital") and does create new capital. In supply side models, it is more important to increase saving. Land taxation helps here, too.

Land taxation, if vigorously applied, tends to reduce the investment value of land through a process called "tax capitalization." There is a diminishing marginal utility of savings to any wealth holder, meaning the more you have, the less you need more. With land devalued, those needing wealth seek substitute assets to replace land in their portfolios. To acquire those additional assets, they must save more and invest the savings in real new capital, rather than land.

The Septuple Effect: Greater Economy and Less Corruption in Government

Georgist taxation tends to reduce the need for public spending in at least two obvious ways. One is to increase job opportunities, which in turn reduces welfare spending. The other is to obviate much of urban sprawl with its costly, wasteful cross-subsidies.

In the longer run, it seems reasonable to expect that more genuine productive job opportunities at home would reduce the pressures for military spending, at least those portions which are strictly boondoggling of a make-jobs nature.

There are city councils and councilpersons who can botch up and corrupt the best system ever blueprinted. But the Georgist program may even help straighten them out. Lincoln Steffens taught us that the troublemaker in Eden was not Eve, nor even the serpent, but . . . the apple! The apples of discord that corrupt city councils are unearned increments to land value, which they create or deny with every decision about extending sewers or changing zoning. Georgist taxation dehydrates those apples by attaching higher tax liabilities to each unearned increment.

Does Renewal Destroy Housing for the Poor?

SOME PEOPLE, RECOGNIZING that George's idea of taxing land values will be effective, fear that it will be too effective. They are reminded of earlier programs of urban revitalization that made victims of those they were supposed to help.

"Slum clearance" in the 1950s had a negative cast, with a name catered solely for middle class consumption. Reuse of cleared land was often at lower density, inevitably throwing an increment of unhoused people on the private market. Federal "Urban Renewal" in the 1960s was better named, but the actual emphasis was all on clearing, not rebuilding. The inventory of cleared, unrebuilt land under the Federal program grew vaster each year. "Bombing Out" and "Negro Removal," the cynics' cracks, were on the mark, although blacks were not by any means the only evictees. Any talk now of demolition and renewal evokes the specters of those tragic, cruel, wasteful public programs.

But George's program *begins* with fostering renewal and intensive use. Clearance is involved only as needed to serve renewal, never a goal in itself. The first land taken would generally be vacant or unused, such as boarded-up buildings. New buildings would draw renters and buyers from old ones, releasing more space. The idea and the impact are to increase supply of rentable and salable floor space. There would also be more stores with more competition in selling, and more employers with more competition in hiring.

How do we know there would be an aggregate increase of supply? Higher density is one test. Untaxing buildings fosters higher density, because density, exemplified by high buildings, is the substitution of capital for land. Untaxing capital obviously makes that more economical.

Higher quality is the other test. The richer the new tenants or buyers, the more space they release elsewhere when they move to new quarters. Now this is the hardest point to see and accept, if you are poor or an advocate for the poor. There will always be specific cases where the rich bump the poor. There is a certain mindset that locks onto such specific cases and makes up contemptuous names like "trickle down" to dismiss effects on the aggregate market. But the aggregate is what should concern us. If we mobilize local tenants to fight new building, we are marshaling a minority with a particular vested interest to fight against the interests of the majority of the poor, and everyone. We will spend our lives straining at gnats and swallowing camels. For the plain fact is that building new homes for the rich, the ones who can afford new homes, is what releases useable space for everyone else.

There are three kinds of slums. Only one kind, the narrowest of the three, is likely to witness evictions for the rich. This is the slum on high-valued land. These slums develop in the van of expanding commerce or high rise apartments, where landowners neglect their buildings because they expect to demolish them soon. These areas are limited. The second kind is on bad land, which will stay bad.

The third and most common is on good land covered with old buildings, which have filtered down to people who generate bad neighborhood effects. Many of these units go vacant. The land value is low. The market will never renew these slums at one stroke, but by nibbling at their fringes. But as it nibbles incrementally in, if it does, it unavoidably creates more space than it consumes, raising the aggregate supply.

Another fear for the poor is gentrification. But this, by definition, is where new gentry displace the poor without renewal, occupying the same old buildings. This is one result of not renewing; renewal as such is innocent. It seems a bit carping to criticize people for maintaining and restoring old buildings. The alternative may be viewed in many ungentrified neighborhoods where buildings simply go out of use, sheltering no one.

An example of what happens when renewal does not occur is Camden, New Jersey, which has the highest tax rate in the state. It's a depressant now and a vicious circle as the high rate drives away capital and further erodes the depleted tax base. But what if the tax were on just land value? The depressant would become a stimulant, the drag a motor, by the simple magic of converting a variable charge into a fixed, unavoidable one. So it is with most other cities in need of renewal, which today look vainly to Washington for salvation and redemption. They do need enabling legislation from their states, on the Pennsylvania model, but given that, they can save themselves. They'd better; no one else is going to do it for them.

But the ultimate end of Georgist policy is to be viewed in terms of the nation, not just single cities. The idea is to pit cities against each other to attract people. Nothing is better for people than to be competed for. It raises their bargaining power as tenants, buyers, and workers.

A Summary of Reconciliations

GEORGIST POLICY HAS been shown as a means to revive dying cities, and in the process to reconcile equity and efficiency, to reconcile supply side economics with taxation, and to reconcile capital formation with taxation of the rich. It can be seen as a means of harmonizing collectivism and individualism, in the most constructive possible ways. I know of no other program whose proponents even make such claims, let alone substantiate them. As you issue forth with cap and gown into a world that has already priced you out of the real estate market, you will find George's program worth your intense study and strong support.

Notes

1. *Editor's note:* This figure comes from 1988, before the Japanese economy—and its land values—plummeted.
2. See also Schwab (1998).
3. A primary concern expressed by environmentalists about land value taxation is that it will cause "overdevelopment," particularly by forcing farmers to sell to developers at the urban fringe. The opposite is the case. The tax encourages more intensive development of the sites with greatest value, leaving sites of lesser value (those at the urban fringe) undisturbed. Nevertheless, if citizens are not persuaded that this principle will be effective in stemming sprawl, it is possible to draw an urban growth

boundary, and apply the land tax more heavily inside it than outside. In a perfect market, with perfect planning of public works, this might not be necessary; but in this imperfect world it may be the best device to recover from the present aggravated condition of urban sprawl.

Site Value Taxes and the Optimal Pricing of Public Services[1]

By WILLIAM S. VICKREY*

Introduction: Pricing Urban Services

CITIES OWE THEIR existence to the presence of activities with economies of scale or density, and to transportation costs. With no transportation costs, activity would be scattered at random. With no economies of scale, all activity would be carried on in hamlets on a household scale to minimize transportation costs. In order to reduce transportation costs and take advantage of economies of scale, people live in dense settlements.

Marginal Cost User Fees

WITH BOTH ECONOMIES of scale and transport costs, it is efficient to organize economic activity unevenly over space, with cities being locations at which economic activity is concentrated.

Decentralization of the efficient allocation requires pricing all goods and services, including public services, at short-run marginal social cost. The competitive free market is justified on the basis that it accomplishes this result for activities without economies of scale or where these economies are exhausted. For activities with economies of scale, pricing at marginal social cost will in general not cover total costs. A subsidy is then required if output is to be pushed to the point of taking full advantage of these economies. What should the source of the subsidy be?

Here, I propose that the subsidy should be covered by a tax on site values—the value of urban locations. Marginal cost pricing of

*1996 Nobel Laureate in Economic Science; former President of the American Economic Association; McVickar Professor of Economics Emeritus, Columbia University, New York.

all goods and services, along with a tax on site values to finance the deficit of increasing returns activities, is both efficient and equitable.

The mispricing of public services will reduce the potential benefits from urbanization. A subsidiary aim of this discussion is to examine how badly distorted the pricing of particular public services is in practice and what marginal cost pricing of these services would entail.

Site Value Taxation

IN ORDER TO permit marginal cost pricing of urban services, a subsidy is required to cover the fixed costs. The best source of that subsidy is revenue derived by taxing the rental value of land or sites.[2] That value is created in part by the very services for which the site value tax will pay. Taxes on site rents are therefore an efficient, equitable, and adequate method of subsidizing services that are priced at marginal cost.

Site value taxation is nothing new. It is already a component of the property tax, which is actually two taxes in one. The property tax combines one of the best and one of the worst taxes we have. The portion of the tax that falls on sites or land values is the only major tax that is reasonably free of distortionary effects and is not intolerably regressive. The taxes on improvements and personal property are more difficult to assess properly. They impose excess burdens through undue discouragement of such investment.

In the next section, I shall show how, under suitable assumptions, these urban site rents (over and above the rent on peripheral rural land) will be just sufficient, no more and no less, to provide the subsidies needed to supplement marginal cost pricing.

Demonstrating the Principle with Models

A Linear City Model

In order to see why site value taxes are just adequate to subsidize urban services that are priced at marginal cost, let us consider a simple one-dimensional model.[3] Imagine a city laid out on a strip of oceanfront of uniform width. Imports can be landed and exports dispatched indifferently on any point on the frontage, but local (coastwise) transportation has a line-haul cost proportional to distance.

Activities with economies of scale can be represented as having a fixed cost consisting of imports, variable costs consisting of imports, local outputs of other activities and land, all varying in proportion to output.

If an activity wishes to increase the frontage it occupies, it will thereby increase the distance freight must be carried past this frontage, and require encroachment on the rural land at the edge of the city. The marginal social cost of its land occupancy is thus equal to the rural rental cost of the land plus the cost of the transportation along its frontage. Total land rents equal line-haul transportation costs plus rural rents for equivalent space.

If the city is in competition with other similar cities, and there is no scarcity of land strips on which cities can be established, competition will drive world prices of its inputs and outputs to the point where it is operating at the minimum point on its average total cost curve, and the city as a whole would just break even. Less favorable prices would cause the city to go out of business, and more favorable prices would stimulate the establishment of new cities.

Urban services providers (whether cities, counties, or special districts) err in both directions by pricing either above or below marginal cost. Some services, such as street parking, are provided at a price well below the marginal cost.[4] This results in a shortage of those services and in congestion. In other cases, such as certain public transit routes, the charge is often well above the marginal cost, contributing to underuse. Finally, a flat-rate structure, for water and sewer services, for example, might mean that some customers will pay more than the marginal cost, while others will pay less. Central city residents might thus cross-subsidize the extension of services into distant suburbs. Not only does that entail a transfer of wealth from cities to suburbs, it also means that services are not supplied where they are most valued. The entire urban economy becomes distorted, as does the spatial structure of cities.

Line-haul distances will vary in proportion to the output and size of the city, as will also freight volumes, so that transportation costs vary as the square of the output of the city.[5] Marginal transportation costs will be twice average transportation costs. Where average total cost is a minimum, marginal cost equals average cost, so that total fixed cost equals total transportation cost equals the excess of land rents over rural rents.

More Realistic Models

A similar, but somewhat more complicated analysis, can show the same result for two- and three-dimensional models, except that for the two-dimensional models excess land rent and fixed costs are equal to one-half of the local transportation costs. Also, if we have such elements as locally produced components of fixed costs, land used in transportation, line-haul transportation costs not proportional to distance, and the like, precise modeling becomes dauntingly complex, but the main result—that site rents in excess of rural values will remain just sufficient to cover the subsidies needed to implement marginal cost pricing—seems reasonably robust. However, if city sites with special characteristics, such as harbors, are limited in supply, this would tend to produce rents exceeding the subsidy requirements.

Application to Specific Services

THE EFFICIENCY OF marginal cost pricing applies to all goods and services. In the context of public services, users should pay marginal costs and site owners should pay the fixed costs through a tax on site rates. In what follows, I illustrate what marginal cost pricing entails for specific public services and how considerably such marginal cost pricing is at variance with current practice.

Fire Protection

Superficially, the beneficiaries of fire protection are the owners of the combustible property. But the cost of providing fire protection of a given grade to a given area is at least 80 percent independent of the number of combustible structures in the area, aside from the pathological cases like the South Bronx. Direct costs of responding to alarms amounts to a relatively small part of the total cost, as does the value of the impairment in the service quality resulting from the possibility that the unit may be out on another call when a new call comes in. Costs are chargeable 80 percent or more to land occupancy, and only 20 percent or less to possession of combustible property.

Utilities

Water mains, sewers, telephone lines, cable services, power lines must all be carried past property whether the occupant uses the service or not, and a large part of the cost is independent of the quantity of the service used. The independent costs comprise the portion that should be paid by property owners. Their property values reflect the availability of those services. The actual per-unit costs should be paid by customers.

Land holders should expect to pay for access to utilities, whether or not they use them, for the same reason that car renters should expect to pay for headlights and windshield wipers, whether or not they use them. One cannot expect to avoid paying for the headlights or windshield wipers on a rental car merely because one is not going to drive at night or in rainy weather. Similarly, tennis players will pay more to play on a court next to a fire house, because it is located in a neighborhood where these various services are available. The tennis court benefits from the provision of fire services even if it can never catch fire. And even if it did not benefit, it would be reasonable to charge the tennis court for appropriating some of the limited land that is served by fire protection. Rents in Westport are what they are because of the subways in New York, even though Westport residents never set foot inside the subway but all work in such places as the Pan Am building.[6]

Postal Service

In the case of mail service, financing of pick-up and delivery services in part from site value taxes would open up the possibility for keeping decisions as to the nature and frequency of such services in local hands, leaving the national postal service with the job of transporting mails between offices and performing some of the sorting operations.

Pricing of Streets, Bridges, and Other Congested Facilities

Congestion pricing of streets and bridges is a more specialized case than the others. The full marginal cost of driving on city streets would include the variable costs of pavement wear, police and emergency services, and accident costs not covered by private insurance. However, the marginal cost is close to zero for most of the physical infrastructure and services provided for street use. Most of the cost should therefore be paid out of site value taxes. The largest portion of marginal cost is the delay motorists impose on each other by creating congestion.[7]

Dramatic congestion relief can be obtained by applying short-run marginal social cost pricing to street networks. For much of the day, traffic densities exceed that for which flow is a maximum. By pricing street use in such a way as to keep accumulation of traffic in the congested area below the maximum flow point, flows at the height of the peak can be significantly increased, and possibly aggregate flows for the day as a whole; speeds will be increased generally, except possibly for brief shoulder periods where traffic is being shifted out of the peak; noise and air pollution will be reduced; and substantial revenues will be obtained that can be used to subsidize transit or reduce other taxes.[8]

In the case of a bridge, the fixed cost should be borne by the property owners in the area at both ends of the bridge, who benefit from the increased activity and convenience. Vehicles at peak hours should be charged a congestion toll—a user fee equal to the external cost a vehicle imposes on other vehicles. The marginal external social cost of a trip is measured by the time from the passage of the bottleneck to the next gap in the flow of traffic. Rather than charging on the basis of the actual duration ex post, one can properly charge on the basis of the expected duration estimated from past experience for comparable recent periods.

If charges are levied according to the rules indicated above, an equilibrium will eventually be reached in which all users reach their destinations with less delay by paying a premium (peak-period) toll approximately equal to the value of the time saved by the marginal driver.[9] If part or all of the revenue from the premium toll is used to reduce the base toll, nearly everyone will be made better off.[10] Airport take-off and landing fees are similar to bridge tolls.[11] Runway charges should reflect the marginal social cost that planes impose by pre-empting valuable take-off and landing times. Auctioning of time slots differentiated by time of day and week is one possibility, though some modifications may be desirable to take account of the differences in the strength of the vortexes produced by lighter and heavier planes. Under some conditions the airspace requirements of a small plane may actually be greater than for larger planes due to the differences in speeds. Some concessions may also be in order for scheduled flights to or from points with which service is relatively infrequent or in smaller planes, due to the stronger economies of scale prevailing under such circumstances.

Transit Fares

Transit fares are badly in need of revision to promote more efficient use of the service provided, including drastically reduced fares for short-haul and off-peak service, and through fares for multi-mode trips. Thus, the first reform that is needed is the limitation of routes to ones that increase site values by an amount greater than the fixed cost of the route. Along the routes that remain, the second reform should be instituted: the application of marginal cost pricing. This might be accomplished either with zone fares or by charging passengers less who ride only a short distance, especially over segments and at times where there are ample numbers of empty seats. The reduction should be around 10 cents per half mile on uncongested segments and perhaps 25 cents per half mile under severe crowding conditions.[12]

Another vital step is to provide for through bus-subway fares to reduce discrimination between transit modes and the use of inefficient routings.[13] At transfer stations, magnetic cards can be used to obtain one-way or two-piece round trip transfers for a suitable charge, without the need to wait for the installation of equipment on busses.[14] Transfers should not be entirely free, to discourage the use of busses for very short segments which often will be the peak load portion of the bus trip.

Starting from an Imperfect World

THE PRICING OF services in actual cities does not come close to the efficient ideal. Businesses are forced to pass on the excess burden of costs associated with the inefficient pricing of municipal services. Prices in the world market generally exceed the minimum average costs that would be attainable in an efficiently run city—one where activities are subsidized by site rent taxation. The way is therefore open for any given city to go ahead with such a program, and, for the time being at least, make a profit until such a time as other cities follow suit and compete the profits away.

In the meantime, in the medium long run, it would be profitable for the landowners of a city to get together and agree to tax themselves to provide the subsidies necessary to bring their local service prices down to marginal cost, thereby increasing the efficiency of the city. In the not too long run they would themselves be the beneficiaries of this increased efficiency: returns to mobile capital are set in regional and national markets, as to a lesser extent are wages; thus it is the landlords, as the owners of the main immobile factor, that stand to gain the most from an increase in the efficiency of the local economy.

Conclusion

CITIES HAVE THE capacity to be fully self-financing without dependence on either federal assistance or on general taxes that are unrelated to benefits received. As I have explained here, in an efficient city the government should price all public services at marginal cost, and finance the deficit from activities with economies of scale through a subsidy.

Even without outright subsidy, changing pricing patterns in the direction of marginal cost plus a premium would produce a vast increase in the efficiency of the city. Road pricing of overcrowded streets (properly applied with electronic techniques) can result in higher speeds and traffic flows, and reduced air and noise pollution. Responsive pricing of electric and telephone services can improve patterns of usage, lower overall costs, and provide increased reliability. Transit fares are badly in need of revision to promote more efficient use of the service provided, including drastically reduced fares for short-haul and off-peak service, and through fares for multi-mode trips.

Ideally, the subsidy to services priced at marginal cost should come from site value taxes, which merely captures the economic surplus produced by urbanization. It would provide revenues to replace taxes having excess burdens, such as sales taxes, wage taxes, and the property tax. Site value taxation is thus the key to a drastic improvement of the economic efficiency of cities.

Notes

1. *Editor's note:* This essay is an edited version of the notes Prof. Vickrey used for two lectures he gave in New York on October 15 and 17, 1991, one at the University Club and the other at St. John's University. The title of his St. John's lecture was "Site Value Taxes and Public Services." The title of the University Club lecture was "Notes on Land, Traffic and Markets." The St. John's lecture was largely theoretical, with few examples, and the University Club lecture was primarily case studies with little theory. Since the themes of the two lectures were similar, and neither was in final form for publication, it seemed appropriate to combine them into a single essay, retaining as much of the original language as possible. Some of the material in this essay was published in Wenzer (1998), which contains three other essays by Prof. Vickrey.

2. Urban site value generated by the availability of various goods and services close at hand in the city is to be distinguished from rural land value related to the "original and indestructible powers of the soil." In other words, site values are a product of location, not of the quality of the land itself.

3. *Editor's note:* The author first expounded his linear city model in Vickrey 1969. At that time he called it the "littoral city." I am indebted to Prof. Mason Gaffney for this information.

4. Charges for street parking should be based on the added difficulty that occupancy of space imposes on others seeking to park. In practice this can be approximated by a rule that whenever, in a given neighborhood, during a given time slot, fewer than 2 to 5 percent vacancies are observed over a suit-

able period, charges should be increased, and whenever vacancies average 10 to 20 percent, charges should be reduced (to zero in some cases).

5. *Editor's note:* An example may help. Tripling output alone causes a tripling of distance traveled (three times as many freight cars filled, traveling the same distance). Tripling the length of the city (and track length) to accommodate the increased output triples the distance traveled *per freight car*. Tripling the units of travel and of distance traveled means a nine-fold increase in transportation costs. Prof. Nicolaus Tideman was helpful in clarifying Prof. Vickrey's meaning here.

6. *Editor's note:* Westport is in southwest Connecticut. From Westport one can take a Metro North train to Grand Central Station, immediately below the Pan Am building.

7. Another cost motorists impose on each other and on third parties is air pollution. A surcharge could be added to capture that cost: it would be adjusted according to each model year's standard emissions rating, where it is driven, and local conditions (such as inversions). A well-maintained vehicle could be submitted for voluntary inspection to show that it performed better than the standardized rating, thereby qualifying it for lower pollution fees. (Testing could then be more stringent and costly, as it would usually be undertaken only when likely to prove worthwhile.) Heavily polluting vehicles that are driven mostly in areas of little pollution would not pay much. An incentive system would encourage rural drivers to buy polluting vehicles from urban owners. This would be much more effective in reducing urban pollution than applying uniform standards to all new vehicles.

8. The simplest implementation consists of units carried by all vehicles operating in the congested area, operating on power beamed from roadside scanners and responding with a signal identifying the vehicle. If the area is divided into zones with scanners at all thoroughfares crossing zone boundaries, charges can be computed based on the trip segment at a given time from the entry point to the exit point of each controlled zone traversed. Systems have been available at least since 1959, and have been since upgraded and thoroughly tested.

More sophisticated methods are being studied involving the use of "smart cards" and moderately elaborate apparatus on the car permitting the driver to be given an immediate indication of charges as they accumulate, as well as providing anonymity for those concerned with the privacy red herring. In some versions the charge would be related to the speed or delay experienced by the vehicle itself, but this seems undesirable both because of the incentive it would provide for aggressive driving and because the relation between delay experienced and delay caused by a particular vehicle is at best loose and indeed often inverse.

9. It is important that the tolls rise and fall gradually. Otherwise, half or more of the benefit will be lost, and difficulties may be encountered with

racing or lagging when tolls change. Adjustments are also needed for casual users. They might be provided with rebate vouchers realizable as lottery tickets or redeemable at service stations.

10. One can guarantee that absolutely no one is made worse off by providing a lay-by in which those who so desire can wait for a period equal to the reduction in the queuing time resulting from the change in regime and obtain a voucher entitling him to pay only the old toll.

11. In addition to auctioning runway rights, additional charges might be imposed on the noise emitted by aircraft (similar to the pollution charges discussed in note 7 above). The charge might vary by time of day (higher at night), but it should not vary according to the runway used, since air traffic controllers can already take noise factors into consideration in assigning runways. An incentive approach is more efficient than uniform regulations. It allows each airline to adjust operations in the least costly fashion: by assigning the noisier aircraft to airports that are less subject to noise constraints, by exchanging planes between airlines, and by retrofitting planes.

12. The ability to differentiate between short-haul and long-haul trips depends on technology. Marginal cost pricing could be implemented without waiting for a full complement of magnetic equipment, however, by providing for the sale by agents to short-haul riders of pre-imprinted magnetic cards for $5, $10, and $20, to be inserted in a magnetic entry turnstile which will deduct the regular fare (possibly plus a small premium to discourage use for regular fares) from the balance and imprint the time and place of entry. Short-haul riders can then insert the card in an adjustment register outside the controls at the destination station to have the appropriate amount rebated. Longer-haul riders would continue to use tokens for the time being. Balances too small for entry could be added to balances on new cards at the adjustment registers.

13. *Editor's note:* It is evident here and in the previous and following notes that Prof. Vickrey was thinking in terms of the subway system in New York City, where he lived. It is harder to imagine how his proposals would work for an urban-suburban bus system in smaller cities such as Denver or Cleveland.

14. It is likely to prove politically unpopular, and in many cases it will be economically inefficient, to differentiate fares between, say, a 6-mile trip on a given train and a trip to the end of the line, cars in most cases having to be carried to the end of the line whether occupied or not. Differentiation can result in inefficient routing where passengers have a choice as to where they will board the train. In some cases a suitable incentive can be provided for passengers to select less crowded transfer points. For example, passengers between Flushing and downtown can be offered a small fare reduction for transferring at Queensboro Plaza, 6th Ave. or Times

Square rather than at Grand Central, implemented by their inserting their magnetic cards in a register in the transfer station with the lower fare.

What Do We Need to Know about Land Value Taxation?

By DICK NETZER*

Introduction

MORE THAN A century ago, Henry George concluded that poverty existed in America's rapidly growing cities in the midst of unparalleled rates of economic growth and prosperity for some people because the owners of land and other "natural opportunities," who do not contribute to the productive process, were appropriating the fruits of labor and capital. His solution lay in the taxation of the rent of land and natural opportunities—that is, the recapture of rent for public use, rather than the taxation of labor and capital. George's insights were foreshadowed in the writings of the classical economists a few generations before him. They, however, had not pressed ahead with the policy implications; in *Progress and Poverty*, George did just that.

The political movement created by that book had some early, partial successes in the form of adoption of various types of differentially heavy taxes on land. But, by World War I, the momentum had given out, and there were some retrograde developments, like reducing the already low taxes on land in some places (notably, the local "rates" in England and Wales). There have been very few political successes since then.

In recent years, more and more public finance and urban economists have had positive things to say about land value taxation, but with no policy effect. That lack of success has always been something of a mystery, and there are various unproven hypotheses to explain away the mystery. At least one explanation that has a degree of plausibility is that land value taxation has an antiquarian flavor about it. From this perspective, it was a good

*Professor Emeritus of Economics and Public Administration, Wagner Graduate School of Public Administration, New York University.

idea in its time (when the only important level of government in the U.S. was local, and the only important tax was the property tax), but the world is so much more complicated today, and its problems call for complicated solutions. So there is an obvious challenge: is land value taxation still relevant to and feasible in today's world? To respond, we need to answer the question in the title of this essay: what do we need to know about land value taxation?

Economists and Land Value Taxation: Then and Now

I AM ABOUT to take some liberties, but the story might best begin by looking, in very general terms, at what we economists knew about land value taxation thirty years ago and what we know now. I choose thirty years ago, because there was little attention by economists—in North America or anywhere else—to the property tax, in any of its manifestations, from about 1930 until the 1960s. In the U.S., most public finance economists had been convinced that the property tax was a dying, anachronistic institution by three factors: 1) decades of savage criticism of the low quality of tax administration, which had not improved much, 2) the collapse in property tax collections during the Great Depression of the 1930s, and 3) its replacement by state-collected sales or income taxes. As late as 1956, a leading economist forecast that, in another 20 years, "the property tax will . . . have become an all-but-forgotten relic of an earlier fiscal age" (Mitchell 1956). Even as he wrote, however, the role of the property tax in American state and local finance had stabilized. A new decline began in the mid-1960s, to be followed by stabilization in the years since 1980, but in the late 1950s, economists began to examine the property tax once again, and an extensive literature emerged.

What did we learn specifically about land value taxation from that literature? As you will see, I do not think we learned a great deal. To me at least, that is reason enough for first-rate scholars to direct their attention to the appropriateness of land value taxation in the contemporary world, which is now being done under the sponsorship of the Lincoln Institute of Land Policy.

Thirty Years Ago

The state of knowledge of land value taxation in the economics profession up through the 1960s can be summarized as follows:

1) The theoretical literature on land value taxation after Henry George was very sparse indeed. In fact, the only noteworthy theorizing was done by Harry Gunnison Brown, a person whose name few recall, who spent his long career at the University of Missouri, in the 1920s. Brown said to me twenty years ago that his main contribution was to put the theory in the language of contemporary economics. I think he went further, by analyzing how *other* taxes (notably consumption taxes) created substantial deadweight losses in the form of distortion of economic choices, to the extent that those taxes are not shifted backward to landowners.

2) The very *definitions* of what precisely, land value taxation is—which was clear enough to Henry George—had been muddled by his critics, particularly the virtually "sainted" Richard B. Ely.[1] Advocates of land value taxation frequently spoke of quite different taxes as if they were truly taxes that recapture the rent of land, and they seemed ready to accept "approximations" that sometimes had little in common with land value taxation.[2]

3) There was almost no scientific evidence on the effects of land value taxation in practice. There were anecdotes about the effects of differentials in the taxation of land and buildings in different places in English-speaking countries, but the anecdotes were utterly unpersuasive. Frequently, they had the character of visions seen by the devout. In part, this was because the real-life cases were few, idiosyncratic, and rather distant from rigorously-defined land value taxation.

4) While all advocates would have agreed in principle that land value taxation required proper valuation of land, many seemed willing to accept extremely bad valuation practices and used data from such practices as arguments in their anecdotes. There was little serious attention to valuation issues.

5) There had been almost no empirical work on the issue of the capitalization of taxes into prices of land, aside from a bit of work on farmland done in the 1920s and summarized in Jensen's splendid 1931 book on the property tax in the United States.

Where Are We Today?

Based on work done in the last thirty years, we know a bit more now than we did in the 1960s:

1) There has been some theoretical work on land value taxation, but not a great deal. One strand of this is within the field of urban economics. William Vickrey, among others (but he most forcefully) advanced the theorem of the optimal system of urban public finance: marginal cost pricing plus land value taxation, the latter to cover services where marginal cost is below average cost and to finance services not suitable for marginal cost pricing (Solow and Vickrey 1971; Vickrey's essay in this volume). The implications of this have had some attention, beyond the virtually universal acceptance of the theorem by urban economists.

2) Another strand has been the theorizing about the effects of land value taxation on the timing of development, which has had some interesting theoretical fall-out (Arnott 1996). The outcome of the timing controversy has been real attention to the definition of land value taxation. Again, Vickrey (1970) had no doubt about this, but the issue of how to define land value taxation was treated properly only after the charge was made that it distorted the timing of development.[3]

3) There has been some serious empirical work on the effects of actual cases of differential taxation of land. The persuasive studies have shown mixed results. The Australian studies show virtually no effects (but in the context of trivial tax rates); the Pennsylvania studies funded by the Lincoln Institute showed strong positive effects for Pittsburgh and no statistically significant effects for the smaller cities (Woodruff and Ecker-Racz 1969; Oates and Schwab 1997).[4]

4) While advocates typically remain airy about implementation with respect to valuation, a number of writers and practitioners have given the issue serious attention. However, I see some retrogression in the advice now being given by American experts to would-be taxers of real property in the formerly Communist countries, along the lines that anything is good enough to start with.

5) Perhaps the biggest change has been the extensive amount of work done on capitalization of tax differentials. Despite the extraordinary difficulty of empirical work in this area, that work has led to a fairly clear understanding of how the process really works, and what impedes rapid capitalization, an understanding that is essential in a newly introduced land value taxation system. (See, for example, Case 1978 and Yinger et al. 1988.)

Future Research Needs

SO, WHAT *DO* we need to know? In order to make land value taxation intellectually and politically acceptable, a number of questions will need to be resolved with further research.

1) The Ethics of Land Value Taxation

To Henry George, land value taxation was the efficient way of raising money for government, but the main argument was an ethical one. It is the ethical argument that spawned a Georgist movement. The fundamental ethical justification proposed by Henry George for land value taxation was, as is well known, the fact that the site value is created not by the individual owners of sites but by the community, acting in two capacities. First, the larger community was the provider of infrastructure (often through private monopoly utilities awarded territorial exclusivity and eminent domain powers by political bodies) and of the legal institutions of land ownership and land use. Second, the community, in the shape of markets, was the means that caused local economies to grow and develop. The ethical conclusion is that the community, not the individual site owners, should recoup the fruits of these community actions.

An important contemporary dimension of this is the ethical appropriateness of taxing land rents where local governments exercise land use controls and continually act to increase land values in their communities. Indeed many local governments act as if their main goal were to maximize land values within the jurisdiction. Under these circumstances, land value taxation may or may not be an ethical improvement. Moreover, land use controls have a mixed press among economists. On the one hand, the existence of land use controls is essential to the one efficiency solution for the local public goods problem that economic theory has offered, the Tiebout solution (Tiebout 1956). On the other hand, land use controls increase the costs of housing and urban public services, and almost certainly have inequitable effects among income groups in urban areas. It is not clear how land value taxation would affect that argument.

There is also need to examine, in the contemporary context, the most common ethical criticisms of land value taxation. One problem is that recent buyers of land unjustly become victims when a new or greatly increased land value tax is instituted. (Is this a more or less serious issue today than it was decades ago?) A second problem is the existence of other types of economic rents that go largely untaxed, which struck the opponents of Henry George as terribly important a century ago. Interestingly, some of the leading scholars in the field of taxation now maintain that the income tax can be truly equitable and efficient only if "income" is defined as ability or capacity, that is, the natural opportunity biology affords individuals. This would convert the tax into one on non-land rents. If we say, crudely, that any wages and salaries earned in excess of $20,000 reflect differential innate ability, then there was about $1.3 trillion in this type of economic rent reported on federal individual income tax returns in 1993 (*U.S. Bureau of the Census 1996*, Table 527), which probably is in excess of the economic rent stemming from land.

2) Efficiency in Land Use

Urban economists generally agree that land value taxation is likely to be neutral in its effects on land use in most respects, unlike other forms of taxation, especially the conventional American property tax. It is, therefore, regarded as more efficient. But there are a host of questions, granted the validity of the theoretical proposition. For example, how dependent is this outcome on the precise definition of taxable land value? Quantitatively, how much improvement in the efficiency of land use can be expected over time? To what extent will imperfect, but still good, administration vitiate the efficiency properties of the tax? In practice, how would a change to land value taxation change or redistribute land uses? How much delay in approaching efficiency can be expected from the existence of long-lived buildings on most urban land?

Also, how would land value taxation interact with land use regulation? One can imagine both complementarity and substitution. What other kinds of taxes or fees are most compatible with land value taxation, that is, would not undo the positive effects of land value taxation? This last question directly concerns the widespread use of so-called impact fees in many parts of the country.

There is little research extant that addresses any of these questions. The empirical research noted above on the impact of land value taxation deals with the question of whether additional investment is elicited by a switch to land value taxation, not with efficiency per se.

3) The Distribution of Income and Wealth

George attracted many followers with the proposition that land value taxation would alleviate poverty and the unequal access to economic resources. Economic theory and even superficial observation suggest that this must be so: poor people are not the important owners of land and other natural opportunities. The illiquidity of such assets and the need for access to large amounts of relatively low-interest credit would guarantee the result. But *how much* is this so, in our world, where two-thirds of households are owners of the urban land under their houses and people of moderate means have substantial ownership, albeit indirect, of corporate assets, including land and other natural opportunities? To the extent that the proposition is true (that the poor own few assets), a shift from a relatively proportional national tax system to land value taxation (if it amounted to a non-trivial fraction of total tax revenue) would make the distribution of tax burdens by income class more progressive.

Another set of questions is how land value taxation would affect the distribution of income and wealth among groups of households measured by characteristics other than income—age, homeownership, and so on. For example, it seems likely that a quantitatively significant amount of land value taxation would reverse the long trend toward relatively low tax burdens on older people.

The answers to these questions call for systematic and logically consistent tracing of the potential impacts. Data on land ownership are anything but explicit, so this effort entails piecing together data to make plausible estimates about the ownership of land and the income and wealth distribution of those owners. And having made such estimates, we need to compare them with estimates of the incidence of the major existing tax sources.

4) Relevance and Feasibility of Land Value Taxation in Rich Countries

The fundamental questions about the efficiency and equity of land value taxation may be answered positively, as they have been over the years, and in convincing quantitative terms, without being any more persuasive than has been the case in the past. Practical policy-makers generally seem to believe that land value taxation is not only politically poisonous, but also irrelevant to current tax policy and administratively infeasible.

As a policy matter, "relevance" means first, whether land value taxation has sufficient revenue potential to be a serious substitute for other sources of revenue and, second, whether it meets the revenue needs of different levels of government. (It has ordinarily been proposed as a local government tax in rich countries.) "Feasibility" involves questions of administrative capabilities. In the few rich countries in which there is substantial use of the conventional property tax as a source of local government finance, notably the U.S., Canada, Japan, and, to some extent, the U.K., the policy question often is posed as conversion of the conventional property tax into one on land only. Feasibility is less in question in such countries, although the administrative issues are far from trivial. In other rich countries, in which there is little or no use of the conventional property tax, the land value tax may be both relevant and feasible, but there is more argument about that. However, even in such countries, there is a lively interest in decentralization, and some forms of "recurring taxes on immovable property" (the OECD term for property taxes) are often suggested as instruments of local fiscal autonomy.[5]

Many poor countries, especially those in transition from Communist systems, also have a lively interest in decentralizing government and, in some countries, in using property-tax-like fiscal institutions that are often rudimentary, but sometimes quite sophisticated. The question of relevance and feasibility in poor countries is noted below. But there are a number of reasons why there is a great deal to be learned from inquiring about the question in the rich-country context, for the following reasons.

- National tax systems have been in place for some time without major changes in nearly all rich countries: in Europe, for twenty years or more; in Japan, North America, Australia, and New Zealand for even longer. Therefore, there is a bias against radical changes, at least in political terms, which is often not the case in developing and transitional countries. So, skeptics might argue that land value taxation has little policy relevance for the rich countries.
- The efficiency costs of the existing tax systems are fairly well understood, and the efficiency gains from moving to the superior tax instrument, land value taxation, can be estimated with some confidence. For example, Martin Feldstein recently estimated that the economic losses to the American economy from an increase in the overall level of taxation (presumably, a proportional increase in all major tax sources) may equal as much as 165 percent of the additional revenue collected (Feldstein 1997, 210–11).[6] Nicolaus Tideman has estimated that, if Feldstein's estimate of the marginal economic cost of public funds is correct, the average economic cost is probably 45 percent of the total revenue collected (Tideman 1997). Thus, a major shift to land value taxation, which has no efficiency costs, would reduce the efficiency losses of the tax system by more than 45 percent of the amount of the shift.
- The effects of tax policy choices on the distribution of income and wealth has been a central concern in these countries for a very long time, certainly for as long as representative political institutions have been important. The advent of relative afflu-

ence, notably in the past fifty years, has made all these countries social-democratic to some extent; one aspect of this ideological transformation is widespread agreement that tax policy should be shaped to attempt some redistribution, even at some cost in economic efficiency. Redistributive land value taxation would be highly relevant to rich democratic countries, if their voters were persuaded that land value taxation is in fact appropriately redistributive.

- Land value taxation seems more feasible in rich countries than in poor ones, because the former generally have decent tax administration, which makes a sophisticated new tax relatively easy to implement. The quality of tax administration varies considerably among the rich countries and in some countries is far from matching best practice, but the situation is far better than in most countries in the Second and Third Worlds.
- Another dimension of feasibility is the presence and quality of legal and administrative machinery for establishing and recording land ownership, rights in land, and transactions in land rights. Once again, the rich countries, whether they operate under common or civil law systems, have land registration systems that work reasonably well. This is true of some poorer countries, but by no means all of them.
- Where there are existing real property taxes in use in the rich countries, those tax instruments—albeit highly imperfect in every such country—usually are serious, functioning ones. That is far from the case with existing land taxes in nearly all formerly Communist countries and most developing countries.
- Local government has varying degrees of fiscal importance in the rich countries, but is real and functioning in most of them. That is not true at all in many of the poor countries. This has to do with the issue of relevance, because of the strong case that can be made for land value taxation as the ideal local tax.

Although the efficiency gains of land value taxation can be achieved by any tax on owners of land (if the amount does not depend on how the land is used or any other actions by the owner), the equity gains are lost if a measure that does not reflect the relative personal wealth of the owner in terms of land is employed. So, we can say that the *feasibility* of land value taxation is likely to be greatest in countries that already have in place:

1) a serious (that is, non-trivial in amount) tax on the real value of property, and

2) the valuations made for this tax are, at least in intent, based on the current market value of real property, because there is little doubt that there is a strong positive correlation between the ownership of valuable land and the income and wealth of the owners of land.

So, the relative importance and nature of property taxation are important variables in considering feasibility. As for *relevance*, the importance of local infrastructure improvements and service levels in determining relative land values, as well as the historic association between property taxation and local government, suggests that land value taxation is likely to be most relevant where:

1) local governments are responsible for provision of most local infrastructure improvements and local services and have a good deal of discretion in making decisions about such expenditure, and

2) local governments with average economic capacity[7] must finance much of their expenditure from revenue they themselves generate, again with some discretion in how they do so.

What *are* the differences in fiscal structure that are used in the 23 "rich" OECD countries (OECD 1996)?[8] We start with the extent of centralization in the tax systems of these countries in 1994. In 18 of the 23 countries, the central government together with the social security systems accounted for 70 percent or more of the total tax revenue, in numerous cases more than 90 percent. Among the five decentralized "sports," three (Canada, Switzerland, and the U.S.) are federal in their formal structures, and two (Sweden and Denmark) are unitary. The three other federal countries (Australia, Austria, and Germany) are significantly less decentralized in their revenue systems than is true of the other federal countries. Some countries, like Belgium, Italy, and the Netherlands, in which there have been professions of interest in devolution, remain only trivially decentralized on the revenue side. The U.K. is now the most centralized among the middle-sized rich countries, after a long history in which it was among the least centralized.

There is no obvious explanatory factor for these differences, aside from the idiosyncratic political history of each country. The smaller countries in land area tend to be relatively centralized, but Switzerland and Denmark are among the smaller countries and quite decentralized. There is no visual or statistical relation between the size of the public sector and the extent of its centralization, although one can posit a plausible hypothesis that suggests that a larger public sector should be more decentralized, and another to the opposite effect. One might argue that, because decentralization of revenue systems probably is more costly administratively than centralization and surely will yield inter-area disparities in revenues, decentralization is a luxury for the richest among countries, but that hypothesis, too, is inconsistent with the data.

As might be expected, in some countries in which local governments are of minimal importance, central governments also make minimal efforts to collect and report data on the finances of local governments, so the OECD documents contain obsolete (or no) data on the nontax revenues and grants received by local governments for eight of the twenty-three countries. For the other fifteen, it is possible to put together a more complete picture of local government finances, in order to understand how land value taxation might be relevant.

Just how important are the revenue collection authority and responsibilities of subnational governments—including their financing by user charges and other nontax revenues—relative to the size of their economies? Own-source revenues of provincial and municipal governments combined are more than 10 percent of GDP in eight of the fifteen countries: three of the Nordic countries and all five of the federal countries. But local (municipal) government, by itself, does not reach the 10 percent level in any of the federal countries and is essentially trivial in Australia, where it amounts to about 2 percent of GDP.

The explanation for this is, of course, twofold: first, the spending responsibilities assigned to local government are very modest to begin with in Australia and Belgium, for example; second, local government spending is financed by grants, overwhelmingly in Ireland, the Netherlands, and the U.K. (In the federal countries, most grants to local government usually come from the intermediate level of government: states or provinces.) In fact, in nine of the fifteen countries, local governments finance less than 30 percent of their direct expenditure. Among the sources of own-source revenue, the variation in the relative importance of nontax revenue is less than the variation for other sources. As for local taxes, property taxes exist in thirteen of the fifteen countries, but they are overshadowed by other types of local taxes in eight of the thirteen.

Local government own-source revenue from the property tax is above 25 percent only in Australia, Canada, Ireland, the U.K., and the U.S. But that may be a misleading indicator of the *potential* for the use of land value taxation to finance local government expenditure. A better indicator may be the share of total general government revenue spent by local government in recent years. That is, if land value taxation, rather than grants from higher levels of government, were the sole or main source of financing local government, what share of total government revenue (all levels combined) would it account for?

In thirteen of the fifteen countries (all but Australia and Belgium), local government consumes 20 percent or more of total general government revenue. Nine reach the 25 percent level, and six reach the 30 percent level. That suggests the possibility of anything but a trivial role for land value taxation in many of the rich countries.

This is a static picture. The federal countries aside, in nearly all of the other rich countries examined here, there has been serious interest in more devolution to subnational governments. The U.K., for example, is developing a modified form of federalism.[9] A relatively small role at present for local government in the provision of public services and/or a very small degree of local financing of local expenditures may be subject to major changes in some countries. Thus, there could be a place for land value taxation in the most unlikely of countries, such as Italy, where devolution until now has simply meant more state grants to local governments to do things that are not very important (and where there are truly spectacular opportunities for the recapture of the rent of land, as in the Centro Storico of the Venetian commune). Still, feasibility and relevance are surely greatest in the more devolved countries in which there is some use of property taxation.

Earlier, I referred to estimates of the efficiency losses stemming from existing tax systems. Properly speaking, those estimates are of losses in output and consumer satisfaction caused by perfectly legal tax *avoidance*, that is, changes in decisions made by consumers and producers in response to taxation.[10] But there are other "deadweight losses," costs that, for the most part, are not measured in the usual estimates of efficiency losses.[11] These losses consist of administrative (collection) costs and compliance costs of taxpayers themselves.

The administrative costs to governments of collecting and enforcing the provisions of the tax law are generally not significant. In the U.S., such costs for income, payroll, and consumption taxes appear to be quite low as a percentage of the taxes actually collected, and that is the case in most of the other rich countries. There are some exceptions, however. Table 1 shows one of them: about one-half of all state governments permit vendors to deduct a specified percentage from the sales taxes they are obligated to remit to the state, as "compensation" for acting as tax collectors. That can increase administrative costs to as much as 4 percent of collections, which is not a small number.

In comparison to income and consumption taxes, property taxes are often considered to have high administrative costs, largely because the determination of tax liability—valuation of property—is done by the tax authorities, not self-reported and subject to verification by the authorities, as in the case of other taxes.[12] For example, in their 1994 survey, Joan Youngman and Jane Malm report that, in the Netherlands, the cost of valuation in municipalities with populations over 50,000 is more than 5 percent of tax collections. They also report a cost of valuation figure of roughly 2.5 percent in Britain, for a system of valuation that is mediocre in its results, to put it kindly.

In the U.S., at least in larger cities and counties, total administrative costs for property taxation have been considerably lower when tax administrators discover that strange innovation, the computer. For example, in New York City, such costs are less than one percent, despite an extremely heterogeneous tax base and a property tax law of unbelievable complexity.

Perhaps more important, valuation for land value taxation has to be vastly easier and cheaper than for conventional property tax. It is true that the location of every parcel of urban land is unique and, therefore, its value must differ a bit from that of adjacent parcels. But the differences are minimal, which is not the case for non-residential buildings. The historic charge, going back to Ely, that valuation for land value taxation *must* be more difficult than that of land and buildings taken together originates in the notion that the value of a parcel of urban land is the market value of the land and building taken together, less the depreciated replacement cost of the building. In fact, following that procedure is unlikely to result in a number that reflects site value accurately. In contrast, developing "contour maps" of site value per square foot or square meter from sales and demolition records is a simple process.[13]

It is also important to keep in mind that the quality of valuation for the existing property tax is not very good, even if we exclude the worst jurisdictions. A high standard of performance is considered to be a coefficient of dispersion of 20 percent of the median assessment-to-market-value ratio.[14] That would be considered an entirely unacceptable result from the standpoint of horizontal equity in income or sales tax administration.

Compliance costs are another dimension of tax efficiency. How much does compliance cost taxpayers? Taxpayer compliance costs are negligible in the aggregate for the existing property tax in the U.S. In some cities, owners of commercial buildings and apartments are required to file income and expense statements for each such property with the assessor.[15] There are some one-time costs where there are exemptions and abatements available, and there will be costs if the taxpayer payments during the year equal the tax levy for the year, because of payment of previous years' taxes. The point is that there is no practical way to evade taxes on real property.[16]

Together, the costs considered here—evasion, administration, and compliance—are massive for the major income and consumption taxes, about 30 percent for the federal income taxes and as much as 20 percent for state sales taxes, but perhaps less than 2 percent for land value taxation. Surely, this has a lot to do with the relevance of land value taxation.

However, because land value taxation in relatively pure form has never been implemented, it is not likely to be adopted in any rich country without some persuasive research into administrative and compliance issues. Realistic scenarios are needed about the likely consequences of adopting land value taxation in each country.

5) Relevance and Feasibility of Land Value Taxation in Developing and Transition (Formerly Communist) Countries

In many Third World countries, there is serious effort to substantially overhaul (and increase in importance) local governments and to provide them with revenue sources of their own. In a few cases, there are existing local property taxes. Sometimes, but not always, feasibility problems with land value taxation would be very great. The relevance, however, is obvious. Few of them can afford the very large efficiency losses that their existing tax systems probably cause. All need to minimize the regressivity of existing or likely tax instruments (that is, bad copies of those in use in rich countries).

The concern for a useful system of local government is, if anything, stronger in most of the "transition countries." The efficiency cost problem is especially severe in most of these countries, such as Russia, in which most of the goods-producing industries have been value-subtractors, not value-addors, for some years. Some seek to resurrect old systems of local government that may have had some utility in the past—in reality or in romantic imagination.[17] Others seek to create systems from scratch where they have never really existed, notoriously, in Russia, Belorussia, and Ukraine. Here, too, there is frequently interest in local reliance on some form of property taxation, which may already exist, though badly designed. This makes land value taxation relevant. In addition, there is often residual hostility to private ownership of land that could be overcome if the rent of land could be largely recaptured for public use. But the feasibility problems can be severe, at least during the extended periods when land markets are developing.

Numerous Western advisers have worked on these issues in the developing countries over the years and in the transition countries more recently. Their findings and the results of their policy recommendations for local government finance in developing countries are fairly persuasive. That is less the case in the post-Communist countries, where much of the technical advice urges those countries to replicate standard OECD country tax systems, and implement property tax systems that promise to be the antithesis of land value taxation. There is a lot more to be known about the likely problems and consequences of implementation of proper land value tax systems in these countries.

6) Consequences for the U.S. of Substantial Reliance on Land Value Taxation

Not since the works of Henry George has there been a systematic examination of what would happen to the U.S. economy as a whole if land value taxation were to substitute for other public revenue in most jurisdictions in the U.S. To examine this requires general equilibrium analysis for the entire economy of a scenario in which land value taxation is a major (though not exclusive) substitute for taxes on income, consumption, and capital. Unlike George's time, this is to be done in an era in which there is a lot of non-local government finance. The scenario I envisage is one in which land value taxation accounts for a significant (10 to 20 percent) share of all public sector revenue in the U.S., and the tax is either national or imposed everywhere at rates that are not wildly disparate. Also, it should be assumed for this analysis that only the U.S. and a few other countries impose the tax, while others are not using land value taxation. This would permit the analysis to take into account the openness of national economies. What might happen to the levels of capital formation, to aggregate incomes, to labor income?

This strikes me as a fairly straightforward analysis, albeit requiring the considerable oversimplification needed for computable general equilibrium models. It is almost impossible to argue the case for land value taxation if the analysis is not made.

7) Relative Merits of Land Value Taxation and Conventional State and Local Taxes

What are the local and national advantages of substituting land value taxation for other taxes? This needs to be determined in jurisdictions that rely heavily on consumption and income taxes: at the local level, particularly in large cities, and at the intermediate (state) level in most rich federal countries (including the U.S.). The substitution of land value taxes for local nonproperty taxes flies in the face of the advice of many American public finance experts, who strongly urge nonproperty taxes on the large cities and more generally. A shift by the state to this form of property taxation would reverse the major shift in state tax systems that took place sixty years ago. It seemed clear enough then, and for some decades afterward, in light of the dreadful (and seemingly unimprovable) quality of property tax administration and what we thought we knew about the economics of the property tax (notably its excise tax character at the local scale), that income and consumption taxes were the preferred alternatives. Henry George and his followers always disputed that conclusion, and they may have been right. In light of current knowledge about the deadweight losses and administrative burdens of other taxes, was the negative view of the property tax ever valid?

8) Land Value Taxation as a Cure for a Variety of Additional Economic Ills

George made a persuasive case that, in the American economy of 1879, reliance on a single tax that recaptured all the rent of land would cure an array of economic ills, especially the business cycle. We think we now know how to avoid wild swings in the economy, collapse of the financial system, and prolonged depression by means that are relatively benign. We also recognize the incredible complexity of the economic world today. As a result, few see the business cycle as one of the gravest of our economic ills. But long-term growth is another question, and one that George was concerned with.

Today it is appropriate to ask what a switch to land value taxation can contribute to sustainable growth, thus including environmental concerns. It is appropriate in this connection to define the tax more broadly, as one on the return from exploitation of any scarce resources that are not the product of human endeavor, but that are appropriable by private parties. Some of the answers to the questions may be implicit in or suggested by the answers to the questions posed earlier in this paper, but some are not.

Conclusion

IN THIS PAPER, I have assumed that most people who attend a lecture named for Henry George are likely to be at least sympathetic to the ideas associated with him. I have not tried to make a positive case for land value taxation, which seemed superfluous. What I have attempted is to deal further with what has always seemed to me a great mystery: why, given the virtues of land value taxation, has there been so little success in persuading governments to adopt it? Some years ago, I propounded the notion that at least part of the explanation, as far as this country is concerned, can be found in the strong antipathy among ordinary Americans against taxing unrealized capital gains, which land value taxation does (Netzer 1984). (We economists see no problem with this, but then we see no case for minimum wages, or for heavy taxation of the income from capital, or for barriers to international trade, or for numerous other things that enjoy wide popular support.)

In this paper, I have taken a different tack, addressing what surely is a less emotional cause for reluctance to adopt land value taxation: uncertainty as to how it would really work out in practice in the contemporary world. I have listed what I see as the reasonable person's hesitations, in the form of questions that researchers should be able to answer. The answers still may not be persuasive politically, but I think that answers that are intrinsically valid can be found. A group of economists, under the sponsorship of the

Lincoln Institute of Land Policy, are right now trying to find those answers.

Table 1

ESTIMATES OF THE COSTS OF TAX ADMINISTRATION, TAXPAYERS' COSTS OF COMPLIANCE, AND THE EXTENT OF TAX EVASION, FOR VARIOUS U.S. TAXES

Administrative costs:	
Percent of tax collections—	
U.S. individual income tax	0.6
State sales taxes	0.4–1.0
vendor compensation, in half of states	1.0–3.6
Taxpayers' compliance costs:	
Percent of taxes paid—	
U.S. individual income tax	9.0
State sales taxes	2.0–3.8
Tax evasion:	
Percent of legal liability not reported on tax returns ("tax gaps")—	
U.S. individual income tax	20.0
U.S. corporation income tax	22.7
State motor fuel taxes	6.5
State cigarette taxes	5.4
State sales taxes (but the mail order tax gap is estimated at 2.4 percent of total state sales tax collections)	< 5.0
State compensating use taxes	40.3
Delinquency rate for reported state sales tax liability (i.e., liability reported, but tax not paid)	13.0

Source: Mikesell (1997) and Murray (1997)

Notes

1. Ely was a co-founder of the American Economic Association and of a long-lived school of policy-oriented University of Wisconsin economists who tended to minimize attention to economic theory.

2. Examples of "approximations" are a) taxes on *increases* in land value, b) land value tax rates that are so low that they can have no discernible effect on behavior, and c) parcel taxes, which are levied per unit of land rather per unit of land *value*.

3. There are dozens of articles on this subject in economics journals. A few of the more important articles contending that land value taxation distorts the timing of development are Shoup (1969), Shoup (1970), Skouras (1978), and Bentick (1979). Tideman (1982, 1995) critiques the non-neutrality thesis, arguing that the authors who take that position have

analyzed a tax on the discounted future income of the planned use of a site, not a tax on the market value of the site, which is the value assessors aim to estimate. In an empirical test of the non-neutrality thesis comparing Wellington and Auckland, New Zealand, Roakes et al. (1994) find no evidence that land value taxation affects the timing of development.

4. Oates and Schwab (1997) is a good source for other empirical studies of Pennsylvania cities. Empirical studies of Australia are also available: Brown (1980) describes a study by Hutchinson (1963) that compared suburbs around Melbourne, which found those taxing land only (not buildings) had twice the value of residential improvements as those using a standard property tax. Edwards (1984) analyzed differences among tax jurisdictions in the Melbourne area with econometric models and found results similar to those of Hutchinson. By contrast, Lusht (1992a and 1992b) found little effect of land value taxation on housing construction around Melbourne, but a considerable effect on industrial development.

5. OECD stands for Organization for Economic Cooperation and Development. It consists of countries in Central and Western Europe and North America, plus Canada, Turkey, Japan, Korea, Australia, New Zealand, and Mexico.

6. Feldstein estimates that if all taxes (income tax, payroll tax, sales tax, property tax, etc.) were raised proportionally by enough to yield an additional (marginal) $100 of revenue, there would be a loss of private real income of not just $100 million, but an additional $165 million. This loss has three principal components: 1.) the loss of output from the fact that people would work less; 2.) plus the loss from a less efficient division of income between saving and consumption; 3.) minus the value of the additional leisure that people have because they work less. The loss from the first or middle $100 million of revenue is less than the last (marginal) $100 million, because when taxes are higher, people go to greater expense to avoid them. Thus the average cost of public funds ($45 per $100 in revenue) is considerably lower than the marginal cost.

7. The specification "average economic capacity" allows for a system of fiscal federalism in which the poorest places may receive so much in grants from higher levels of government that they do not in fact finance much of their spending from local taxes.

8. The OECD member countries excluded are the three recent Central European adherents (the Czech Republic, Hungary, and Poland) plus Mexico, and Turkey. The poorest member country included is Greece.

9. Scotland held a referendum on home rule in September 1997. Legislative bodies with specified responsibilities now exist in Scotland and Wales.

10. Tax avoidance affects decisions to invest, to work, and to save and choices made among inputs and consumption of goods and services.

11. A deadweight loss means costs not compensated by benefits, useful activities that would have taken place but did not, or activities that people must undertake that do not contribute to the total value of the economy's output of goods and services.

12. In the U.S., most states also subject non-real property in the form of business machinery and equipment and, less often, inventories, to property taxation. That is done on the basis of self-reporting, with minimal attempts at verification in almost all of the states. The result is that, in practice, the value subject to tax is rarely as much as 50 percent of the value that should be reported according to economic data.

13. Some writers have developed quite different methods of estimating land rents, but using methods that are quite expensive or entirely impracticable outside the pages of economics journals.

14. For those not familiar with the coefficient of dispersion, a simple example may clarify it. Suppose five houses have been sold in an area. The first one was assessed at $28,000, but it sold for $100,000. Thus, the assessment-to-market-value ratio for that house is 0.28. The ratios for the other four houses are 0.35, 0.40, 0.46, and 0.49. The median (middle) ratio is 0.40. The differences (treating negative numbers as positive) between the median and the other ratios are 0.12, 0.05, 0.06, and 0.09. The average of those differences (0.08) is their sum (0.32) divided by 4. The coefficient of dispersion is the average difference divided by the median (0.08 divided by 0.40), which is 0.2 or 20 percent.

15. For taxpayers who own only one such building, the marginal cost of compliance is the price of a postage stamp, since the appropriate federal income tax schedule is acceptable.

16. This is not true of personal property taxes, however.

17. I recall reading some 30-odd years ago in the leading Bogotá newspaper one of a series of essays by an economist who was about to be inaugurated as President of the Republic. The central point of the essays was the proposition that the "genius" of Colombia lay in its 880 *municipios*. I had just calculated that 850 of them did not have enough revenue to provide any public services at all, beyond the salaries of the *alcalde* (mayor), municipal clerk, and municipal tax collector.

SECTION 3

International Trade

Protection or Free Trade

An Analysis of the Ideas of Henry George on International Commerce and Wages

By THOMAS L. MARTIN*

Introduction

THE PROTECTIVE TARIFF became a divisive national issue in the United States with the nullification movement in South Carolina in the early 1830s. Fifty years later, when import competition increased following the recession of 1873–1878, reform of the tariff again became a critical national issue. As imports increased in the early 1880s, so did the political pressure to provide more protection from the growing import competition. At the same time, the opposite pressure to reduce tariffs was created by a persistent federal budget surplus. Reduction of revenues through lower tariffs became the Democratic solution, while the Republicans favored increased spending. This conflict of interests set the stage for the rise of the tariff issue to primary importance in national politics.

During this critical period, Henry George spoke out often and emphatically for free trade, although he was not a free trader from the beginning. As he explained,

> I was educated a protectionist and continued to believe in protection until I came to think for myself and examine the question (George, *TS*, 9/29/1888, IV, 13:1).

When he examined the question for himself, he concluded that tariff protection did not actually protect the workers of America because it failed to raise wages. In *Progress and Poverty*, George (*P&P*:18) stated his position clearly: the fallacies of protectionism have "a tenacious hold, in spite of their evident inconsistencies and absurdities." The survival of the mistaken idea, according to

*Associate Professor of Economics, University of Central Florida.

George, was due to the inappropriate acceptance of the wages-fund theory. This theory implied that since the total of all wages is fixed, the competition of foreign products or foreign labor would only further subdivide this fund and reduce wages. The answer was not protection, but the replacement of all taxes, including taxes on imports, with the single tax on increases in land values.

After the success of *Progress and Poverty* and his increased opportunities to speak on the issues of the day, George was eager to spread his ideas on import tariffs and the interests of labor. The protectionists in Congress had "so long held sway," according to George (*PFT*:205, 214), that for decades the protected industries had enjoyed it "all their own way." The time was right for popular education on the issue of taxation and tariffs, and with it, the means of bringing "the whole social question, into the fullest discussion" (George *TS*, 2/18/1888, III, 7:1).

To help promote such popular education, George published in 1886 his book *Protection or Free Trade: An Examination of the Tariff Question, with Especial Regard to the Interest of Labor.*[1] In addition to this book, he attacked what he called the "protectionist delusion" in a series of articles appearing in the *North American Review* in 1886 and 1887 entitled "Labor in Pennsylvania." Finally, he argued for free trade as the editor of *The Standard* from January 1887 until December 1890.

This paper demonstrates that George's ideas on protection and wages contained in these works were fundamentally sound. As Cord (1965:241) has suggested, Henry George "received less mention than is his due" in the field of history of economic thought, and this paper provides evidence from the field of international trade theory by examining George's analysis of the effects of free trade on relative wages. Section I examines George's thought on the trade issue within the setting of the political economy of the 1880s. Section II examines George's two factor trade model and compares it with the modern theory. Finally, Section III offers conclusions on the effects of George's work and the tariff reform efforts of the 1890s.

I

The Political Economy of Protection in the Early 1880s

NOT LONG AFTER *Progress and Poverty* appeared in 1879, interest in the tariff issue increased as the 1880 presidential campaign reached the party conventions. Garfield and the Republicans reaffirmed previously established beliefs that the tariff "levied for the purpose of revenue should so discriminate as to favor American labor" (Stanwood [1903] 1967, Vol. 2:199). George opposed this Republican doctrine because he believed it was not in the best interests of American labor, the Republican pronouncements notwithstanding. Instead, he would support the Democrats, who reaffirmed their belief in a tariff "for revenue only." The Republicans under Garfield went on to keep both the White House in 1880 and their majority in the House of Representatives. As a result, they also kept the primary responsibility for the reform of the tariff.

Despite the strong support for the protective tariff on the part of domestic producers in many states, there appeared to be room for optimism concerning the possibility of a downward revision of the tariff. President Chester A. Arthur appointed a Tariff Commission in 1882 to recommend a solution for the conflicts of interest involved in the reform of the tariff necessary to lower the budget surplus (Stanwood [1903] 1967, Vol. 2:204). The commission members were all favorable to the principle of protection, and as a result, the recommended tariff reforms did not seriously threaten the interests vested in the protective system (Stanwood [1903] 1967, Vol. 2:221). The resulting Tariff Act of 1883 lowered slightly the average rate of the tariff, while the tariff was increased on selected imported products which had domestic competition (Taussig [1885] 1893:249–50).

Despite the lack of true reform in the 1883 tariff, there remained room for optimism. After the new Congress was seated in the spring of 1883, the Democrats proposed a 20 percent across-the-board reduction in tariffs. This proposal was narrowly defeated (Stanwood [1903] 1967, Vol. 2:221). With the arrival of the presidential election season in 1884, even the Republican platform proposed to "correct the irregularities of the tariff" and reduce the federal surplus. According to the Republicans, this was to happen, of course, without "injuring the laborer" that received protection from the tariff (Stanwood [1903] 1967, Vol. 2:222).

The election of Democrat Grover Cleveland to the Presidency in 1884 provided hope for Henry George and many others that protectionism might be reversed through a judicious reform of the tariff. George wrote from England that the election of Cleveland must ultimately bring back the reality of the tariff question into national politics. The tariff question, George hoped, would be forced on the politicians after capturing the attention of the masses (Stanwood [1903] 1967, Vol. 2:204). It was during this optimistic time that Henry George began *his* work on *Protection or Free Trade*.

Unlike the Republican administrations, Cleveland appointed no protectionists to his first cabinet. In addition, Cleveland stated that a "certain reduction should be made in our customs revenue" within limitations, such that the industries and interests which have been encouraged by such laws "should not be ruthlessly injured or destroyed" (Nevins 1933:283, 282). After one year in office, President Cleveland made it clear that such limitations would be politically important:

> The question of free trade is not involved. Nor is there now any occasion for a discussion of the wisdom or expediency of a protective system. . . . (Stanwood [1903] 1967, Vol. 2:224–25)

Henry George worked to encourage such discussion. To that end, *Protection or Free Trade* was published in 1886.[2] With his book and his articles, George wanted to convince labor that his free trade philosophy was consistent with his previously held positions. George offered practical and philosophical arguments against the tariff in what Lissner (1980:xi) calls a "weapon worth an armory full." The actual tendency of the protective tariff, argued George (*PFT*:225), was "to lessen aggregate wealth, and to foster monopolies at the expense of the masses of the people." This was, of course, the message of Adam Smith and many of his followers.

"What protection teaches us," explained George (*PFT*:47), "is to do to ourselves in time of peace what enemies seek to do to us in time of war." George worked to prevent the protectionist war that was impending in the United States.

In January 1886, Cleveland stated that he would not use his influence to help pass tariff reform bills in Congress (Nevins 1933:287). As the year progressed, however, President Cleveland changed his mind, much to the pleasure of Henry George. In April, Cleveland stated his belief that workingmen felt "discrimination in favor of capital as an object of government attention" (Richardson 1896–1899, 1909:394). By June, he was talking to Republicans to urge them to support tariff reform efforts. Later that month, however, the tariff reform bill and Cleveland's position were rejected in the House of Representatives. Rather than ending the issue, however, this began the next great tariff struggle in American history. By December 1886, Cleveland had threatened Congress with a special session to discuss tariff reform. In his annual message that month, Cleveland declared that the popular demand for a lower tariff "should be recognized and obeyed" (Richardson 1896–1899, 1909:510). This was a "battle call" to Henry George, and the next section examines the tools of analysis George used to win the battle (DeMille 1946:545).

II

George's Analysis of Free Trade and Relative Wages

As a supporter of both unionization and free trade, George tried to convince his readers that there was no inherent contradiction in his position. To his critics, one could not oppose import tariffs and monopolies in output and land markets while simultaneously supporting efforts to reduce competition in the case of unionization of labor markets. One critic suggested that George "betrayed the direction from which he had come," and indicated the undesirable direction in which he was going (Rose 1968:170). Henry George, of course, thought otherwise.

After methodically exposing the logical fallacies of protection, George then asked why such exposures were of limited practical importance. If the "protective theory is really so incongruous with the nature of things, and so inconsistent with itself," how does it survive and even thrive? (George *PFT*:225).

George's answer was two-fold. First, the leading classical theory taught that free trade moved factors of production from less productive into more productive employment. To many laborers in the 1880s, like in the 1980s, this abstract idea about allocative efficiency translated into actual workers losing actual jobs in the short run, while job creation took longer to be felt by workers. According to the traditional labor view, trade destroyed jobs and did not raise wages. George understood the difficulty of his task.

> The idea of tariff protection commends itself to the masses of workingmen, because to them it seems to have at least the merit of "keeping work in the country" (George *LP*, Pt. IV:92).

In 1888, George would explain that the confusion between work and wealth was at the heart of the problem. The strength of protectionist ideas "lies in the habit of thought which regards the necessity of work, not the results of work, as desirable . . . " (George *TS*, 10/27/1888, IV, 17:6). The damage of specific jobs lost was highly visible and influential even before the age of television advocacy. With this prevailing attitude toward trade, it is not surprising that free trade did not inspire the support of the masses of the working people.

The second reason for a lack of support for free trade, according to George, was the lack of a satisfying new theory to replace the embattled classical theory.

> I do not think induction employed in such questions as the tariff is of any use. What the people want is theory, and until they get a correct theory into their heads, all citing of facts is useless. (Quoted in Barker:449)

Then, as now, the effect of free trade in commodities on the distribution of income was one of the most important questions in economics. But the existing classical model could not give a satisfactory answer to the question of trade and the relative payments to different factors of production because it was based on a single factor of production: a labor theory of value. The marginalists were beginning to solve the problems of wage and interest determination during this time. The neoclassical trade model would take decades beyond George's death to provide a satisfactory theoretical explanation of the effects of protection on the relative wages of labor.

It was precisely this issue of the effects on wages that Henry George addressed in his 1880s writings. George, in fact, anticipated certain important aspects of the logic of the neoclassical theory on trade flows and relative factor payments. Specifically, the important aspects were the relative factor endowments in the trading nations and the relative factor intensities in the production functions. The neoclassical model explains that even with identical technologies, a country will have a comparative advantage in the product which uses intensively in production the country's relatively abundant resources. On the other hand, domestic production which competes with imports must use intensively the country's relatively scarce resources. Based on this reasoning, the Stolper-Samuelson theory predicts that in each country free trade will increase the prices of the abundant factors of production relative to the prices of the scarce factors. Protect some industries against import competition through tariff or quotas, and a nation's relatively scarce, relatively expensive factor of production will benefit. In addition to consumers, those who pay the costs of "protection" are owners of the relatively abundant, relatively inexpensive factors of production (Chacholaides 1981:85).

In summary, Henry George's model assumed that the United States had a relatively scarce endowment of capital in the 1880s and 1890s relative to England, and a relatively abundant endowment of land to labor when compared to the smaller, crowded England. Furthermore, the protected industries in the United States were capital intensive, not labor intensive. Labor was not gaining by protection. George's argument was consistent with the logic of the 20th-century neoclassical theory when he examined the two critical issues of the nations' relative factor abundances and relative factor intensities in production as a part of his "satisfactory new theory."

George first considered relative factor abundance much in the spirit of the modern theory, computing the relative factor endowments.

> England is a little island on which nearly 40,000,000 people are begging for opportunities to work, while the United States, with its vast area of land, has but 60,000,000 people within its borders (George *TS*, 8/25/1888, IV, 8:1).

He went on to compute relative factor endowments, stating that in England "there are but one and one-third acres to the individual, whereas in the United States there are thirty-two and one-fifth" (George *TS*, 8/25/1888, IV, 8:1). This fact, rather than the absence of a tariff in England, explained George, was the reason why labor in England was relatively less expensive than the relatively more scarce American labor.

> That their condition is not so good, and as an average it is not, is due to our greater and cheaper opportunities for work, which we enjoy not as a result of protection but because of our more extensive area and varied natural resources relative to our population. (George *TS*, 8/25/1888, IV, 8:1).

England was relatively labor and capital abundant, while land was scarce. The United States was relatively scarce in its endowment of labor and capital, while land was the abundant factor. There was a persistent flow of financial and physical capital from England to the United States throughout the 1880s and 1890s, indicating ample opportunity for gain in America. As the 19th century moved toward a close, the American capital stock had expanded significantly, and would be both wider and deeper than in the middle of the century. Capital intensive industries took longer to develop in the United States than in England, but they did develop (Field 1983:425).

George would argue that the protected industries typically were capital intensive, and he concluded that capitalists would be protected by an import tariff on capital intensive imports. Labor would be relatively worse off. Industries with small holdings of capital are not those which are protected, as it is the large stocks of capital that are granted tariffs. According to George, the industries the tariff aimed to protect were those "in which the mere workman, or even the workman with a small capital, is helpless" (George *PFT*:204). The protected industries, those competing with the imports, used unskilled labor and large amounts of America's relatively scarce factors of production.

> As for the great mass of those engaged in the protected industries, their labor can hardly be called skilled . . . but consists of the mere tending to machinery . . . (George *PFT*:210).

The businesses which were helped were the "large establishments" using "costly machinery, great amounts of capital, or the ownership of natural opportunities which bear a high price" (George *PFT*:204). These natural opportunities included the ownership of land and the rapidly developing transportation systems, including especially the railroads. Therefore, according to George, American import tariffs benefitted the landowners or the capitalists, depending on the industry, but not labor.

> Could anything more clearly show that the real motive of protection is always the profit of the employing capitalist, never the benefit of labor? (George *PFT*:206)

Tariffs on iron ore benefitted the owners of the mine, but not the workers. Laborers were mistaken when they failed to support tariff reductions since

> the whole aim and spirit of protection is not the protection of the sellers of labor but the protection of the buyers of labor, not the maintaining of wages but the maintaining of profits. (George *PFT*:204)

Protection bid up the value of the scarce land and maintained profits, but did not help raise the wages of labor. Labor should not, therefore, have supported the protectionist plans developed in the Congress.

George analyzed the coal industry in Pennsylvania, which had received tariff protection for years. Based on the same logic as his iron ore example, George reached a similar conclusion. "Whomsoever the tariff may protect," stated George, "it does not protect the coal miners" (George *LP*, Pt. IV:86). The benefits of the coal tariff

> such as they are, certainly do not go to either the miners or to their immediate employers, the coal operators. If anyone at all is benefited, it is

> the owners of coal land and the monopolists of transportation (George *LP*, Pt. IV:89–90).

Abundant labor was not helped by protectionism. In fact, those workers in unprotected industries were made relatively better off.

> As a matter of fact, where no monopoly exists, wages and profits in the protected industries of Pennsylvania are not higher, but, I am inclined to think, rather lower than in the unprotected industries (George *LP*, Pt. IV:91).

The decrease in wages relative to the return to capital is exactly what the modern Stolper-Samuelson theory would predict. The reverse result for England is a true test for a grasp of the logic of the modern theory, and this, too, George had. Suggesting a false protection, George stated that the "condition of miners has for some time been growing worse in Pennsylvania" while the condition of the miners in Great Britain has gotten better. England's freedom of trade benefited its relatively abundant factor, labor, which was used intensively in its land-scarce methods of production for export. Calling them his "principles," George claimed that his results from the mining industry generalize to all other Pennsylvania industries (George *LP*, Pt. IV:91).

George argued that to protect the interests of labor, unionization rather than protectionism was the answer. Competition on the supply side of input markets, not import competition in output markets, was what kept wages from rising.

> What American workmen have to fear is not the sale in our goods markets of the products of cheap foreign labor, but the transference to our labor-market of that labor itself. (George *PFT*:201)

International factor movements and the competitive nature of labor markets, according to George, kept wages from rising. The level of wages in any occupation can be increased above the general level only by "restricting the competition for labor" (George *PFT*:201–202).

George recognized, however, that not all kinds of labor were abundant, and therefore that free trade may not always benefit all labor. Furthermore, labor might enjoy "such special skill or ability as make[s] a particular demand for his services" that wages could be increased with protection but "only to a small extent and for a short time" (George *PFT*:209). The increased domestic production resulting from a tariff "suddenly increases the demand for a certain kind of skilled labor" which temporarily increases the wage rate

> to an extent and for a time determined by the difficulties of obtaining the skilled laborers from other countries or of the acquirement by new laborers of the needed skill. (George *PFT*:209)

George argued that it would be much better for labor if the aspiring monopolists were paid directly, instead of indirectly through import tariffs. As if quoting from the modern theory of the second best, George suggests that it would be more efficient to "pay our protected infants directly from the public treasury what we now allow them to filch from the people" (George *TS*, 9/15/1888, IV, No. 11:1, col. 5). By taxing all instead of just some people, that would be the "most economical and efficient way of 'protecting' those who are now protected" (George *TS*, 9/15/1888, IV, 11:1, col. 5).

This analysis forms the heart of the income distribution implications of George's trade model. Here, in George's attempt to dissuade labor from the support of protectionism, is the heart of Stolper-Samuelson logic. Protectionism reverses the movement in relative factor prices, reducing the demand for the relatively abundant factor of production, the workingman. Enriched are the owners of capital, land, or other scarce resources.

III

Political Economy after *Protection or Free Trade*

GEORGE THOUGHT THAT labor was losing on the tariff issue and the immigration issue, and he was right. The tariff would not be lowered, but would, in fact, be increased. By March of 1887, when Congress had adjourned, no reduction in the surplus had been achieved and no tariff reform had been achieved. In December, Cleveland devoted his entire annual message to the issue of tariff reform. In this speech he stated that the surplus should be reduced by a reduction of import tariffs, not a reduction of internal taxes.

Had Cleveland's message come sooner, perhaps his supporters might have had enough time to rebut the onslaught of attacks. Instead, Cleveland's message hurt his re-election effort and tariff reform more than it helped (George *TS*, 9/29/1888, IV, 13:2).[3]

In March 1888, another tariff reduction bill was proposed which suggested a reduction on the tariffs on raw materials, on finished iron and steel products, and on sugar. The interests of labor were brought into the debate. Protectionists were sending their opinions to every iron mill to reach labor and increase their fear of the results of the passage of the tariff reduction bill (Nevins 1933:377). Nevertheless, Henry George remained optimistic that labor would support free trade.

> I know that they will respond to an aggressive attack on protection when they will turn away from a timid one. The only element of danger I see in the political situation is the half-hearted and treacherous timidity of Democratic politicians manifest in the doubtful states. (Quoted in Nevins 1933:423)

In June, he appealed to Cleveland to waste no time in putting tariff reform in the front of the national campaign. By September, George was declaring that Cleveland shared his belief that the "sweeping away of restrictions would be for the benefit of industrial enterprises and the benefit of labor" (Nevins:416–17).

In the Presidential election of 1888, the positions of the two parties were firmly established and gave the voters a definite contrast. Cleveland wanted all tax reduction to come from reductions in the import tariff. The Republicans, on the other hand, reversed positions on their 1884 platform and now declared that they favored the "entire repeal of internal taxes," rather than surrender any part of the protective system (George *TS*, 9/15/1888, IV, 11:1). Much to the dismay of Henry George, the protectionist Republicans were back in office with Harrison in 1888. The outgoing president stated again his reform position in his annual December message, a message which contained some "remarkably sharp words on the inequalities of wealth in America," which, according to one historian, were "so radical in tone that they might have been written by Henry George" (Nevins 1933:398).

The Republicans wasted no time in further raising, not lowering, the tariff with the passage of the McKinley Tariff in 1890. By 1892, the Democrats were back in the White House with Cleveland and held a majority of seats in both houses of Congress. They tried to lower the tariff, but the effort was in vain. Henry George was disappointed that there had been no special session called to discuss and reform the tariff, as the silver issue had by then taken hold of the attention of President Cleveland (Nevins 1933:444). By 1893 there were wage reductions and bread lines. By the spring of 1894 labor protests were blossoming.

With the passage of the Wilson-Gorman tariff in 1894, tariffs were increased to the highest level yet. As Cleveland summarized,

> Every true Democrat and every sincere reformer knows that the bill in its present form . . . falls far short of the consummation for which we have long labored. (George, Jr.:576)

George and Cleveland had both labored long only to be disappointed at the outcome. The great tariff battle which had begun in 1885 was about to be finished, with George and the free traders coming out on the losing political side. The Democrats lost, too, as their party was now weakened and would remain out of the White House for almost two decades. The Republicans gained the Presidency and control of both houses of Congress in the elections of 1896. Two days after his inauguration, McKinley called a special session of Congress to discuss increasing the tariff in order to raise revenues. The year 1897 would see the approval of the Dingley Tariff, which would raise nominal tariff rates to a still higher level. In that same year, Henry George would die. The protectionist tide would be slowed by the administration of Woodrow Wilson, but not reversed until after the Second World War.

In the turbulent decades of the 1880s and 1890s, Henry George anticipated key elements of the modern theory concerning the impact of trade on relative factor prices. In many significant ways, George understood that tariffs pitted the interests of the small, highly-interested group of producers and governing officials against the interests of the larger and only generally interested group of consumers and producers of non-import competing products.

Beyond anticipating elements of the modern theory, George's writings added to the moral foundation of the free trade argument. George argued that protection is "repugnant to moral perceptions and inconsistent with the simplicity and harmony which we everywhere discover in natural law" (George *PFT*:30). Trade, on the other hand, has always been "the extinguisher of war, the eradicator of prejudice, the diffuser of knowledge" (George *PFT*:52). This was the result of trade because "prejudices are worn down, wits are sharpened, language enriched, habits and customs brought to the test of comparison and new ideas kindled" (George *PFT*:54).

Above all, George believed in free trade because he believed that human freedom led to human progress. "When we consider the question from facts to principles," he asked, "do we not find the better condition where there is greater freedom?" (George *TS*, 9/22/1888, IV, 12:2, col. 1). If we get over this "mean spirit which teaches us that foreigners are our enemies," and the zero-sum idea that "men can only benefit themselves at the expense of other people," he believed that a time would come when all people could enjoy leisure, luxury, and, perhaps most importantly of all, the "opportunities for developing the highest part of man's nature" (George *TS*, 9/29/1888, IV, 13:2, col. 3).

In the preface to the 1980 edition of *Protection or Free Trade*, Lissner states that the book's unique contribution is in the way it shows how the campaign for free trade is "an essential element of the crusade for human freedom. . . . The campaign for justice and liberty cannot rest until these ideas prevail everywhere" (Lissner 1980:x–xi). Henry George would, no doubt, be pleased with that assessment, as George believed in freedom, and thought it should be practiced. He favored free trade

> not merely that she shall be rich, not merely that she shall be great, but that she shall lead the world to freedom. . . . I am a free trader because I believe in freedom . . . (George *TS*, 8/11/88, IV, 6:3, col. 2).

At this time in our history, an examination of George's thought can help discussion of these issues which remain highly divisive.

Notes

1. The book was published by the new firm of Henry George and Company, which included Henry George and his son.
2. Barker (1974:424) states that George was "bedeviled by obstacles and misfortunes" while writing the book. The half-completed manuscript was lost in 1883, but was completed by the presidential election season of 1884.
3. This article was based on a speech George delivered at Cooper Union on September 21, 1888.

Why the Preaching Must Never Stop

Henry George's and Paul Krugman's Respective Contributions to the Free Trade Debate

By LAURENCE S. MOSS*

Introduction

THE TINBERGEN ARCHIVES in Los Angeles, California are a monument comprised of books, lectures, and films—a monument that exists for the sole purpose of honoring the dead. Established to inform succeeding generations about this "century's greatest crime," the destruction of most of Europe's Jewish community, it "preserv[es] the history of the Holocaust and the blessed memory of the Six Million who lost their lives so cruelly and unjustly." Mr. Cal Tinbergen, the Director of the Archives, has assembled media of all types to fortify "the fight against bigotry and hatred."[1] In this never-ending battle Tinbergen and others are driven to spread ideas about tolerance and understanding over bigotry and hatred, so that peace and respect for human dignity someday might prevail in the world.

I admire the clarity of Mr. Tinbergen's vision about who he is and what he does. I imagine he is a man who gets up each morning and sets out on a business routine calculated to fight bigotry and hatred and keep the memory of the victims of the Nazi genocide alive. I, myself, get up each morning, but with less clear goals. My college hires me to teach students how economic theory helps to make the world intelligible, especially for business decision makers. Along the way, I must qualify extreme principles in various ways and then challenge my students with examinations and term paper reports about my lectures. Deep down, however, I

*Editor, *The American Journal of Economics and Sociology*; Professor of Economics, Babson College, Massachusetts.

want to preach tolerance as well, but economists are not supposed to preach at all (Stigler 1982).

Indeed, there is a long tradition in economic theory that promotes tolerance—based not on religious and moral duty, but on the value of capturing the gains from open trade and exchange.[2] That tradition exalts the middleman or entrepreneur, who discovers new and more valued combinations of resources and legal rights and sees nation-states as administrative regions that can provide frameworks for interregional trade, without themselves becoming salespeople for the trading groups and firms in their regions. When I get this message across to my students, I do indeed teach my students something worthy of comparison with Mr. Tinbergen's crusade against bigotry and hatred.

I teach the gospel of free trade. As a member of a discipline that dates back more than 300 years, I manage to advance several steps beyond Mr. Tinbergen's call for mere tolerance of other peoples, races, and regional cultures. I use a variety of arguments to encourage government officials, politicians, business leaders, trade unionists, and even spiritual leaders to appreciate the importance of commercial exchange and to stop punishing people for engaging in trade and exchange. The Nazi round-up of the Jewish merchants and shop owners for supposedly profiting at the expense of the German people, the slaughter of the Armenian merchants during the first World War for their middleman activities, which had long aroused suspicion among Turks, and the current tensions in Indonesia directed against the Chinese business community accused of causing the Asian currency crisis—all are examples of merchant hatred.[3]

As a student of the market process, I have kind words for the middleman trader who pioneers new trade routes and profits from integrating regions (Block 1976:186–191; Sowell 1998; Lerner 1961:41–48). As an economist, I take the work of the Tinbergen Institute one important step further: I address what happens to living standards in each respective region when trade and commerce are allowed to emerge and take shape in market settings. To an economist it is not enough that the inhabitants of Region A stop slaughtering those of Region B. For people to live dignified lives, they must have comforts. They must have materials to fuel their creative labors so that new shapes can emerge, and they must connect with each other for mutual interest and gain. Because free trade and exchange are so obviously advantageous, officials should tolerate economic activity and not tax, prohibit, or crush the improvements it makes possible.[4]

Economic science admits that from the efficiency point of view there are exceptions to the general rule that free trade is a universal good. The best reasoning in economics uses sets of assumptions to demonstrate that "wisely chosen but always moderate" interventions can result in surprising net gains.[5] Indeed, the study of the exceptions to free trade—the mainstay of the modern trade theory course at a university—sometimes swamps an entire semester's work in trade theory, making the simple case for free trade less obvious and somewhat obscure. Exceptions to any rule should not pile up until they bury the general rule completely (Krugman 1996a:117–125). Free trade is a distinctively human practice. A person's right to trade with others is an important, if not sacred, human right. Governments and others have a correlative duty not to interfere, except to prevent the most egregious forms of behavior.[6] This important point—a point about deontology or moral duty and not merely about efficient exchange—has to be reemphasized in every generation: the preaching for free trade must never stop.

I shall now demonstrate the virtuous character of mainstream economic theory by taking a close look at two important books on the subject of commercial policy. The first was written in 1886 by the great American iconoclast Henry George and appeared under the title *Protection or Free Trade*. It was published at a time in American history when tariff reform was high on the political agenda; in fact, tariff reform was the leading issue in the presidential election debate of 1888 (Reitano 1994). George tried to persuade organized labor that free trade and not protectionism was in its interests. I shall spend the most time on George's work, outlining its scientific arguments.

The second book about which I have something to say is *Pop Internationalism*, published more than 100 years after George's book, by the prolific American economist Paul Krugman (1996a).[7] In this book, Krugman does battle with the appalling ignorance of our most prominent political and business leaders and their consultants who were (and still are!) advising the U.S. president in a manner and with language destined to foster a global intolerance of other peoples and their values. Krugman's book, much like George's important book of a century earlier, is a veritable milestone in a continuous tradition of preaching economics. Through his writing, Krugman hopes to battle the ignorance, intolerance, and nativism of those who pretend to watch over the political and economic interests of the community. When joining in this intellectual crusade, students and professors are every bit as sincere and ennobling as the people at the Tinbergen Institute.

Indeed, students and professors wedded to the free trade idea may even surpass the Tinbergen Institute in the area of human rights and tolerance. Whereas Tinbergen asks for tolerance and respect only—a request consistent with economic isolationism and legal geographic segregation, with strict prohibitions on immigration—the discipline of economics has for 300 fertile years broken down the segregation barrier by pointing to the importance of interregional integration as the key to ending war and building wealth (Mises 1963:821–832). In the context of political turmoil and ignorance, leading economic writers have risen up with fine books, manifestos, articles, and speeches to do battle with those actively opposing free trade. In so doing, the profession of economics has ennobled itself. As professionals, economists cannot help but preach the gospel of tolerance in a world that is all too willing to forget tolerance and lapse back into the ethical norms of an age that is older, more violent, and filled with tribal superstition and hatred (Hayek 1988).

From this point, I take a careful look at Henry George's 1886 presentation of the free trade idea both in terms of its scientific merit as well as the political context in which it was developed. Then I review Paul Krugman's treatment of the free trade doctrine, although more briefly. In the concluding section I offer some thoughts about the future of toleration. I think a case can be made in favor of unrestricted migration of any people and its culture. In a borderless world, trade would remain a substitute for migration, and migration would become a substitute for trade itself. I argue that it is both fitting and ennobling for economists to take leadership roles in this important plan for development. Again, economists must never stop preaching free trade. The preaching provides a deeper and more detailed background for the strictly scientific account of how trade and exchange promote mutual gain.

George's Contribution to the Free Trade Argument

IT IS DIFFICULT to find any decisive factor in George's background that would explain his appreciation of economic reasoning and his commitment to free trade.[8] George was born in Philadelphia in 1839, but his economic thinking was not of the Philadelphia protectionist variety. George was quite cosmopolitan. He dropped out of school at age 15 and took to the sea as a sailor. After voyages to India and Australia, George became a newspaperman in California during the gold rush period (Barker 1991:3–104). There he saw fortunes won and lost in the speculative gamble over property rights in land and mineral rights. He took up the racist cause of those who wanted to restrict Chinese immigration as well (Barker 1991:122–3). Yet despite his racism, George published an outstanding defense of free trade in 1886, based on the best scientific thinking of his day.

The full title of George's book is *Protection or Free Trade: An Examination of the Tariff Question, with Especial Regard to the Interests of Labor*. Its purpose was to reach a "common conclusion on [the] subject" of how to raise the wages of labor (George *PFT*:ix). To many citizens and their political leaders, it seemed obvious that the best way to create jobs was to limit foreign imports. By making imports to the United States scarcer, U.S. families would be induced to purchase domestic products, thereby sparking job creation in the import-competing industries. How could any rational person disagree with this analysis? But disagree we must.

It is wasteful and destructive of liberty to discourage imports. As Adam Smith explained, the purpose of production and trade is to promote consumption (Smith 1976, II: 660). Furthermore, imports are paid for mostly by exports and it is these exports, reflecting a region's comparative advantage, that also create valuable jobs.

This point was argued so clearly by the early 19th-century British economists—the list includes David Ricardo, Robert Torrens, James Mill, Mountifort Longfield and others (Viner 1964).

In America there has been a long and professionally acclaimed political tradition opposing free market exchange. I shall lump together this collection of myriad interventions, proposed and implemented, under the rubric "protectionism." Trade policy was a "contentious political issue throughout American history" (Reitano 1994:xxi). The American colonists fought the British because they objected to British mercantilist trade policy, partly on the grounds that it prohibited the fledgling American colonies from installing their own mercantilist policy. In the late 18th century, Alexander Hamilton's *Report on Manufactures* advocated the use of a protective tariff and other subsidies to build up the industrial (manufacturing) base of the then-developing United States.[9] America was then and remained well into this century a predominantly agricultural region with only a meager sprinkling of urban centers. The tariff crisis of Andrew Jackson's presidency and the conflicts over protecting Northern industry prior to the Civil War combined to make tariffs an extremely controversial issue. Next to the continuation of plantation slavery there was no other issue that so divided America in the 19th century.

As I remarked, Henry George's book was published in the midst of the tariff debate leading up to the Presidential election of 1888. This was the first "national election [in American history to focus] primarily on the tariff question" (Reitano 1994:107). The Republican Party was openly protectionist and insisted that supporting taxes on imports was both profitable and patriotic. The Republicans claimed that such interventions were necessary not only for financing government but also for protecting domestic industry and jobs. It was argued that the common worker should vote for the Republican candidate and reject the "free trade" ideas of the Democratic Party. Indeed, Republican presidential candidate William McKinley demonstrated an absolute ignorance of the theory of comparative advantage when he extolled high taxes on imports because tariffs kept out all "foreign products the like of which [we] are capable of producing at home" (Reitano 1994:103). The Republican Party characterized the Democratic Party and its free trade liberalism as a sinister plot. Free trade, the Republicans said, would pauperize the American worker not only by allowing imports to replace domestic products but also by allowing more Chinese and Eastern European immigrants to enter the United States and lower (real) wages (Reitano 1994:49).

In George's day, the bastion of protectionist thought was Philadelphia, Pennsylvania. Here a large iron and steel manufacturing complex prospered during the Reconstruction period following the Civil War. The Philadelphia factory owners were interested in keeping out those nasty lower-priced imports, and they staunchly backed the protectionist platform of the Republican Party (Reitano 1994:51). But campaign contributions and votes were only parts of the story I am retelling.

The Trustees of the University of Pennsylvania wanted to alter their curriculum to reflect these protectionist sensibilities. As early as the 1869–70 academic year, students had to study protectionism as a graduation requirement. In 1881, the rich businessman Joseph Wharton founded a special school at the University of Pennsylvania to educate future business leaders about the virtues of protectionism. It may be said that "with the founding of the Wharton School [of Business in the 1880s] the [protectionist] views of the Philadelphia business community gained in influence over economics teachings at the University of Pennsylvania" (Sass 1993:229). In 1881, Robert Ellis Thompson was hired to teach the social science course at Wharton. To accompany that course of study, Wharton financed Thompson's main book, *Social Science and National Economy* (1875). Indeed, the Wharton school and its influential Philadelphia protectionist community remained a bastion against the teaching of free trade up to and after the 1888 election. Needless to say, with the Republican victory of William McKinley in 1896, protectionism won out over free trade.[10]

George quite properly identified the mission of the Wharton School of Business and its pundits as the enemy. He made the faculty the target of his preaching. He wrote that when presenting the protectionist position he would not attack a weak thinker but instead quote directly from the writings of University of Pennsylvania Professor Thompson "who is the latest writer who seems to be regarded by American protectionists as an authoritative exponent of their views" (George *PFT*:x).

George's principled opposition to protectionism was not without severe costs to his own political career. In fact, George's commitment to free trade over protectionism led to his dismissal by the proponents of various U.S. organized labor movements. For example, the Knights of Labor (KOL) initially endorsed George's ideas in the early 1880s because he supported Irish tenant-farmers in their battle against absentee landlords. Manifestations of such support were his 1881 *The Irish Land Question* and his correspondence from Ireland with several leading U.S.-based Irish newspapers. But even as George spoke more and more about the merits of free trade, most trade unionists were protectionist. They especially feared that the admission of more immigrants would mean lower wages. Not only did the unionists wish to guard the borders against newcomers, but they also wanted to exclude foreign goods and services. George's advocacy undoubtedly cost him support among the Knights who, after a brief honeymoon with George, lost interest in his economic ideas (Weir 1997:426).

George had long been disgusted with the immoral ways in which wealth could be won at the expense of the common laborer, based in part on his early experiences during the California gold rush. As a result, in 1879, he wrote one of the most popular and inspired books that has ever been written in economics and in any language, the lovely, and indeed at places lyrical, *Progress and Poverty*. "[It] was the most widely read of all books in economics; in the English-speaking world in the last quarter of the nineteenth century, [in fact,] it was not [Karl] Marx but Henry George who was the talking-point of all debates among fiery young intellectuals" (Blaug 1986:84).

The thesis of *Progress and Poverty*, which played an important part in George's advocacy of "true free trade" in 1886, was an explanation of why poverty should coexist with such vast aggregation of wealth as was proceeding apace in America in the 19th century. According to George, those who possessed the exclusive rights to land and other natural formations such as minerals, waterfalls, even picturesque hamlets on majestic mountains, should not unjustly profit from these possessions (Backhaus 1997:453–

474). If they worked hard to improve the nature-given structure, they were entitled to their hard-earned wages and even entrepreneurial profits. They were not entitled to profit from the mere rise in the scarcity value of the unimproved land. Speculative passive gains were, for Henry George, unjust. According to George, the wild bull-market frenzy of American land policy, combined with the never-ending quest for monopoly privilege, had brought about a tendency in America for the overall national income to rise and for the share of the national income going to workers to fall. Poverty coexisted with plenty because the land and other natural resources were being held in speculative hoards that promoted an artificial scarcity that inured to the benefit of the monopolistic landlords.

One remedy for this inequality was for the state to assess land (but not improvements) and then levy a tax on owners equal to its annual rental value. The rents, explicit and implicit, would then become part of the public troves. Other taxes, such as the inheritance or capital gains tax and the various specific taxes on industrial output, which discourage entrepreneurship and creativity, could be eliminated once the tax on the unimproved value of the property was in place. The best tax, according to George, encourages economic progress, and a tax on the unimproved value of natural resources would accomplish that goal. Today, few other taxes have been devised with as small a negative effect on incentives as what has come to be known as Henry George's "single tax." Indeed as late as 1978, Nobel Prize winner Milton Friedman stated that "in [his] opinion the least bad tax is the property tax on the unimproved value of land, the Henry George argument of many, many years ago" (cited in Blaug 1986:86). With Friedman's endorsement, *Progress and Poverty* may yet prove to be a bombshell for fiscal reform with a slow fuse.

From Henry George's point of view, poverty in America could hardly be blamed on cheap imports. It was, rather, the result of the private appropriation and subsequent monopoly ownership of nature's legacy. George's *Protection or Free Trade* is a curious amalgam. First, it contains the leading scientific arguments from the French and English economists of his day supporting free trade. Second, it ties these arguments together with his ideas that poverty is caused by those who claim not only exclusive rights to land and other resources but to their market value as well.

George's Scientific Arguments

THE SCIENTIFIC ARGUMENTS Henry George offers in *Protection or Free Trade* can be summarized as follows:

1. Trade is not a zero sum game. George recognized that voluntary trade is mutually advantageous. It is not a one-way street in which only the rich get richer and the poor get poorer. In response to those American protectionists who insist that free trade is a "good thing for rich [developed] countries but a bad thing for poor [less developed] countries [because it] enables a country of better-developed industries to prevent the development of industry in other countries," George harked back to the insights of the English classical school of political economy. He reminded his readers, as David Hume had done in 1742, that "free trade is voluntary trade. It cannot go on unless to the advantage of both parties, and, as between the two, free trade is relatively more advantageous to the poor and underdeveloped country than to the rich and prosperous country" (George *PFT*:148–149). In other words, the solitary Robinson Crusoe on a tiny island and the rest of the world both would gain by trade. The advantage, as George noted, "would [however] be far greater to Robinson Crusoe than to the rest of the world" (George *PFT*:149). This is the first scientific principle of modern commercial policy, which holds that allowing some trade is always preferable to prohibiting it. Indeed, the exact logic of this claim was nicely laid out in a classic paper by Paul Samuelson (1938).

2. Trade expands the mass of commodities available for distribution. George understood that free trade encourages the increase in the total mass of commodities and services available to a region through specialization and the division of labor. "Trade," he said, "by permitting us to obtain each of the things we need from the locality best fitted for its production, enables us to utilize the highest powers of nature in the production of them all, and thus to increase enormously the sum of various things which a given quantity of labor expended in any locality can secure" (George

PFT:57). Here he follows the approach that David Ricardo and the English economists proposed. He distinguishes the effect that trade has on the size of the gross domestic product from the related issue of how trade affects the distribution of the gross domestic product.

3. Middlemen raise living standards, rather than reducing them. The prejudice against middlemen, retailers, and brokers seems to be all but universal in popular culture. Since the intermediaries and brokers do not produce anything tangible and permanent, their profits are always viewed with suspicion and alarm. They appear to sneak their profits out of someone's pocket. George spoke out against this point of view and the intolerant attitudes associated with it. He demonstrated that the one who stands behind the buyers and the sellers helps create markets by facilitating mutually advantageous trade. In George's words, the middleman "transports things" and brings them to where they are wanted in time (George *PFT*:63). Out of this surge in values come whatever amounts of money competition allows the middlemen to retain. In modern terms, the middleman creates wealth by lessening the transaction costs the buyers and sellers would otherwise incur (North 1990). George confessed that "I am only concerned in pointing out that the trader is not a mere 'useless exchanger,' who 'adds nothing to the real wealth of society,' but that the transporting, storing, and exchanging of things are as necessary a part of the work of supplying human needs as is growing, extracting, or making" (George *PFT*:63).

4. Importation makes export sales possible. George recognized that a region cannot continue exporting without also importing. By importing the goods and services from foreigners, the foreigner obtains the power to purchase that country's exports. Foreign trade cannot be sustained without importing. In George's words, "exports and imports, as far as they are induced by trade are correlative. Each is the cause and complement of the other. . . . And so far from its being the market of a profitable commerce that the value of a nation's exports exceed her imports, the reverse of this is true" (George *PFT*:116).

At another point he insisted that a trade surplus can never be a measure of "increasing wealth" (George *PFT*:13). The trade or merchandise surplus may correlate with a nation's effort to pay off unjust liabilities to foreign claim holders. A case in point is 19th-century Ireland. As George observed, "for many years the exports from Ireland have largely exceeded the imports into Ireland, owing to the rent drain of the absentee landlords. The Irish landlords who live abroad do not directly draw produce for their rent, nor yet do they draw money. Irish cattle, hogs, sheep, butter, linen and other productions are exported as if in the regular course of trade, but their proceeds, instead of coming back to Ireland as imports, are, through the medium of bank and mercantile exchange, placed to the credit of the absent landlord, and used up by them" (George *PFT*:118). The net savings achieved by Ireland when it successfully ran a trade surplus with England, and thereby reduced its outstanding liabilities to absentee landlords (who did not reinvest their funds in Ireland), did not make Ireland richer.[11] Ireland would have been much better off if it had received tangible imports for all of its exports. If the Irish peasants had repudiated their tenancies and claimed the land to be theirs, they might have attracted foreign direct investment followed by rising productivity and the discovery of new areas of comparative advantage.

5. Specialization and export are based on comparative, rather than absolute, advantage. George understood that the gains from unencumbered trade are attributable to comparative rather than absolute trade advantage. Individuals in a region gain from commerce when they specialize and export those goods and services in which they have the greatest comparative production advantage. This reallocates world resources to where they are most urgently needed, where urgency is expressed by comparative world prices.

The zealous advocate of protectionism and celebrated American journalist, Horace Greeley, was fond of pointing out that if the United States were to lay a heavy duty on Chinese tea they could end up producing that same tea at a lower cost than in China mostly because of the saving in shipping and packing costs. But Greeley's view is surely myopic.

Henry George offered a broader understanding of the pattern of trade and its possibilities, which showed that the U.S. benefitted by importing tea and having its workers apply their skills to other tasks: "there are other things, such as the mining of silver, the refining of oil, the weaving of cloth, the making of clocks and watches, as to which our [United States] advantage over the Chinese is enormously greater than the growing of tea. Hence by producing these things and exchanging them directly or indirectly for Chinese tea, we obtain, in spite of the long carriage, more tea for the same labor than we could get by growing our own tea" (George *PFT*:148).

6. Export advantage does not depend only on wages but also on productivity. George understood that high wages are not a necessary barrier to mutually profitable trade, because the comparative advantage, which forms the basis of all trade, depends not only on the cost of scarce factors of production but also on their relative productivity. According to George, "it is not true that the products of lower-priced labor will drive the products of higher-priced labor out of any market in which they can be freely sold, since, as we have already seen, low-priced labor does not mean cheap production, and it is the comparative, not the absolute, cost of production that determines exchanges" (George *PFT*:198–99). In response to the protectionist claim that tariffs are needed to preserve high wages, George remarked, "We have seen that low wages do not mean low cost of production, and that a high standard of wages, instead of putting a country at a disadvantage in production, is really an advantage. This disposes of the claim that protection is rendered necessary by high wages, by showing the invalidity of the first assumption upon which it is based" (George *PFT*:144).

7. Trade opportunities function like labor-saving technological innovations. George recognized that foreign trade or exchange is in fact a "mode of production" that affects the economy in exactly the same way as does the invention of a new machine. According to this author, "the use of machinery enormously increases the production of wealth [and] we should see that the increased power given by invention inures primarily to labor, and that this gain is so diffused by exchange that the effect of any improvement which increases the power of labor in one branch of industry must be shared by labor in all other branches" (George *PFT*:254). The introduction of labor-saving machinery can disrupt existing busi-

ness routines or result in some labor unemployment. The introduction of free trade, like the introduction of new methods of production, also can have these very same effects.

Just as no rational monarch would have taxed improvements in the steam engine because its use lowered wages and decreased opportunities in the coal mines, so also no prudent national authority should tax international trade. The importation of certain cheaper commodities and services will diminish job opportunities in the import-competing sector. However, these adjustment costs are no greater or more mysterious than those that arise by processes of technological change that augment the productivity of labor. We should not prohibit technological innovation, and, for the same exact reason, we should not vote out free international trade.

So far, we have outlined "free trade" arguments in George's writings that parallel the best of the free trade arguments found in the writings of the classical school. There is more to George's ideas about trade. I should now like to highlight how he tied free trade to his larger call for land reform.

True Free Trade and the Land Question

EVEN THOUGH FREE trade can, in principle, raise living standards in the same manner as the introduction of labor-saving machinery, under present conditions the introduction of more productive machinery often leads to unemployment and falling wages for a small group of displaced workers. Here George tackled with renewed creativity the famous "machinery question" that had interested David Ricardo and others. He pointed out that the "division of men into a class of world-owners and a class who have no legal right to use the world explains many things otherwise inexplicable," including why machines now have the surprising tendency to "destroy independence, to dispense with skill and convert the artisan into a 'hand,' to concentrate all business and make it harder for an employee to become an employer, and to compel women and children to injurious and stunting toil" (George *PFT*:264).

Free trade is not a panacea for the social problem. At first free trade expands the mass of commodities and services available to the consumer. This increases living standards for common workers who are able to enjoy higher real wages out of which they can save and perhaps someday go into business themselves. However, under current conditions in the United States, monopoly ownership of critical rights to natural resources and to unique spatial locations frustrates most people's entrepreneurial efforts. They are forced to bid against each other for critically important rights to locations that are kept artificially scarce. The rental price of the rights is high and most of the entrepreneurial gain is captured by the privileged landowners at the expense of these creative common laborers. According to George, if the rent of land were collected as public revenue, the "great cause of the present unequal distribution of wealth would be destroyed, and that one-sided competition would cease which now deprives men who possess nothing but power to labor of the benefits of advancing civilization, and forces wages to a minimum no matter what the increase of wealth" (George *PFT*:285; Whitaker 1997, 1901). While there is a "tendency" for free trade and labor-saving inventions to benefit labor, that tendency is "in some way aborted and this connection is especially noticeable in our age" where land and other resources are monopolized (George *PFT*:285).

Now let us turn our attention to protectionism, that is, taxes and other barriers imposed on imports. George pointed out that "the primary purpose of protection is to encourage producers . . . to increase the profits of capital engaged in certain branches of industry" (George *PFT*:166). This elevation of profits will attract the entry of other industrial competitors since profits must reach a common level throughout any industry. Here George invoked a variant of the famous "competition of capitals" argument presented by Adam Smith in his *Wealth of Nations* (Hollander 1973:182–189). George explained, "The first effect of a protective duty is to increase the profits in the protected industry. But unless that industry be in some way protected from the influx of competitors which such increased profits must attract, this influx [of competitors] must soon bring these profits to the general level" (George *PFT*:170).

The influx of competitors might be prevented, however, if the protected firms in that industry enjoy some sort of unique or non-replicable commercial advantage. That advantage could be a rare resource, a special location, or a patent monopoly. In these cases the elevated profits will persist and inure to the industrialists but only so long as the non-replicable advantage persists. In the long run, the landowner will somehow capture the elevated profits in higher rents.[12] In other cases, the competition of capital will destroy the surplus returns as soon as the legal barrier to entry disappears or is removed—for example, when a patent expires. Thus, there is a long-run tendency for the benefits of protectionism not to remain with the owners of capital but either to disappear altogether or else be bid away by the owners of the natural resources and be incorporated into higher rents.

Notice the interesting symmetry in the scientific argument. With either free trade or protectionism, only the privileged property owners stand any chance of gaining in the long run. The policies of protectionism and free trade differ only in their short-run effects on wages and profits. According to George, in the short run, free trade favors the workers. In the short run, protectionism favors the factory owners. In the long run, both capital and labor lose as their extraordinary gains get competed away or else captured by the monopoly land owners. The monopoly interests at large in society capture these gains in the form of higher rent payments. Why favor free trade under present-day land monopoly conditions? George favored ordinary free trade because it was an important first step toward a broader and more radical free trade that he termed "true free trade."

True free trade for George meant not only the "abolition of protection but the sweeping away of all [distorting taxes]—the abolition of all restrictions (save those imposed in the interests of public health or morals) on the bringing of things into a country or the carrying of things out of a country" (George *PFT*:286). True free trade means the "abolition of all indirect taxation of whatever kind, and the [exclusive] resort to direct taxation for all public revenues" (George *PFT*:286). George concluded that there is "no conflict between labor and capital; the true conflict is between labor and monopoly. . . . No matter how rich an employer might be, how would it be possible for him to squeeze workmen who could make a good living for themselves without going into his employment? The competition of workmen with workmen for employment which is the real cause that enables, and even in most cases forces, the employer to squeeze his workmen, arises from the fact that men, debarred of the natural opportunities to employ themselves, are compelled to bid against one another for the wages of an employer" (George *PFT*:306).

In this analysis, George is an early anticipator of the famous Stolper-Samuelson theorem that was first presented to the economics profession in 1941 (Stolper and Samuelson 1941; Martin 1989). That theorem holds that free trade will lower the real wage of the scarce factor and raise the reward of the abundant factor compared with what they would otherwise have been if all trade were forbidden. Protective tariffs will have the opposite effect and raise the reward of the scarce factor. The proof of that theorem only holds tightly in the two-factor, two-commodity case and cannot be maintained in a multifactor and multicommodity world unless strong additional assumptions are made about the nature of technology and technological relationships (Deardorff and Stern 1994:7–34).[13]

The importance of the Stolper-Samuelson argument is that if labor were the relatively scarce factor of production and land the relatively abundant factor, then the movement toward free trade would lower the real wage of labor and raise real rents. This analysis surely resembles 1886 America, which had unbounded land and depended on waves of immigrants to feed its hungry manufacturing sector. Yet, when we read George we learn the opposite: the gains from free trade at least in the short run will benefit the laborers and not the landowners. For a while, free trade brings higher wages and relatively lower rents.

Could George be claiming that in America it is land and not labor that has somehow become scarcer? I think he was maintaining exactly this point. George insisted that, under the social conditions of his time, the creation of exclusive property rights in land and the sport of trying to make speculative profits made land scarcer and that this is the source of the great social injustice that harms labor in the long run (Whitaker 1997). This argument suggests that George's approach can be illuminated with the aid of the modern Stolper-Samuelson theorem.[14]

In summary, George favored free trade in commodities and services as a method of getting workers to recognize their interest in true fair trade, which "leads not only to the largest production of wealth, but to the fairest distribution" (George *PFT*:290). The elimination of unjust monopoly and privilege will secure "justice in distribution . . . and the great inventions and discoveries which the human mind is not grasping can be converted into agencies for the elevation of society from its very foundations" (George *PFT*:290). George ended his remarkable 1886 book with this overall assessment about the utility of free trade and its relation to labor: "True free trade will emancipate labor" (George *PFT*:290).

Krugman and Pop Internationalism

I NOW DIRECT your attention to 1986, one hundred years after George published *Protection or Free Trade*. President Ronald Reagan's Commission on Industrial Competitiveness, consisting of distinguished business executives, trade union leaders, college professors, and former government officials, already had reported back to the Executive Office about the supposed reasons that once profitable and mighty American industries were losing out to international competition. The nation was greeted with calls for a new type of mercantilist trade policy in which Congress would pick and subsidize winning industries and phase out losers. This form of protectionism was named "industrial policy" (Audretsch 1998). As the 1988 elections indicated, a skeptical American public did not greet these calls for a new industrial policy very kindly, perhaps recalling the awful waste and special interest character of earlier well-meaning government programs. Discredited, industrial policy soon gave way to the rhetoric of competitiveness.

In December 1992, a month before his inauguration, President-elect Bill Clinton hosted a conference in Little Rock, Arkansas. Among those invited were the heads of America's largest corporations, such as John Sculley, then CEO of Apple Computer, and several of America's most prominent economists, including Paul Krugman (Krugman 1996a:vii–viii).[15] At the Little Rock conference, Krugman learned that many of America's best political leaders, captains of industry, and smooth consultants had no real understanding of the fundamentals of international trade theory. He heard that international trade was essentially a zero-sum competition between nations and that lost export sales to an American airplane manufacturer meant American jobs lost to foreign competition. Current account deficits meant that our nation's consumers had defiantly created more jobs abroad for foreigners than those foreigners had created here for Americans. It was clear that the Clinton administration was bent on viewing the world as one in which "nations, like corporations, are engaged in fierce competition for global markets" (1996a:vii–viii). The Clinton administration needed a good preaching.

According to Krugman's assessment, from 1985 and 1995, a "deeply misconceived ideology of international trade had taken hold of much of the public discussion of trade issues in general" (Krugman 1996a:114). Krugman went on to call "quintessential" President Clinton's statement that "the United States is like a big corporation in the world economy." This remark, more than any other, summarized the bankruptcy of the modern public debate about commercial policy. Again the popular public debate, completely uniformed by 300 years of economics, had taken an ugly turn. It was time to start preaching free trade again and that is exactly what Krugman has done. He presented his case against the barbaric ideas of the policymakers in many important forums. (See note 7, infra.)

The dangerous intolerance manifest in pop internationalism—the idea that a nation must be managed like a corporation and export sales encouraged—was brought out most clearly in 1992 in the rhetoric of presidential hopeful Ross Perot. This candidate heard a "giant sucking sound": the elimination of jobs that would occur in the import-competing sectors of the United States economy if the remaining small tariffs against Mexican goods were finally removed. Perot urged the United States to continue its protectionist policies and to scuttle the proposed North American Free Trade Agreement (NAFTA).[16]

Perot and Clinton both view trade as a device to increase jobs in the United States. President Clinton, in his 1998 State of the Union Address, spoke about "240 trade agreements that remove foreign barriers to products bearing the proud stamp, 'Made in America'"

(Clinton 1998:A-19). This is important because "high exports account for fully one-third of [American] economic growth." Clinton went on to remind Americans that the "world's economies are more and more interconnected," but this brief recognition of the mutually advantageous nature of voluntary trade among regions quickly is replaced with confusion, when he asked, "Why should Americans be concerned about [serious financial problems in Southeast Asia]?" The answer to this question is that "these countries are our customers, and if Asia sinks into recession, they won't be able to buy the goods that we want to sell them. They are our competitors, and if their currencies [fall in exchange value vis-à-vis the dollar] the price of their goods will drop, flooding our market and others with cheap goods, making it tougher for us to compete" (Clinton 1998:A-19). What is amazing about this rhetoric is that in just a few short sentences, nations have been described as both customers and competitors. Nations are like corporations fighting for market share—or are they?

According to Krugman, it is a great error to think of nations as corporations (Krugman 1996b; Krugman 1996a:106). The United States does not sell goods and services; rather, people and businesses located in the United States trade with people and businesses in other regions. The President must show an understanding of basic economics here and emphasize that interregional trade and specialization swells the mass of commodities and services available to all for distribution. Krugman explained that trade functions like processes of technological change to expand potential wealth to all Americans. Admittedly, under Stolper-Samuelson, free trade might lower the real wage of our relatively scarce factor of production (nothing in modern economic theory permits us to rule out such a redistribution of wealth), but to limit or prevent international trade would be analogous to taxing and prohibiting processes of technological change. In the past, technological innovations have produced enormous changes in the ways that we work and live. For the same reason we accept technological change we must tolerate international trade and exchange based on comparative advantage (Krugman 1996a:119–230). Here Krugman is resorting to the same exact reasoning we detected in Henry George's writings of one hundred years ago.

Krugman is especially upset with several of the President's academic advisors, some of whom were trained as economists, but who, in their lust for power and influence, have eschewed the fundamental principles of economics and embraced pop internationalism. Krugman offers a blistering attack on Lester Thurow's bestseller *Head to Head: The Coming Battle Among America, Japan, and Europe* (Thurow 1993). This book managed to receive an endorsement from President Clinton himself! My softcover edition contains Senator Paul Simon's endorsement.[17]

Thurow's polemic severed its ties with the two-centuries-old free trade tradition. *Head to Head* misdirects attention from the myriad ways in which a nation or region of the world differs from a large corporation. For a country, encouraging export sales to create jobs when taken to extremes could seriously lower regional productivity and real income. Exports are what we need to pay for our imports: living standards rise because of imports. Why would the people in a region be joyous about paying extra amounts for the things they import? Rather, a nation or region is not a corporation that sees sales of its goods and services as a source of shareholder value. A nation is itself a region comprised of numerous corporations and individual households. It does not speak with one loud voice but with a plethora of individual voices, interests, hopes, and aspirations.

According to Krugman, a large region resembles a closed system, and certain accounting relationships must hold true in the current international financial system. These necessary accounting relationships operate differently for regions than for large corporations (Krugman 1996b). That is why if one region of the world is attracting enormous amounts of capital, then (a) it will necessarily run a trade deficit (current account deficit) with its partners, and (b) its aggregate domestic investment will exceed its aggregate domestic savings.[18] The trade deficit is merely the other side of a region being a net seller of bonds, stocks, and other property rights assets to individuals outside that region. Someone who advocates policies that, under flexible exchange rates, are intended to achieve a simultaneous increase in foreign direct investment and a surplus on the trade account is trying to accomplish the impossible. Modern accounting guarantees that this cannot happen.

Krugman, like George 100 years earlier, sounds the clarion trumpet of free trade out of a love of liberty and tolerance and with the 300-year-old insights of modern economics. Economists are the pillar of the intellectual crusade to teach all nations about the benefits of cooperation and international exchange.

Conclusion

I HAVE EXAMINED the two important books that draw upon core economic ideas and principles to address important political issues of their respective time periods and to preach the gospel of free trade. As I said at the beginning, that preaching amounts to a call for tolerance. Not only should people be allowed to live peacefully and unharmed, they should also be left alone to freely trade and exchange goods and services on a mutual basis with others in different parts of the world. George and Krugman treat protectionism, as do I, as something often sinister and inconsistent with broader issues of social justice.

For George, the war against protectionism extended to broader and more far-reaching problems of social organization. In his judgment, monopoly restrictions limiting access to land and raw materials must be removed. For Krugman, the battle against protectionism takes the form of flatly denying the curse of pop internationalism and returning to fundamentals, emphatically denying that international trade is some sort of strategic competition such that when one nation-state loses another one thereby gains. Both authors demand that we understand the fundamental mechanisms and processes of comparative advantage, from which toleration and free trade will follow.

The challenge of social justice will not disappear in our lifetimes. One hundred years from now, in 2101, few of my 20th-century readers will be around. Still, it will be fun to find among the books or cyberspace treatises that special free-trade text harking back to Krugman and George and others who, like the Tinbergen Archives, keep the torch of tolerance alive in a different age and a different context.

I have my own imaginative thoughts about what the latest advances in preaching will be about. The central issue will have to do with the free movement of individuals from one region of the world to the next. Many nations will use military force to keep the "foreign devils" off their lands. Policymakers will allege that there is only so much work to be done and that if more people enter the country to work, they will push locals out of jobs.

The doctrine of free trade assumes that when real wages differ among regions, only goods and services travel and not the services of individual laborers themselves. Indeed, it is a theorem of modern international trade theory—the factor-price-equalization theorem—that open-market exchange of goods and services will equalize "factor prices world wide just as unrestricted factor mobility would do" (Humphrey 1996:69). Free trade in goods and services serves as a substitute for the free movement of laborers and their families (Deardorff and Stern 1994:9–10). Differences in the real wage of labor and other factors tends to narrow without the reshuffling migrants and asylum seekers.

As the bulk of the world shifts from free trade areas with pockets of protectionism to a veritable common market, our concept of tolerance must be broadened even further from the acceptance of free trade and the unimpeded exchange of goods and services to the acceptance of immigrants and wanderers experimenting with new designs for living and working together. Free trade ideas will become more evident in another sense as well. With open regional borders and free travel, the free trade doctrine will be applied both to the services of labor as well to the families of the laborers who may have a preference for living in one place rather than another. This extension of the free trade doctrine to the whole idea of freedom to associate, to travel, to work, without the threat of interventions to disrupt, derail, and detract from those associations is the next frontier in free trade doctrine. Economists, along with organizations like the Tinbergen Archives, can take pride in the fact that they have moved the world closer to an even more thoroughgoing notion of tolerance. The economics of a world without immigration laws and tolerant of the mobility of men and women is most properly a topic for a sermon.[19]

Notes

1. The Tinbergen Archives is located at 1800 South Robertson Boulevard, Suite 206, Los Angeles, California 90035. In a note thanking me for my recent purchase of the film "Nuremberg," Mr. Cal Tinbergen summarized the goals and objectives of his archives as I have stated in the text.

2. Douglas A. Irwin (1996) offers a coherent and interesting history of the free trade doctrine. Its links to a broader cosmopolitan conception of economic life are better found in the works of the Austrian economist Ludwig von Mises (1963). Other efforts to persuade critics that middlemen perform important and valuable services can be found in Lerner (1961:32–48) and more recently (Landa 1994).

3. It is not easy to generalize and point to any single cause for genocide. It seems to me that at least some bigotry and hatred of social groups can be linked in large part to profit-making middleman activities and the ignorance surrounding those activities. On the causes of hatred against the European Jews, see Goldenhagen (1996:90–91). On the Armenians and Jews as parasitic "races" that survive parasitically by dealing in money changing see Alfred Marshall (Marshall 1961, I:244). Marshall's remarks were published only a few years before the shocking Armenian massacres of 1894 in Asia Minor by the Ottoman army but he allowed this remark to stand in each successive edition of his text. The Armenian slaughter of 1915 also failed to catch his attention. On the 1998 Indonesian crisis and its links to the long-standing hatred of the diaspora Chinese in Southeast Asia, see Seth Mydans, "Indonesia Turns Its Chinese Into Scapegoats," *New York Times* (February 2, 1998): A-3.

4. The West grew rich because free trade and exchange occurred in an environment that encouraged innovation and entrepreneurship. This means that the text must be qualified to read that free trade and exchange will produce these progressive results in a legal environment that participants find to be "legitimate" and that encourages trust and long-term private planning. For accounts that largely support my statement in the text see Rosenberg and Birdzell (1986), Steckel and Floud (1997), and Mokyr (1990).

5. There are "exceptions" to the rule that free trade will always be to the advantage of a region. See Irwin (1996), Krugman (1996), and Maneschi (1998). According to Maneschi, "protection for infant industries had been advocated since mercantilist times, and . . . because of the careful and plausible way [John Stuart] Mill rephrased the argument . . . he insured its respectability among mainstream economists for over a century. The only other argument for protection accepted as valid (from a nationalist viewpoint not sanctioned by Mill himself) was the terms of trade argument, whereby a country with monopoly power in trade can use a tariff to improve its terms of trade" (1998:141). Maneschi goes on to say, "advocates of protectionism such as Henry Carey identified rising

living standards with industrialization anticipating 'new trade theory'." The NTT holds that dynamic factors promote comparative advantage. This leads to the policy insight that comparative advantage "can actually be created with the assistance of policy makers who wish to advance their country's economic standing" (1998:143). These are the principal exceptions to free trade that I refer to in the text.

6. Rights talk is now unpopular among scholars. Certainly, it was the language of Adam Smith's day and used by him to attack various state-imposed limits on human behavior. Consider Smith's response to the policy of removing poor people from the parish where they chose to reside. Smith argued that such government action is "an evident violation of natural liberty and justice" (Smith, I: 157). To extend these claims about justice requires that we decide what to allow in the commonwealth: (a) the types of trade and exchange and (b) the types of commodities and services. Most civilized nations have outlawed ownership and exchange of slaves and certain types of pornography. I shall not attempt a defense of this approach here except to say that such an approach is consistent with Henry George's general approach to policy questions.

7. Krugman's book culled together important and interesting papers on trade and international competition that he had published in leading journals and magazines during the 1990s: "Competitiveness: A Dangerous Obsession," *Foreign Affairs* (March\April 1994): 28–44; "Proving My Point," *Foreign Affairs* (July\August 1994): 198–203; "Trade, Jobs, and Wages," *Scientific American* (April 1994): 22–27; "Does Third World Growth Hurt First World Prosperity?" *Harvard Business Review* (July\August 1994): 113–121; and "Myths and Realities of U.S. Competitiveness," *Science* (November 1991): 811–815.

8. Barker (1991) tries to link events in George's life with the emergence of his ideas about land reform. See especially chapters 6 and 7.

9. Hamilton and the Federalists were opposed by Thomas Jefferson, who extolled in his early writings the benefits of agriculture. It is not well known that Jefferson opposed immigration "on the grounds that European morals are depraved" (Grampp 1965:117). This is ironic given the recent DNA evidence that Jefferson himself parented children out of wedlock with one of his slaves. This is a controversial topic but one worth mentioning here.

10. The Wharton school would continue to uphold interventionism until the apostasy of the famous Wharton economist Simon Patten. He came to Wharton a "scientific representative of [protectionist] policy" but later turned against "unbridled big business" and monopoly business after 1900 and became a promoter of progressivism and reform. The University of Pennsylvania's Wharton School eventually drove Patten out, but that was not until 1917 when most of his best work had been accomplished (Sass 1993:238–240).

11. As a general rule, when the inhabitants of nation A are paying off loans or repatriating profits to the inhabitants of nation B, this constitutes net foreign disinvestment for nation B and a "capital account deficit" for nation A. A capital account deficit in a regime of flexible exchange rates necessarily implies a current account trade surplus for nation A. Nation A is in effect "saving" by consuming less than its potential output and using the net exports to "buy back" foreign financial claims on the future productivity of the region.

12. What I have in mind here is simply that when the business's lease comes up for renewal, the landlord will demand higher rent. The tenant can afford to pay higher rent so long as it does not go beyond the profits and chew away part of his capital (his equity "tied up" in the business). If the landlord claims rent up to this limit and no more, then the value of the property will increase as the higher rent is capitalized into a higher land price.

13. Rogowski (1989) argues that the experience of the United States (along with Germany and Britain) in the nineteenth century confirms the logic of the Stolper-Samuelson theorem where this theorem now serves as a historical law. Since the United States has abundant land and much less labor and capital, it follows that the United States would become protectionist. According to Stolper-Samuelson, protectionism raises the real returns to the relatively scarce factors of production. Labor and capital "therefore" were led by their private interests to agitate for protectionism. Ironically, Henry George took the position that it was land that had become "artificially" scarce and that protectionism would ultimately benefit the landlords at the expense of labor and capital. I discuss this problem below.

14. Compare my treatment with Martin (1989:489–501). Rogowski (1989) uses the Stolper-Samuelson theorem in a "three factor case" to explain political alignments. Also see note 13 above.

15. At the time of the invitation in 1992, Krugman had already published his *Rethinking International Trade* in which he established what has come to be known as "new trade theory" (NTT). NTT holds that the comparative advantage enjoyed by any region or nation can be shaped by the active involvement of the government. It is obvious that Krugman was invited to the Little Rock conference because he was expected to endorse government interventions designed to improve U.S. competitiveness. This may have been a miscalculation by the political forces, because Krugman was already actively putting warning labels on his scientific work. In subsequent writings, Krugman sounded a note of caution. He warned that "new thinking about trade does not yet provide simple guidelines for policy" (Krugman 1986:18). Krugman's arguments for abandoning free trade were fair game for the interest groups. They would seize upon his or

any scientist's texts and use them to "advocate policies that are not likely to benefit the nation as a whole" (Krugman 1986:19).

16. According to Krugman, the Clinton administration's entry into NAFTA was not based on any systematic understanding of free trade and its importance as an extension of a basic political vision of tolerance for other regions and its people. More likely than not, the U.S. administration simply felt that the supposed one-sided advantage given to Mexico by the agreement is just the cost of helping Mexico's government remain in power (Krugman 1996a:155–65).

17. U.S. Senator Paul Simon hopes that "this book . . . [will] have impact in the halls of Congress, in the workplace, and in the boardroom. That's why I have put a copy on each senator's desk" (Thurow 1993, rear cover).

18. A region may be attracting capital because its wages are low in relation to its laborers' productivity or because some investors may simply wish to withdraw investments from more unstable political environments.

19. Indeed, I was surprised to discover that among philosophical libertarians and more so among political libertarians, unlimited migration of peoples of all colors and cultures remains controversial. See however the refreshingly consistent and principled writings of Walter Block who cares little for nation-state building (Block 1998).

SECTION 4

PHILOSOPHY OF JUSTICE

Peace, Justice, and Economic Reform

By NICOLAUS TIDEMAN*

Introduction: Peace—More Than Tranquillity

THERE IS A bumper sticker that says, "If you want peace, then work for justice." At a superficial level, this simple slogan contains an important half-truth. At a deeper level, it contains a more profound half-truth. To understand these half-truths and why they are only half true, we need to know what peace is, what justice is, and we need to understand the relationship between the two. So in this talk I want to explore the meanings of peace and justice, their relationship, and the role of economic reform in attaining both.

"If you want peace, then work for justice." The more obvious and superficial meaning of this slogan is that people who are treated unjustly will prevent the attainment of peace until the wrongs to which they are subject are righted. Demonstrators shout: "No justice. No peace." The apparent meaning of peace in this case is tranquillity, the absence of strife. And if this meaning of peace is accepted, the slogan is true. You cannot expect to end strife as long as people have unresolved grievances. But the reason that this is only half true is that this meaning is only a shadow of what peace really is.

Peace is more than armistice, more than the cessation of violence. Peace is unity and harmony. In a peaceful world, people are all pleased to cooperate with one another. When we have attained true peace, there will be no person who has any purpose that any other person seeks to thwart. In a peaceful world, everyone will feel the truth of John Donne's meditation:

> No man is an Island entire of itself; every man is a piece of the Continent; a part of the main; if a clod be washed away by the sea, Europe is the less, and well as if a promontory were, as well as if a manor of thy

*Professor of Economics, Virginia Polytechnic Institute and State University.

> friends or of thine own were; any man's death diminishes me because I am involved in Mankind; therefore never send to know for whom the bell tolls; it tolls for thee (Meditation XV).

Is it imaginable that we might ever attain a world where everyone felt so? And if we do so, what will be the role of justice in that world? What is justice?

The Image of Justice

THERE ARE SO many conflicting, strident claims for different conceptions of justice that a person might reasonably despair of ever finding a meaning of justice that people would agree upon. Any conception of justice may seem to be no more than one person's opinion. And yet there are things that we all know about justice. If I tell you that I stand before you as justice, you know that across my face you will find—a blindfold. In my left hand I hold aloft—a pair of scales. You know that in my right hand I have a sword that I will use if necessary. And my gender is female.

The blindfold, the scales, the sword, and the feminine gender. These features of the traditional symbol tell us much about justice.

The blindfold might seem out of place, since it prevents justice from either seeing what the scales say or wielding the sword effectively. But we know that the blindfold has a distinct and essential meaning. The blindfold ensures that justice will not be swayed by any visible characteristics of those who plead before her. Justice is not concerned with whether you are black or white, short or tall, beautiful or ugly. Every person receives the same treatment from justice.

The scales have at least two possible interpretations. The first interpretation is that the disputants at the bar of justice each place their arguments in one of the pans of the scales, and justice determines who has the weightier arguments. Our language supports this interpretation with references to the scales of justice tipping in one direction or another. But there is different use of the scales that is particularly relevant to questions of social justice, as opposed to personal disputes. The scales can be used to achieve an equal division. Justice is done when the contents of one pan of the scales are exactly balanced by the contents of the other. This is the meaning of the scales that I shall apply.

And then the sword. The sword represents the fact that justice is prepared to use the threat of force, and force itself, to see that her decrees are carried out. In a world where men have so often used weapons to achieve selfish dominance, the feminine gender helps make credible the claim that the sword is used only to achieve justice, and not to advance the selfish interests of the person who wields it.

Thus if we know that justice is the blindfolded woman with the scales and the sword, then we know that justice is the principles of equality and evenhandedness that command and prohibit the use of force in resolving conflicts.

Consider what this tells us.

It tells us first that if we wish to claim that justice authorizes the force we wish to use, or that justice forbids the force that others wish to use against us, then we must be able to show that our claim is consistent with equality and evenhandedness. The slogan "might makes right" is an oxymoron, a misuse of language. An autocrat like Genghis Khan who imposes his will on others, without any reference to principles, does not operate in the realm of justice.

Second, the blindfold tells us that we are not in the realm of justice if the principles we offer to explain why our use of force is justified are of the form, "Because I am better than you," or Hitler's, "Because Aryans are better than Jews." Justice compels us to acknowledge the equality of all persons. Claims of individual or group supremacy cannot be accepted by justice.

Third, not only are all persons equal in the blindfolded eyes of justice, but their different goals in life all deserve equal respect. Lenin's claim that all power should be in the hands of the Central Committee of the Communist Party, because the Party was the unique source of true understanding of the historical dialectic, cannot be accepted by justice. Even if the Party is the unique source of true historical understanding, that is not a sufficient reason to give all power to the party. Justice provides equal treatment for those who wish to pursue lives that are inconsistent with the advance of the historical dialectic. And any other elitist claim that some particular goal provides the basis for favored treatment must similarly be rejected by justice.

Even the utilitarian proposal that conflicting claims should be settled in the way that yields the greatest possible utility must be rejected as an elitist imposition of a particular goal on people who may have other plans. If I choose to pursue a life that can be guaranteed to lead to depression and despair, I have as much claim to the protection of justice in that pursuit as if I choose the path that leads to bliss. Justice must be neutral in its evaluation of people and their goals. As Bruce Ackerman (1980:11) has said in defining neutrality,

> No reason [justifying the exercise of power] is a good reason if it requires the power holder to assert:
> (a) that his conception of the good is better than that asserted by any of his fellow citizens, or
> (b) that, regardless of his conception of the good, he is intrinsically superior to one or more of his fellow citizens.

Conflicting Definitions of Justice

IF WE COMMIT ourselves to neutrality, does that provide a unique definition of justice? No, it doesn't. There are a number of definitions of justice that might claim to satisfy neutrality, although the claims of some definitions are dubious, and other definitions can be rejected on other grounds.

Conservatism: Justice as Tradition

Consider first the conservative claim that justice is defined by traditional rules. The conservative says, "I don't say that I'm better than anyone else, nor do I say that my conception of the good is better than anyone else's. I may not even like what tradition demands. But if you want to be just, you will follow the rules that have traditionally been followed."

I have seen one drawing of justice that reflects this conservative view by portraying justice as a seated woman, with a book in her lap. The book is clearly the received law, the source that justice cites as the foundation of her decrees. But this is not the standard image of justice.

There is an important virtue of conservatism. It eliminates the waste of resources in fighting over who has what rights, the waste from what economists call rent-seeking. Furthermore, there will be some situations where there is no time to secure agreement on anything other than the status quo. Thus there is reason to have at least some element of conservatism in the procedures by which disputes are resolved. But conservatism cannot be the ultimate rule of a just society. It would perpetuate slavery, the selling of daughters as brides, racial and sexual inequalities in civil rights, and every other historical injustice that, through our moral evolution, we have overcome. The neutrality of conservatism is superficial. Conservatism cannot claim to offer either the evenhandedness that the blindfold promises or the equality that the scales require.

Justice as Majority Vote

Next, consider the claim that justice is defined by what the majority wants. The majoritarian says, "If you want to know who should prevail in a conflict, take a vote." As appealing as majoritarianism may be on the surface, it cannot provide a coherent theory of justice.

If one wishes to make sense of majoritarianism, one must first specify the perspective from which voters are expected to vote. Are voters to vote as proponents of their selfish personal interests, or are they to vote as disinterested judges of what is best?

Suppose first that voters vote on the basis of their selfish personal interests. Then voting is incoherent as a basis for justice. If voters always vote selfishly, then at any time when you might think that the voting was over, there will always be some measure that can be proposed that will benefit a majority at the expense of a minority, which could therefore be adopted by selfish voting. The process of deciding by voting will never end if any proposal can be advanced at any time and people always vote selfishly. Selfish voting can be used to decide between any two proposals. And it can be used in more general settings if there is some more or less arbitrary stopping rule to keep the process from going on indefinitely. But selfish voting as a general mechanism for determining what is just is incoherent.

Now suppose that voters behave as unselfish, disinterested judges of what is best. In this case, voting as a mechanism for determining what is just is incomplete, because it leaves unanswered the question of what is meant by "best." Does "best" mean "creates the greatest total utility" or "comes closest to preserving the expectations of the status quo" or "maximizes the rate of growth of the population" or something else? How would you know what best means? If the Supreme Court knows that what is best is what comes closest to preserving the expectations that have developed from our Constitution and traditions, then the justices can employ voting to decide cases and establish new precedents. But to say that what is just is what is voted to be best by unselfish, disinterested judges without specifying what best means is to decline to answer the question of what justice is. Thus neither selfish voting nor unselfish voting serves to define justice, although there can be an element of voting in our efforts to resolve disagreements about what an agreed definition of justice requires in particular circumstances.

Justice as Contract

If voting cannot be used to define justice, one might entertain the possibility of using a contractarian formulation: What is just is the rules to which people would have agreed if they did not know their personal circumstances. In "Justice as Fairness," John Rawls said,

> [Suppose that a group lets] each person propose the principles upon which he wishes his complaints to be tried with the understanding that, if acknowledged, the complaints of others will be similarly tried, and that no complaints will be heard at all until everyone is roughly of one mind as to how the complaints are to be judged. . . . [E]ach person will propose principles of a general kind which will, to a large degree, gain their sense from the various applications to be made of them, the particular circumstances of which being as yet unknown (Rawls 1958:171–72).

This is a reasonable recipe for implementing the Golden Rule and a fine idea for seeking agreement about the principles by which complaints shall be judged. If people were to follow this suggestion and achieve the agreement that is described, they would achieve fairness.

However, this does not make Rawls's suggestion a good way to identify justice. The critical difficulty with his suggestion is that those who mete out justice cannot afford the luxury of securing complete agreement on principles. They must bring their judgment to bear on those who have not agreed on principles. In this context, the closest that a person can come to Rawls' suggestion is to ask himself, "Are the principles that I propose to apply ones that I would agree to if I did not know how I would personally be affected by them?" This is a dangerously weak criterion.

In later writings, Rawls (1971:75–83) claims that in the original position, people would choose the rules that maximized the well-being of the representative member of the least advantaged class. John Harsanyi (1975:594), on the other hand, has said that in the original position people would choose the rules that maximized average utility. Someone else might say that in the original position people would choose the rules that provided the greatest stability. How can we know what people would choose?

No matter how a contractarian answers this question, there will be the difficulty raised by Ackerman, in *Social Justice in the Liberal State*. Describing the attempt to apply the Rawlsian criterion, Ackerman (1980:330–31) says:

> Despite my best efforts, I shall be defenseless . . . the moment I try to make it clear to another person why it is right that I, rather than he, should establish a claim over a disputed thing:
>
> I: When I look into myself, I am sure that I would have insisted upon this right as a condition for entering society with you.
>
> You: You haven't the slightest idea what you would have insisted on in a presocial state. You're simply using the idea of a potential entrant as a screen upon which to project the deepest desires of your socialized self. But I too have desires; why should mine be sacrificed to yours? And if you insist, it is possible that I too may delve deep into my psyche and find a transcendent grounding for my desires.

The sword of justice is too momentous to be constrained only by the requirement that those who judge be able to convince themselves that their judgments satisfy principles to which they would have agreed, if they had not known how they would be affected by those principles. The contractarian approach may be a good way to seek consensus. It may be a good guideline for those who are called upon by disputants to arbitrate between them. But it is not a good way to define justice.

Justice as Equality

Next, consider egalitarianism. The egalitarian says that justice is equality. There is a conceptual difficulty in specifying how beings as different from each other as humans are could ever be equal, unless we create a society where all humans are female clones of one another. (This should be technologically feasible within a few decades, if it is not already.) But I do not think that egalitarians want a society of clones.

Ackerman (1980:113–20) has offered a suggestion for determining whether any persons among a genetically diverse group are genetically disadvantaged. His suggestion is that, to be genetically undominated, a person must possess a set of abilities that permit him to pursue some life purpose that some persons have, with as much facility as any other person is able to pursue that life purpose. Ackerman also asserts that every person has a right to be genetically undominated.

I doubt that we have the technological capability yet to ensure that every child who is born will be genetically undominated, and until we have that capability and decide to use it, any egalitarian will need to deal with the question of how genetic inequalities are to be rectified.

John Rawls (1973:338) has proposed that the talents that individuals possess be regarded as a common pool and that those who have more than an average share have an obligation to compensate those who have less than an average share. Ronald Dworkin (1981:283–345) has made the contractarian suggestion that people can justly be required to pay an income tax that represents the insurance against being untalented that they would have desired to purchase before they knew what talents they would have.

Dworkin acknowledges that his suggestion would not produce equality. If we believe Harsanyi's claim that people who did not know their personal circumstances would want to maximize their expected utility, then, even in the absence of adjustments for incentive effects, Dworkin's suggestion leads not to equal utilities, but rather to equal marginal utilities of money, which generally implies unequal utilities when people have different capacities to get utility from money.

Ackerman (1980:132–33) suggests that each person who is genetically dominated is owed compensation by those who dominate him.

All of these suggestions should be rejected. Talents are not a common pool from which some persons have taken more than their shares. If we are all fishing in the same pond, the fish that you take will diminish the quantity that is available to me. But the talent that you have in no way diminishes the quantity of talent that is available to me. Your talent is not acquired at the expense of my talent.

From the perspective of peace, no man is an island; each of us is a part of mankind. Any of us who has been graced with an extra measure of talent should recognize that often the best use of our talent is to provide for others. Nevertheless, from the perspective of justice, each of us must be allowed to act like an island if he wishes.

Suppose that a bone-marrow transplant from me would save your life—or at least prolong it. And suppose that there is no other person whose tissue type matches yours. Would you assert that you have a right to receive such a transplant whether or not I want to give it? Would you suggest that the sword of justice should be used to force me to give it? An egalitarian ought to be prepared to require me to provide the transplant, for if I refuse I am denying the possibility of continued life to another person, when I have continued life for myself, and the cost to me would be relatively modest.

If you do not mind requiring a bone-marrow transplant of me, then what about a kidney? Suppose that, through no fault of your own, both of your kidneys have failed, and I am the only person who has a kidney that is compatible with your tissue. Would you force me to donate a kidney? And if you call yourself an egalitarian and you would not, then why not? After all, I have two working kidneys and you have none. What could be more equal than requiring us to divide the available working kidneys equally?

If you do not mind requiring me to donate a kidney, then what about my heart? Suppose that I have lived for 50 years and you have lived for only 25. Your heart has been damaged by an illness, through no fault of your own. I have the only heart that matches your tissue, and it would be good for another 25 years. One of us will have to die. Why shouldn't we put the one available heart in your chest, so that we might divide the available years of life equally between us? A good egalitarian should require me to part with the one available heart after I have had my share of years.

But I don't think you would. I don't think anyone would. We are not egalitarians. We recognize the sanctity of the boundaries of the human body. In a peaceful world I will gladly give a spare kidney to anyone who needs it. But in a just world, no one will forcefully extract a kidney from me, even to save someone else's life. Justice is not egalitarianism.

Just as I own my kidneys, so do I own my talents. In a peaceful world I will use them for the benefit of all mankind. But the sword of justice should not be used to force me to compensate those with less talent. Nor should it be used to force me to abide by the insurance contract that you believe I would have signed, if I had had the chance, before I knew what talents I would have. Nor, in Ackerman's framework, should I be held responsible for the fact that someone else decided to have a child that turned out to be genetically dominated by me. If anyone is held responsible for the fact that a genetically dominated child is brought into the world, it should be the child's parents. And if the parents are irresponsible, then the parents' parents, or the parents' teachers should be held responsible.

If would-be parents are too poor to provide for the children that they ought to be able to have, then we should ask whether their parents provided inadequately for them, or whether they were unjustly deprived of resources that ought to have been theirs. But it is not a reason to levy assessments on those who have talent. An egalitarian redistribution to compensate for differences in talent is as unjust as an egalitarian redistribution of kidneys. Egalitarianism is not justice.

True Justice

A PROPER DEFINITION of justice begins with the principles of classical liberalism. In a just world each person is permitted to determine the purposes to which his or her body is put—the hands and the brain no less than the kidneys. We each have rights of self-determination. This includes the right of ownership of what we produce, at least, as John Locke (*Second Treatise of Government*, § 27) said, when we leave as much in natural opportunities for others as we appropriate for our own productive activities.

We have the right to co-operate with whom we choose for whatever mutually agreed purposes we choose. Thus we have the right to trade with others, without any artificial hindrances, and we have the right to keep any wages or profit that we receive from such trading.

These components of the classical liberal conception of justice are held by two groups that hold conflicting views on a companion issue of great importance: how are claims of exclusive access to natural opportunities to be established?

John Locke qualified his statement that we own what we produce with his famous "proviso" that there be "as much and as good left in common for others." A few pages later, writing in the last decade of the 17th century, he said that private appropriations of land are actually not restricted, because anyone who is dissatisfied with the land available to him in Europe can always go to America, where there is plenty of unclaimed land (Locke, *Second Treatise of Government*, § 36). Locke does not address the issue of rights to land when land is scarce.

One tradition in classical liberalism concerning claims to land is that of the "homesteading libertarians," as exemplified by Murray Rothbard, who say that there is really no need to be concerned with Locke's proviso. Natural opportunities belong to whoever first appropriates them, regardless of whether opportunities of equal value are available to others (Rothbard 1982).

The other tradition is that of the "geoists," as inspired if not exemplified by Henry George, who say that, whenever natural opportunities are scarce, each person has an obligation to ensure that the per capita value of the natural opportunities that he leaves for others is as great as the value of the natural opportunities that he claims for himself. Any excess in one's claim generates an obligation to compensate those who thereby have less. George actually proposed the nearly equivalent idea, that all or nearly all of the rental value of land should be collected in taxes, and all other taxes should be abolished (George 1981:328–46; 403–07). The geoist position, as I have expressed it, emphasizes the idea that, at least when value generated by public services is not an issue, rights to land are fundamentally rights of individuals, not rights of governments.

There are two fundamental problems with the position of homesteading libertarians on claims to land. The first problem is the incongruity with historical reality. Humans have emerged from an environment of violence. Those who now have titles to land can trace those titles back only so far, before they come to events where fiat backed by violence determined title. And the persons who were displaced at that time had titles that also originated in violence. If there ever were humans who acquired the use of land without forcibly displacing other humans, we have no way of knowing who they were or who their current descendants might be. There is, in practice, no way of assigning land to the legitimate successors of the persons who first claimed land. And to assign titles based on any fraction of history is to reward the last land seizures that are not rectified.

The second fundamental problem with the position of the homesteading libertarians is that, even if there were previously unsettled land to be allocated, say a new continent emerging from the ocean, first grabbing would make no sense as a criterion for allocating land.

It would be inefficient, for one thing, as people stampeded to do whatever was necessary to establish their claims. Still, that is not decisive because, if we are concerned with justice, it might be necessary for us to tolerate inefficiency. But the homesteading libertarian view makes no sense in terms of justice. "I get it all because I got here first," isn't justice. Justice—the balancing of the scales—is the geoist position, "I get exclusive access to this natural opportunity because I have left natural opportunities of equal value for you." (How one compares, in practice, the value of different natural opportunities is a bit complex and worthy of a separate lecture.)

Justice is thus a regime in which persons have the greatest possible individual liberty, and all acknowledge an obligation to share equally the value of natural opportunities. Justice is economic reform—the abolition of all taxes on labor and capital, the acceptance of individual responsibility, the creation of institutions that will provide equal sharing of the value of natural opportunities.

Real Peace

GETTING BACK TO where we started, is it true that, "If you want peace—real peace—you should work for justice"? And if so, why? Well, it's half true. To see why, consider what peace is, and how one might create it.

Peace is unity and harmony. Peace is people recognizing that we are all parts of one another, that it is always for ourselves that the bell tolls.

What keeps us from attaining peace? One of the greatest hindrances to the attainment of peace—real peace—is the resistance that so many of us feel to tolerating oppression and injustice. When we know that we, or others we care for, have been treated unjustly, it is ever so difficult to attain a state of unity and harmony with others. The leap to peace is so much easier from a position of justice. So, even though peace and justice are very disparate things, and peace is much the more attractive one, still it make sense, if you want to help people reach peace, to work for justice.

But the reason that this is only half true is that, in fact, justice is not actually necessary to your attainment of peace. If you want peace for yourself, you can have it, at any time, in any circumstances in which you find yourself. Whether you are treated justly or not, you are a part of the being that is all humanity. Each person's joy is your joy. Each person's grief is your grief. You don't have to wait until you are treated justly to see this.

So if you want a peace for others, then work for justice. Work for freedom. Work for the elimination of all taxes on the productive things that people do. Work for equality in the right to benefit from natural opportunities. These things will make it easier for people to make the leap to peace.

But if you want peace for yourself, simply have it.

The Economics and Ethics of Idleness

By JAMES BUCHANAN*

I

Introduction

I PROPOSE TO use this occasion to explore, in an admittedly speculative fashion, a subject that has come increasingly to occupy my own interest and which also, in a special sense, is related to the interest and efforts of Henry George, whom this lecture series commemorates. I want to concentrate attention on *idleness* in the use of potentially productive resources, and particularly on the ethical aspects of individuals' choices concerning the margins of productive employment. This subject matter has been neglected in modern macroeconomic analysis, which has embodied the presumption that potentially productive resources will be employed optimally, within the constraints faced by individual resource owners, so long as the choice of employment is voluntary. The whole Keynesian macroeconomic emphasis, which came to occupy the attention of economists in mid-century, and which did have profound political impact, was centered on involuntary unemployment, or, to use my terminology in this paper, on idleness that is not chosen or preferred by resource owners.

Furthermore, the modern emphasis of economists, to the extent that they have concerned themselves at all with idleness in resource use, has been almost exclusively confined to labor; little or no attention has been given to possible idleness in the utilization of non-labor resources, something that did concern Henry George a century ago, at least indirectly.

*1986 Nobel Laureate in Economic Science; Professor Emeritus of Economics, George Mason University, Virginia. A somewhat different version of this chapter with a slightly different title was published in Buchanan, James M. *Ethics and Economic Progess*. Norman, University of Oklahoma Press, 1994:112–128.

It will first be necessary to define idleness, which I shall do in Section II. I shall then proceed, in Section III, to show that there are ethical implications of individual choices in resource utilization. Initially, I shall develop the analysis in application to labor or work input. In Section IV, I shall briefly sketch out the outlines of an argument that I have developed more fully elsewhere, an argument to the effect that voluntary choices made by resource owners need not be optimal, an argument that directly counters the conventional wisdom in economic theory. In Section V, I shift attention from labor to non-labor resources, which was, of course, the central focus of the efforts of Henry George, especially as applied to land. Finally, in Section VI, I suggest some interesting policy implications that seem to follow from the whole exercise.

II

Idleness Defined

PRECISELY WHAT DO we mean when we say that a resource, or resource unit, remains "idle"? We define idleness by its opposite; a resource is idle when it is not "at work," when it is not "employed." More generally, we can say that a resource is "idle" when it is not being used to produce value that it might otherwise produce. Such generalized understandings are satisfactory for most purposes, but they are not sufficiently specific for my purposes here.

Note, in particular, that the definition suggested could be used in application to the activities of Robinson Crusoe, all alone on his island, and totally outside any nexus of interaction, economic, political, or social, with other human beings. Crusoe may, of course, work hard and employ his own talents and time to produce something of value to himself. In some descriptive sense, we could measure Crusoe's idleness as distinguished from his work. But his choices in this respect could not carry ethical content since there are no others who could possibly be affected. And Crusoe might, for example, spend his time and energy, his "work," building sandcastles that are swept away by each evening's tides.

I want to introduce a more useful meaning of idleness by opposing this use of resources to "work in an interactive relationship with others" or "employment in producing value for others." In this more restricted, but more useful, definition, a person is idle when and to the extent that he or she withholds work effort from the market, even if, on some "private island," non-marketable and impermanent sandcastles are constructed. A resource, or resource unit, that can produce value when placed on the market, that is withheld from the market, or from own production that allows consumption purchases on the market to be replaced, is *idle*. The subjective value that may be produced for the resource owner is irrelevant.

I also want to rule out of consideration any non-voluntary idleness in the use of resources. Involuntary idleness may be important in many settings, but this sort of idleness is not my concern in this paper. I shall presume, for the analysis and discussion that follows, that all owners of resources may, if they choose to do so, place such resources in employment. There exists a parametric price per unit of resource supplied to the market and the owner-supplier may adjust amounts to this price, from zero to some employment maximum (or idleness minimum).

As noted, I shall initially develop the argument in application to labor, but I do not restrict the analysis, as such. Idleness can characterize the utilization of any resource, labor or non-labor, and no matter how classified. I shall make the appropriate extensions as required. There are differences between labor and non-labor resource units that are worthy of notice, however, differences that offer some explanation of economists' concentration on labor. The presumption is that, for any non-labor resource, under the assumption that resource owners face parametric prices in the market, voluntary choices will always lead to maximum resource utilization, or, stated conversely, to minimum idleness. I shall demonstrate that this conclusion does not follow if we are careful to remain with the definition of idleness stated above.

III

Is It Unethical to Loaf?

CONSIDER A SIMPLE example. There is a highly trained, professionally competent radiologist who is, at age forty-five, at the height of his career. He can secure an income, post-tax, of $200,000 annually. In January 1990, this person chooses, voluntarily, to work no more. He opts for the life of leisure; he "retires"; he lives off his accumulated savings, plays golf and tennis, and socializes. He undertakes no further productive effort. Henceforth, he remains idle.

How would the modern economist evaluate this choice? The foregone payment of $200,000 would have reflected, in some rough and ready sense, the net contribution to value in the economy that was made by the radiologist in question. The value of the national economic product will fall by this total upon the radiologist's choice to retire. But the economist would also note that the $200,000 also measures the pre-retirement income received by the radiologist. Hence, the person who makes the choice between productive work and idleness bears the full burden of payment. No one else in the national economy is affected, at least in any directly measurable economic sense. The choice made by the radiologist is the same as if he were, indeed, a Robinson Crusoe on his private island. There seems to be no ethical content in this choice, no ethical implications that result, because others than the one who chooses for himself find themselves in the same positions whether or not the radiologist chooses work or leisure.

There are some qualifications to this conclusion that must be made. First, if taxes are levied on measured money income, then the choice made by anyone to earn less income and to take more leisure will reduce public-goods benefits and/or increase taxes on others in the fiscal system. I shall simply acknowledge the effects of this fiscal interdependence here, and I shall neglect further discussion because I do not want to base my central argument on this point. Second, if resources are specialized, as is always the case for transitional periods, the change in relative prices will generate gains for some groups and losses for others. In some long run sense, however, these effects disappear and, under the conditions presumed necessary for a workably competitive economy, the primary conclusion seems to stand up. There seems to be no important spillover effect on others that stems from the choice made by one income earner, even a high income earner, to loaf rather than to continue to supply productive effort to the economic nexus.

This apparent result squarely contradicts one of the first principles of economics, a principle first enunciated clearly by Adam Smith in 1776. There exist mutual gains from trade; all parties gain from exchange, and these gains increase with extension in the size of the trading network. As the network of exchange expands, increasing advantage emerges from the increased specialization that is made possible. What has happened when the radiologist in our example decides to work less is that the market has been reduced in size. There will be less prospect of fully utilizing the advantages of division of labor, at least for some area of production in the economy. There will be permanent changes in the price vector for outputs; inputs will earn less than before; the purchasing power of an input in terms of potentially purchasable output will fall. If this hypothesis holds, then the choice made by the radiologist in the example does, indeed, exert spillover effects on others in the whole system of interaction. This choice on the part of one person will necessarily harm others in the system. And, if harm to others is the criterion for unethical or immoral behavior, the choice to loaf rather than to continue to offer productive work to the economic nexus can legitimately be classified to be unethical or immoral.

IV

Increasing Returns

I HAVE EXPOSED what I consider to be a rather glaring contradiction between two parts of the conventional wisdom in modern economics, a contradiction that seems to have been largely, if not completely, overlooked. The tone of my discussion in the preceding section conveys my own analytical preferences, so to speak. I want to argue in support of the basic principle that all members of the inclusive production-exchange-consumption nexus tend to secure gains as the effective size of this nexus expands and that these gains are inexhaustible. That is to say, increases in specialization are always possible as markets are extended, producing, in turn, increases in economic well-being for participants.

But acceptance of this principle requires that the standard conditions for the attainment of equilibrium in a competitive economy be modified in some way. The vulnerable assumption in the model of competitive adjustment is that which postulates that, at equilibrium, firms operate everywhere in the range of constant returns to scale of operation. Note what happens under this postulate. In our simple example, the radiologist chooses to work no more. The competitive adjustment process insures that, after a transitional period, the price of radiology services will return to the same level as that prevailing prior to the decision made by the single supplier to cease productive effort, the services previously provided by the man who chooses to smell the flowers will now be generated by some expansion in the scale of operation of other radiologists or by the entry of newly-trained professionals. In either case, after the gains and losses over the transitional period are damped and a new equilibrium established in the industry, the first result identified emerges. The choice between idleness and productive effort on the part of any input supplier does not permanently affect the economic well-being of others.

To generate a result consistent with the inexhaustible gains-from-trade story, we must allow for the presence of increasing returns (decreasing costs) somewhere in the economy. In our example, the size of the measured nexus is lower by $200,000 annually than it was before the shift in preferences on the part of the person in question. Somewhere in the system, at some location, in some industry, there is now a specialist producer or supplier, of some input or some output, who finds that the market he or she faces is no longer sufficient to allow his or her trade to remain viable. Production is forced into a higher-cost mode of operation because the market will no longer support the specialization attained under the extended market. There will be an increase in the real price of the product or service that is ultimately produced under increasing returns.

V

The Idleness of Non-Labor Resources

TO THIS POINT in my argument I have introduced analysis and material that I have discussed in somewhat more detail elsewhere (Buchanan 1989). I now propose to enter virgin territory, so to speak, and to extend the same analysis to apply to non-labor resources. It is relatively straightforward to discuss the choice between idleness and productive effort in application to labor. The picture becomes cloudy when non-labor resources are treated. In my radiologist example, it is meaningful to think about the shift in preferences that caused the person to cease supplying productive effort to the marketplace and to supply, instead, hours of leisure to himself. There is nothing incoherent about a utility function that shifts in such a way as to make this choice take place. Leisure, or the uses to which leisure may be put, yield utility values to the individual, values which must in all cases be compared with those that emerge from the ultimate purchasing power over consumable goods and services that income from productive work effort makes possible.

But what is the equivalent to the utility value of leisure for non-human resource units? Recall that we must always remain within an individualistic calculus of choice here. Resource units do not, in themselves, take on characteristics that allow us to attribute values directly to them. We must remain with the utility calculus of those persons who own and control the utilization of non-human resource units. But why should an individual, as owner-supplier of a non-human resource unit, secure any potential utility value from withholding this unit from the market nexus?

It is relatively straightforward to understand why the owner of a resource unit would place such a unit on the market. The resource unit, if it is productive, yields a market price that provides the owner with income that may be used for the purchase of desired goods and services from other markets. But why should such an owner ever choose to withhold or to withdraw a unit from the marketplace (Buchanan 1989)?

For this result to occur, idleness in resource use must yield direct utility to the owner, analogous to that yielded by leisure to the supplier of potential work effort. Again, consider an example. A person accumulates under his personal ownership and control several thousand acres of marginally productive agricultural land. This land is leased/rented out to farmers who produce and market crops. The lease or rental value to the owner is $10,000 annually, which is approximately the value of the increment to product attributable to the land itself. The owner receives the $10,000 in annual rental value and returns this value to the income stream in either consumption goods purchases or investment in capital goods.

Let us now assume that the owner of the land experiences a shift in preferences concerning the usage of the land. He chooses voluntarily to withdraw the land from active production of crops and to utilize this resource in its natural state, say, as a hunting preserve. The land becomes idle, in my usage of terms here. To the owner, the choice can be fully rational; the owner withdraws the land from production for the market in the full knowledge that he or she is sacrificing $10,000 annually in rental or market value. The utility value now placed on the idleness of the land must be anticipated to yield more than the utility yielded by $10,000.

The example seems in all respects analogous to the labor-supply example of the radiologist discussed earlier. The inclusive economic nexus is made smaller by the decision of the landowner to withdraw the resource from production for the market. A market value of $10,000 could be produced with the resource, but this value is now replaced with a utility yield that is enjoyed exclusively by the owner of the resource. Other persons in the production-exchange-trading nexus are placed in a less preferred position due to the shrinkage of the size of the market, due to the failure to exploit fully the scale advantages that the potentially available specialization might make possible.

VI

Implications

RECOGNITION OF THE ethical content present in choices between placing resource units on the market and withholding them in idleness does not imply that they need be replaced with a utility yield that is enjoyed exclusively by the owner of the resource. Other persons in the production-exchange-trading nexus are placed in a less preferred position due to the shrinkage of the size of the market, due to the failure to exploit fully the scale advantages that the potentially available specialization might make possible.

If work is praiseworthy and loafing is blameworthy, if there is positive economic content in an ethic of work, as I have argued above and elsewhere, then there must also be comparable normative implications for the employment of non-labor resources. If non-labor resources are capable of producing value on the market, or value that is a direct substitute for goods that would otherwise be purchased from the market, there are external or spillover effects of decisions made by resource owners concerning the way in which these resources are used.

Note that the emphasis here is not explicitly distributional, although distributional implications may be derived indirectly. The owner of the land in our example does not exert a negative externality on others in the polity because he has extensive holdings. The negative externality stems exclusively from the owner's use of the holdings, from the withholding of potentially productive resources from the market nexus. Indeed, it is the owner's decision to forego measured money income, the rental value of the land, that imposes the costs on others. Because the owner does not earn this income and return it to the economy's circular flow as effective demand, the gains-from-trade that might otherwise be possible are not exploited.

VII

Conclusion

RECOGNITION OF THE ethical content present in choices between placing resource units on the market and withholding them in idleness does not imply that there need be some all-or-none commitment. Recognition that the radiologist, in the first example, does indeed provide spillover benefits to others in the economy as he produces value that he, in turn, spends for his own purposes, does not allow us to infer that the radiologist is immoral if he supplies anything less than the physically determined maximum number of hours of work. Additional work supply involves disutility to the supplier, and this decrement to value must be measured against (1) the utility value of the income earned to the radiologist, plus (2) the spillover value to others in the nexus. Beyond some point, the disutility of additional work surely offsets the value, both internal and external, of this work, even in the idealized felicific calculus. The point of my whole discussion here is to stress that there should be some recognition given to the value to other than the work supplier in the choice made between productive effort and idleness.

Much the same logic applies to the landowner's choice in the second example. The landowner does indeed impose costs on others in the economy as he withdraws land from the production of marketable value. But there need be no normative inference to the effect that land, or any other non-human resource, should always be utilized so as to yield maximal marketable product value. The hunting preserve presumably yields utility to the owner, and this utility (like leisure to the worker) should not be left out of account. Again the point to be noted is only that the effects on other than the choice maker, the landowner in this example, should not be overlooked.

In a paper written for another purpose, I have argued that it would be extremely difficult if not impossible to internalize or correct for resource-use externalities by ordinary economic or political adjustments. I suggested that such internalization that exists enters the calculus of choice makers by way of ethical constraints, which may or may not be conscious to the choosers. The radiologist may feel guilty when he does not work, and the landowner may feel a guilt of sorts when he converts the land into a hunting preserve.

Recognition of the interdependencies discussed can, however, lead to agreement on institutional changes that will, at the least, remove perverse incentives. The potentially useful changes are perhaps most evident in tax policy. The radiologist who chooses to forego income for leisure should be required to pay more, not less, in taxes. Yet, as we realize, most tax systems that are based on income would allow the radiologist's tax liability to be reduced. In this respect alone, the substitution of a consumption or expenditure base for an income base of tax would represent a major welfare-enhancing step. The landowner of our second example, who withdraws land from productive use to a purely private use, should be required to pay higher, not lower, taxes in any fiscal system that embodies a conceptually agreed on structure of incentives.

As we move beyond fiscal incentives, perhaps the most serious distortions in incentives are to be located in the failure of effective decision-makers on resource use to be confronted with relevant opportunity costs, even to the extent faced by genuine resource owners in our two examples. At the very least both the radiologist and the land owner make choices to withdraw resources from the market in the full knowledge that they will, privately and personally, suffer the loss of measured product value. In many cases, however, and especially in the modern economy-polity, resource use decisions are made by political agents, presumably acting on behalf of citizens. And these agents do not face the incentives of the marketplace at all. The coalition in the legislature that approves the withdrawal of productive land for preservation of "wilderness areas" or "wildlife habitats" loses neither the direct opportunity cost of lost market value nor the spillover harms generated by the necessary reduction in the size of the inclusive trading nexus along with the effects of the lowered tax base. If public policy analysts could incorporate the elementary principle that "resource use matters" for the ultimate size of the market, some corrective offset to the modern prejudice against the production of market value might be introduced.

Let me end with a private, personal, story. In May 1989, I visited Prudhoe Bay, on the Alaskan North Slope, where I toured the oil-producing facilities. Let me state categorically that there could be no place more desolate than this north slope in the absence of facilities—a barren, frozen, non-inhabitable desert. There exists another section of the North Slope that is anticipated to yield oil, but development has been prevented because of the misguided and confused judgment to the effect that such pristine wilderness should be preserved. This judgment is, to my mind, grossly immoral and especially so in that those who pronounce such judgment, and who do, indeed, exert political influence, do not stand to suffer any of the adverse consequences of the smaller economy that must result as we fail to take advantages of our opportunities.

The main thrust of my argument has been to the effect that the market, as it operates, does not fully take into account the advantages of production for the market because some share of these advantages accrue to other than those who make choices directly. But the argument is strengthened manyfold in application to politics, where those who make ultimate resource-using decisions share almost none of the costs of the sacrifice of opportunities that are foregone.

Idleness for private aesthetic purposes comes at a cost that even the hard-nosed economists have not properly reckoned. Should we be surprised at all by the relative decline in the productive record of the United States economy after the flower children of the 1960s came to work and the romantic environmentalists mounted their efforts to make us return to a natural state? Idleness is idleness is idleness, no matter what the dress.

SECTION 5

Religious Foundations of Social Policy

The Earth is the Lord's

By ROBERT V. ANDELSON*

GEORGE BERNARD SHAW, in a letter written in 1905 to Hamlin Garland, describes how, more than twenty years earlier, he had attended Henry George's first platform appearance in London. He knew at once, he said, that the speaker must be an American, for four reasons: "Because he pronounced 'necessarily' . . . with the accent on the third syllable instead of the first; because he was deliberately and intentionally oratorical, which is not customary among shy people like the English; because he spoke of Liberty, Justice, Truth, Natural Law, and other strange 18th-century superstitions; and because he explained with great simplicity and sincerity the views of the Creator, who had gone completely out of fashion in London in the previous decade and had not been heard of there since."

George's magnum opus, *Progress and Poverty* (the centenary of which occurred in 1979), is characterized by the same moral and religious emphasis remarked by Shaw in its author's London lecture, an emphasis that rises in the final chapter to the noble declaration of a faith revived. It is, I think, therefore entirely appropriate that I focus today on the moral and religious aspects of his basic proposal for economic reform—his proposal to lift the burden of taxation from the fruits of individual labor, while appropriating for public use the socially-engendered value of the land.

For land value taxation is not *just* a fiscal measure (although it *is* a fiscal measure, and a sound one); not *just* a method of urban redevelopment (although it *is* a method of urban redevelopment, and an effective one); not *just* a means of stimulating business (although it *is* a means of stimulating business, and a wholesome one); not *just* an answer to unemployment (although it *is* an answer to unemployment, and a powerful one), not *just* a way to

*Professor Emeritus of Philosophy, Auburn University, Alabama; Dr. Andelson is also an ordained Congregationalist minister.

better housing (although it *is* a way to better housing, and a proven one); not *just* an approach to rational land use (although it *is* an approach to rational land use, and a non-bureaucratic one). It is all of these things, but it is also something infinitely more: it is the affirmation, prosaic though it be, of a fundamental spiritual principle—that "the earth is the Lord's, and the fulness thereof."

It is the affirmation of the same principle to which Moses gave embodiment in the institution of the Jubilee, and in the prohibition against removing ancient landmarks, and in the decree that the land shall not be sold forever. It is the affirmation of the same principle to which the prophets of old gave utterance when they inveighed against those who lay field to field, and who use their neighbor's service without wages. It is the affirmation of the same principle to which Koheleth gave voice when he asserted in the fifth chapter of Ecclesiastes that "the profit of the earth is for all."

The earth is the Lord's! Consider what this means. It means that our God is not a pale abstraction. Our God is not a remote being who sits enthroned on some ethereal height, absorbed in the contemplation of his own perfection, oblivious to this grubby realm in which we live. Our God is concerned with the tangible, with the mundane, with what goes on in the field, in the factory, in the courthouse, in the exchange. Our God is the maker of a *material world*—a world of eating and sleeping and working and begetting, a world he loved so much that he himself became flesh and blood for its salvation. In this sense, then, our God is eminently materialistic, and nowhere is this more clearly recognized than in the Bible, which, for that very reason, has always been a stumbling-block and an offense to those Gnostics, past and present, whose delicacy is embarrassed by the fact that they inhabit bodies, and for whom religion is essentially the effort to escape from or deny that fact.

Our God is not a dainty aesthete who considers politics and economic subjects too crass or sordid for his notice. Neither is he a capricious tyrant who has enjoined an order of distribution that condemns retirees after a lifetime of toil to subsist on cat food while parasitic sybarites titillate palates jaded by the most refined achievements of the *haute cuisine*. It is men who have enjoined this order in denial of his sovereignty, in defiance of his righteous will.

The earth is the Lord's! To the biblical writers, this was no mere platitude. They spelled out what it meant in concrete terms. For them, it meant that the material universe which had been provided as a storehouse of natural opportunity for the children of men was not to be monopolized or despoiled or treated as speculative merchandise, but was rather to be used reverently, and conserved dutifully, and, above all, maintained as a source from which every man, by the application of his labor, might sustain himself in decent comfort. It was seen as an inalienable trust, which no individual or class could legitimately appropriate so as to exclude others, and which no generation could legitimately barter away.

The earth is the Lord's! With the recognition of this principle comes the recognition of the right of every man to the produce which the earth has yielded to his efforts. As the Apostle Paul says in his first letter to the Church at Corinth, if the ox has a right to a share in the grain which it treads out, surely a human being must have a right to the fruits of his labor. For the exercise of this right, he is, of course, accountable to God—but against the world, it holds.

To one who takes seriously, as I do, that insight about human nature which is expressed in the doctrine of original sin, there can be nothing self-evident about the rights of man. In the words of my friend, Edmund A. Opitz, "the idea of natural rights is not the kind of concept which has legs of its own to stand on; as a deduction from religious premises it makes sense, otherwise not." The French Revolution and its culmination in the Reign of Terror demonstrated that humanistic assumptions afford no secure foundation for the concept of human rights. That concept, for the believer, can be neither understood nor justified except in terms of what Lord Acton so eloquently speaks of as "the equal claim of every man to be unhindered in the fulfilment by man of duty to God."

This is what it comes down to: How can a person be "unhindered in the fulfilment of duty to God" if he be denied, on the one hand, fair access to nature, the raw material without which there can be no wealth; and on the other, the full and free ownership of his own labor and its earnings?

You who have studied the history of the Peasants' Revolt in 16th-century Germany know that in calling for the abolition of serfdom and the restoration of the common lands, the peasants were simply voicing demands which were logically implied by Luther's doctrine of the priesthood of all believers—that the service of God to which all the faithful are elected requires, as I have said, access to the land and its resources, and the free disposal of one's person and of the guerdon of one's toil. Despite the excesses that accompanied this uprising, Luther's part in the suppression of a movement which stemmed logically from his own teaching must always be a source of pain to those of us who revere him for his spiritual genius and integrity.

The earth is the Lord's! The same God who established the just authority of governments has also in his providence ordained for them a just source of revenue. Allow me to quote from Henry George:

> In the great social fact that as population increases, and improvements are made, and men progress in civilization, the one thing that rises everywhere in value is land, we may see a proof of the beneficence of the Creator. ... In a rude state of society where there is no need for common expenditure, there is no value attaching to land. The only value which attaches there is to things produced by labor. But as civilization goes on, as a division of labor takes place, as men come into centers, so do the common wants increase and so does the necessity for public revenue arise. And so in that value which attaches to land, not by reason of anything the individual does, but by reason of the growth of the community, is a provision, intended—we may safely say *intended*—to meet that social want. Just as society grows, so do the common needs grow, and so grows the value attaching to land—the provided fund from which they can be supplied (George 1889).

On another occasion he wrote:

> The tax on land values is the most just and equal of all taxes. It falls only upon those who receive from society a peculiar and valuable benefit, and upon them in proportion to the benefit they receive. It is the taking by the community, for the use of the community, of that

value which is the creation of the community. It is the application of the common property to common uses (George *P&P*:421).

And yet, my friends, in the topsy-turvy world in which we live, this provided fund goes mainly into the pockets of speculators and monopolists, while the body politic meets its needs by extorting from individual producers the fruits of honest toil. If ever there were any doubt about the perversity of human nature, our present system of taxation is the proof! Everywhere about us, we see the ironic spectacle of the community penalizing the individual for his industry and initiative, and taking away from him a share of that which he produces, yet at the same time lavishing upon the non-producer undeserved windfalls which it—the community—produces. And, as Winston Churchill put it, the unearned increment, the socially-produced value of the land, is reaped by the speculator in exact proportion, not to the service, but to the disservice, done. "The greater the injury to society, the greater the reward."

We hear constantly a vast clamor against the abuse of welfare. I do not for a moment condone such abuse. Yet I ask you, who is the biggest swiller at the public trough? Is it the sluggard who refuses to seek work when there is work available? Is it the slattern who generates offspring solely for the sake of the allotment they command? Or is it the man—perhaps a civic leader and a pillar of his church—who sits back, and, with perfect propriety and respectability, collects thousands and maybe even millions of dollars in unearned increments created by the public, as his reward for withholding land from those who wish to put it to productive use. Talk about free enterprise! This isn't free enterprise; this is a free ride.

But if that same person were to improve his site—if he were to use it to beautify his neighborhood, or to provide goods for consumers and jobs for workers, or housing for his fellow townsmen—instead of being treated as the public benefactor he had become, he would be fined as if he were a criminal, in the form of heavier taxes. What kind of justice is this, I ask you? How does it comport with the Divine Plan, or with the notion of human rights?

Let me make this clear: Acquisitiveness, or the "profit motive," if you will, is a well-nigh universal fact of human nature, and I have no wish to suggest that the land monopolist or speculator has any corner on it. Even when I speak of him as a parasite, this is not to single him out for personal moral condemnation. He is not necessarily any more greedy than the average run of people. As my late friend, Sidney G. Evans, used to say: "If you have to live under a corrupt system, it's better to be a beneficiary than a victim of it." But the profit motive can be channeled in ways which are socially desirable as well as in ways which are socially destructive. Is it not our duty to do everything we can to build an order without victims—one in which the profit motive is put to use in such a way that everybody benefits?

I do not harbor the illusion that the millennium is going to be ushered in by any program of social betterment. My theological orientation does not happen to be one which minimizes the stubbornness of man's depravity. Yet to make the depth of human wickedness an alibi for indifference to the demands of social justice is to ignore the will of him who said:

> Take away from me the noise of your songs;
> To the melody of your harps I will not listen.
> But let justice roll down like waters,
> And righteousness like an ever-flowing stream.
> (*Amos* 5:23–24)

To some of you, the promotion of specific programs for social justice is seen as part of the responsibility of the institutional church; to others it is not. But all of us, I am sure, can agree that the individual Christian (or Jew or Muslim, Hindu or Buddhist, as the case may be) has a solemn moral obligation to study the issues carefully, and then involve himself strenuously in whatever social and political efforts his informed conscience tells him best advance the cause of right.

> O shame to us who rest content
> While lust and greed for gain
> In street and shop and tenement
> Wring gold from human pain,
> And bitter lips in blind despair

Cry, "Christ hath died in vain!"
Give us, O God, the strength to build
The city that hath stood
Too long a dream, whose laws are love,
Whose ways are brotherhood,
And where the sun that shineth is
God's grace for human good.[1]

The earth is the Lord's!

Note

1. From "O Holy City, Seen of John" by Walter Russell Bowie. Copyright, 1910, by A. S. Barnes and Company. Quoted by permission.

Liberation Theology and Economic Development

By James M. Dawsey*

Introduction: Economic Disorder

Latin American liberation theology has earned the world's admiration for its heroic stand on behalf of oppressed, marginalized people. But also, from its incipience around 1968, liberation theology has been surrounded by controversy because of its often-unabashed association with Marxist analysis. Today, twenty-five years of oversimplified economic rhetoric, especially concerning dependency theory, the recent disintegration of the Soviet bloc, and the loss of confidence in command economies, even in Cuba, have caused liberationists to re-evaluate the economic theories that underpin much of their thought (Ellis and Maduro 1990:10, 77–93, 209–210). In the following pages, I plan to address this small and, I think, fortuitous crisis by suggesting that the American economist Henry George has much to offer liberation theology.

Liberation theology is rooted in commitment to the poor, not just in Latin America, but throughout the world. The greatest poverty in the world today is in Africa. Africa's share of the Gross World Product is a paltry 1.2 percent. Moreover, Africa's share of GWP has dropped since 1980, from 1.9 percent to 1.2 percent. In that time, Sub-Saharan Africa's external debt has tripled to $174 billion (Morrow 1992:42). This translates into devouring poverty for hundreds of millions of people and extreme hunger and malnutrition during periodic famines.

Even the United States, which accounts for 25 percent of the Gross World Product, faces tremendous problems (*Time*, June 1, 1992: 42).[1] An uncrossable gulf separates those who are destitute from those who are rich in American society. While a few sports

*Provost and Dean of Faculty, Emory & Henry College, Virginia; former Alumni Professor of Religion, Auburn University, Alabama.

stars bring in millions of dollars each year, a survey shows that 27 percent of the dwellers of East Los Angeles go to bed hungry at night because they do not have enough to eat (Harter 1993). In fact, according to a 1991 study, approximately 20 percent of U.S. children went hungry sometime in 1991, the worst hunger rate being 34 percent, in Mississippi (Smith 1993:A-3).

These are just a few of the massive problems that this generation faces. And with them in mind, we have a proper backdrop against which to trace the connection between the North American economist and social reformer Henry George and Latin American liberation theologians. Let me posit two similarities between Henry George and Latin American liberation theologians and argue for a third. They agree (1) that there is something basically wrong with the way that society is structured, and 2) that unjust institutions cause much suffering among people. They also have a similar view 3) that concentrated land ownership lies at the heart of social injustice.

The Injustice of Social Structures

BOTH HENRY GEORGE (in the late 1800s) and Latin American liberation theologians (since the late 1960s) have concluded that there is something unjust about the way that society is structured. Thus, much of people's poverty, George and liberationists have reasoned, results from an oppressive, dehumanizing, enslaving, evil economic system.

The structures of injustice can be found in any society. They are most visible, however, in societies that are undergoing major transitions, especially on a new frontier where the rules are changing. As the following example shows, when the Brazilian government decided to develop the Amazon Basin, the result was not only ecological disruption, but the displacement of millions of people from their homes:

> Between 1967 and 1985, the Brazilian government's Superintendency for the Development of Amazonia (SUDAM) opened 8.4 million hectares for new development in the Amazon. "The most recent tally has 631 ranches, whose average size is 24,000 hectares, given the go-ahead by SUDAM. The biggest ones were Liquigas (678,000 hectares), Suia-

> Missu (560,000), Volkswagen A.G. (139,000), and the Armour-Swift/King Ranch (72,000). Most of these were Brazilian subsidiaries of multinational corporations. The income from their Amazonian projects was not repatriated abroad, to foreigners, but went instead to Brazilians in the South." (Shoumatoff 1990:79)
>
> These companies, for the most part, cleared the trees off the land. In one municipality alone, Xapuri, 25,000 acres were burned annually in the late 1970's, with the result that over 320,000 people who had lived there were displaced by 130 new landowners who had come to control title to the land. The clearing proved to be a human and ecological disaster. Many of the displaced people are now not only homeless, but jobless, having migrated and been forced into city slums. Many of those who remained in Xapuri now earn subsistence wages. While a family of rubber tappers and nut gatherers earned approximately $1,300 a year, a family of farmers and ranchers makes less than $800 from the same land. Meanwhile, the destruction of the Amazon is partly responsible for the global warming experienced in the 1980's, with accompanying droughts, widespread starvation, and epidemics of amoebic dysentery and typhoid fever. (Andelson and Dawsey 1992:8–9)

Many of those displaced *nordestinos* ended up in the large cities in the south of Brazil. Soon after the time that this displacement occurred in Xapuri, I visited São Paulo. At that time, the summer of 1989, I was told that the population of São Paulo was 16.5 million people. Of that number, 6.5 million were *favelados* and over 2.5 million were abandoned street children.

While in São Paulo visiting the Escola de Teologia, I was shown several special projects aimed to help the *favelados*. For instance, there was a literacy school for adults and a toy factory employing 200 homeless children. While I consider such projects well intentioned and even heroic, they do not reach the root cause of society's problems—in this case, what was happening at Xapuri. At most, such humanitarian efforts only ease society's pains. Certainly, they do not tell us how society should be re-created if indeed its structures are to be less chaotic.

The Ability to Change Oppressive Institutions

LIKE HENRY GEORGE, Latin American liberation theologians are activists. They agree that people are called to re-create society and make it more just. One of George's more famous lectures was entitled "Moses." In the lecture, George reminded his hearers that while "it is true that 'institutions make men,' . . . it is also true that 'in the beginnings men make institutions'" (George 1878:1). And as Moses, "revolting from [the Pharaohs'] tyranny, strove for the elevation of his fellow-men, is yet a beacon light to the world," George thought, so too he and others should not sit on the sidelines, but strive for a more just society (George 1878:15).

The Exodus theme and its leader are, of course, of great significance to liberation theology. As did George, liberationists hold dear figures from the past who struggled against enslaving institutions. Thus, for example, besides the figure of Moses, liberation theologians point to Bartolome de Las Casas and some other Dominicans of the 16th century who protested the cruelty of the conquest by their precursors. Las Casas, whose father had been part of Columbus' second voyage, came to Hispaniola in 1502 and became a Dominican priest in 1512. His conversion occurred when he read Ecclesiasticus 34:22: "the man who takes away his neighbor's living murders him, And the man who deprives a hired man of his wages is guilty of bloodshed." Although he had at one time held Indian slaves, Las Casas from then on devoted himself to the cause of the Indians, arguing that they should be conquered by the gospel and not by the power of arms, and that in fact, "the Indians were better off as living pagans than as dead Christians" (Berryman 1987:10).

A more contemporary model of activism is found in the archbishop of San Salvador, Oscar Romero, who was assassinated while celebrating Mass on March 24, 1980 in that city. Romero's gradual realization that he must take sides, either for the poor and the oppressed of his country and against a repressive government, or for the government and against the people, is powerfully told in the movie *Romero* and in his own book (Romero 1985).

Toward a More Just Society: The Land Problem and the Bible

IN ADDITION TO a common concern with structural injustice and a conviction that people are called to resist it, liberation theology also shares with the thought of Henry George a belief in the centrality of the land problem.

For example, we can be certain that George would have been as appalled by current conditions in Brazil as liberation theologians have been. According to 1987 reports, 10 percent of the landowners own 80 percent of Brazil's land, with 1 percent owning 48 percent of all cultivable land. Meanwhile, one million peasants are forced off the land each year (Daniher 1987:1–3; Langfur 1987:19). Another report states that "4.5 percent of Brazil's landowners own 81 percent of the country's farmland, and 70 percent of rural households are landless" (Cord 1993:1).

This problem is not limited to Brazil. As stated by Susan George, "the most pressing cause of the abject poverty which millions of people in this world endure is that a mere 2.5 percent of landowners with more than 100 hectares control nearly three quarters of all the land in the world—with the top 0.23 percent controlling over half" (Susan George 1976:24).

Whereas Henry George directly addressed the inequities that arise from private ownership of land, this has been a more implicit theme for liberation theologians, who have focused more on the meaning of the Bible to the poor than on general economic considerations.

Liberation theology has been defined as "an attempt to read the Bible and key Christian doctrines with the eyes of the poor" (Berryman 1987:4). When the poor are given a chance to read the Bible for themselves, they are far more likely than church hierarchies to read it as a document about the present struggle against injustice, and not as a message of other-worldly salvation.

If the message of the Bible is not spiritualized, one is struck by how many of the Hebrew laws really concern the rights of ownership and the preservation of social justice. The most dramatic was the establishment of the Jubilee Year, which stipulated that at the end of every fifty years, any lands that had passed out of a family's hands were to be restored to the original holder (*Lev.* 25:8–17).

Other laws granted free men ownership of themselves, of their households, and of the fruits of their labor. These could be forfeited, of course, as when a Hebrew male sold himself into slavery or when a person committed a crime (*Exodus* 22:2–4). But, even in these cases, people retained certain rights of ownership. For instance, the Hebrew slave was to serve six years and go free in the seventh. If he were married when he came into slavery, then his wife followed him also into freedom (*Exodus* 21:2–3). When a law was broken, society sought restitution for the grieved party, even if a slave. Thus, for example, if the owner of a slave were to knock out the tooth of a male or female slave, the slave was to be let go, a free person, to compensate for the tooth (*Exodus* 21:27).

Although the old Hebrew laws were similar to our modern laws in affirming that people had the right to own themselves and the fruits of their labor, they were very different in another aspect. It was God, and only God, who had the right to be the sole and absolute owner of the land. Or as phrased by Psalm 24:1, "The earth is the Lord's and all that is in it." Justice occurred only when the people recognized that God owns the land and intends its use for everyone's benefit.

All of the people of Israel were to benefit from God's land, and the Mosaic law provided for each Israelite generation and family the equal right to the use of the land. Thus, before entering Canaan, the Israelites took a census of all of the tribes and families, and a council headed by Joshua and Eleazar divided the land in shares of equal agricultural value (Josephus, *Antiquities*, v. 76–78).

Stewardship Rather than Ownership

INDIVIDUAL ISRAELITES WERE not so much asked to be owners of the land as stewards of it. Ancient Hebrew law sought to establish a very different society than those around it by not allowing the division of society into landed and landless classes. To this end, also, the Mosaic law made provisions for widows and orphans and travelers.

God intended his land also to provide for those people who had not been allotted land. According to the law, a tithe was set aside for the tribe of Levi, the priests who were not allotted land. Also, a tithe of the produce from the land was to be placed in storage in each town, and the resident aliens, the orphans, and the widows were to be allowed to go and eat their fill (*Deuteronomy* 14:22–29). In fact, the Hebrew law states that if the people would diligently observe the commandments of God concerning land, then God would bless the people and there would "be no one in need among you" (*Deuteronomy* 15:4–5).

The Hebrew prophets reiterated this concern for proper stewardship of land and a just division of the produce of land.

They especially emphasized the social dimension of *tsedaqah* (justice) by claiming that a right relationship with God is possible only when people act justly toward each other. *Tsedaqah* indicates a right relationship between the people and God, a proper balance or right order. According to the prophet Amos, this meant that God would not revoke punishment from a society that allowed the righteous to be sold for silver and the poor to be trampled into the dust of the earth (*Amos* 2:6–7).

Doing justice not only entails right relationships between neighbors, but entails a right relationship with the land itself, and indeed with all of creation. As the Mosaic law protects slaves, it protects the land and animals from overuse. Thus, in Exodus 23:10–12, the law requires periods of rest for people and animals every seven days and for land every seven years.

Justice or *tsedaqah* brings forth abundant fruits from the land. According to the prophet Hosea, when the relationship between Israel and God is as it should be, then the earth answers with grain, wine, and oil (*Hosea* 2:22). According to Isaiah, *tsedaqah* lives in the fruitful field (*Isaiah* 32:16).

Justice brings *shalom*, a peace much greater than absence of war. Hosea refers to that ultimate day of justice not only as a time when God abolishes war from the land, but as a time when people enjoy a covenant with "the wild animals, the birds of the air, and the creeping things of the ground" (*Hosea* 2:18). Isaiah adds that the ox and the donkey will range freely, while people plant beside every stream (*Isaiah* 32:20). In another passage Isaiah claims that "The wolf shall live with the lamb, the leopard shall lie down with the kid." (*Isaiah* 11:6)

Thus, justice in the Hebrew Bible is a comprehensive term denoting much more than compliance with codified strictures. Being just entails being right with one's neighbor, being right with society as a whole including future generations, and being right with animals. More comprehensively, being just entails being a good caretaker for God's land.

The Papal View of Property and Justice

LIKE MANY CHRISTIANS before him, Pope John Paul II has identified correctly, I think, the idealized Christian view of property that is rooted in the Bible and in Christian tradition. In *Centesimus Annus*, he articulates his vision of property and justice.

> The original source of all that is good is the very act of God, who created both the earth and man, and who gave the earth to man so that he might have dominion over it by his work and enjoy its fruits (Gn. 1:28). God gave the earth to the whole human race for the sustenance of all its members, without excluding or favoring anyone. This is the foundation of the universal destination of the earth's goods. The earth, by reason of its fruitfulness and its capacity to satisfy human needs, is God's first gift for the sustenance of human life. But the earth does not yield its fruits without a particular human response to God's gift, that is to say, without work. It is through work that man, using his intelligence and exercising his freedom, succeeds in dominating the earth and making it a fitting home. In this way he makes part of the earth his own, precisely the part which he has acquired through work; this is the origin of individual property. Obviously he also has the responsibility not to hinder others from having their own part of God's gift; indeed he must cooperate with others so that together all can dominate the earth (Pope John Paul II 1991, paragraph 31.1).

Centesimus Annus ultimately relies on moral persuasion to effect a change in the world (Pope John Paul II 1991, paragraphs 53–62). But most liberation theologians are of the opinion that appeals to conscience and good will do not go far enough. From a liberationist reading of the Bible, the most fruitful way that Christians can work for a more just society is to institute structures that safeguard the welfare of God's land. For, unless through its laws society becomes a proper steward of the land, the rich will continue to rob the poor and this generation will continue to rob the next until the world itself becomes an uninhabitable desert (Andelson and Dawsey 1992:90).[2]

Liberation Theology and Henry George

ANCIENT HEBREW LAWS did a better job of establishing justice than do our laws in that they recognized society's right to the use of the land and put limits on the individual's ownership of it. But the Hebrew laws, devised for an ancient agricultural, nomadic society are not adequate today. More appropriate, I think, is an updated version of the Biblical principle that was offered by the economist Henry George in the late 19th century. George believed that God intended the world's land to benefit all of creation. He also believed that the value that attaches to land "is not by reason of anything the individual does, but by reason of the growth of the community" (George 1889). Thus, it is only fitting that society as a whole should benefit from the value of land.

Let me offer a short description of how society might appropriate the value of land and at the same time make sure that it was looked after properly. George advocated leaving land titles in private hands but appropriating land values via taxation.

> I do not propose either to purchase or to confiscate private property in land. The first would be unjust; the second, needless. . . . It is not necessary to confiscate land: it is only necessary to confiscate rent (George *P&P*:405).

A small percentage of the rent would be left to the landowner, enough to facilitate a market in land titles, thus avoiding the burden and expense of auctioning and leasing lands through government agencies. Louis Wasserman explains how this would work:

> The machinery of property assessment and taxation, George points out, is already everywhere at hand. In those states where the value of land is now assessed separately from its improvements, no further preparation is needed; elsewhere, a separate assessment would be undertaken as a first step. Then, in accordance with the enacted legislation, the tax *rate* on the raw land would be increased by stages until, on completion of the program, approximately the full annual ground rent would thus be recaptured as public revenue. . . . Coordinately with each stage, other existing taxes—those on improvements, personal property, commodities and services, private and corporate income, and so on—

> would be commensurately reduced until [ideally] they were eliminated entirely (Wasserman 1979:36–37).

In our book on a Georgist approach to liberation theology, Robert Andelson and I elaborated on the processes involved in levying a tax on land values:

> The mechanics are simple, in theory and in practice. . . . Land assessments, in accord with the best accepted professional standards are determined by the market—what people are willingly paying for land. No owner or tenant is expropriated or evicted. No limit is placed on the quantity of land one may hold, as long as the annual tax is paid. As under most property tax systems, tenure is at risk only if tax delinquencies occur. Landowners are not compensated for the loss of their prior practice of taking the lion's share of socially created values; but neither are they obliged to reimburse the public for previous gains at society's expense.
>
> Once laws are enacted to carry out this approach, no technical or administrative barriers block the full collection of land rent in states where the tax on land is now low or nonexistent. To avoid economic disruption and minimize opposition, a system of land-value taxation may be instituted gradually. (Andelson and Dawsey 1992:89–90)

By appropriating for itself land values via taxation, society both takes back from the individual what rightly belongs to all of the community, and puts in place a strong economic incentive for land users to keep the land profitable.

Notes

1. *Editor's note:* In addition to the brief article from *Time* cited in the text, those interested in up-to-date statistics about every country in the world on national income (GDP), income distribution, and changes in income will find that the World Bank is a good source. A complete list of World Bank statistical tables can be found at the following URL on the Web: <http://www.worldbank.org/data/databytopic/databytopic.html>.

2. Land here includes all forms of natural resources, including not only locations on the earth's surface but also "sub-surface mineral deposits, radio frequencies, television channels, air rights, waterways, seabeds, wind and solar power, and so forth" (Andelson and Dawsey 1992:90).

Moses—Henry George's Inspiration

By AHARON H. SHAPIRO*

The "Essence" of George's Social Philosophy

IN JUNE, 1878, Henry George delivered his "Moses" lecture to the Young Men's Hebrew Association of San Francisco. His address was later repeated in Scotland, England, and New York. According to Edward J. Rose (1968), the "Moses" Sermon expresses the essence of George's social philosophy. It was delivered while George was in the midst of committing to paper the already well formulated views of his masterwork *Progress and Poverty*.

George was highly critical of contemporary institutionalized religion. He felt that it subordinated the pressing needs of the here and now to the less relevant concerns of the hereafter. He contended that present day Christianity had strayed from the original social objectives of the religion's founders. George argued that "the Christianity that ignores this social responsibility has really forgotten the teachings of Christ" (George 1887:252).[1]

In contrast, George finds great kinship in the pristine and untainted teachings of the Hebrew codifier, Moses (Rose 1968:54–59; Barker 1955, 248–51). George demonstrates in his "Moses" lecture how the social program of Moses, the emancipator, is consonant with his own philosophy and economics. Like Moses, George had hoped to set free a people whom he considered to be in modern industrial bondage.

This article will attempt to enhance the reader's understanding of how the teachings of the Law-giver, Moses, served as a major inspiration to George's own thinking. We shall find that three aspects of Moses' personality impressed George: Moses the revolutionary against the conventional wisdom, Moses the political reformer, and Moses the social and economic reformer.

*Professor of Economics, College of Business, St. John's University, New York.

Moses, the Revolutionary

WE START WITH George's observation that the Hebrews populated Egypt for perhaps two centuries and should have totally assimilated the views of their taskmasters. Yet, says George, "What is remarkable is the dissimilarity." After all, was not Egypt the dominant civilization of the world "ere Abraham looked upon them?" (George 1878:8)

We might add that even Patriarch Abraham, the first Hebrew, on his visit to Egypt had been repelled by Egyptian immorality. He was compelled to deny that Sarah was his wife. He feared that he would be murdered since it was common practice for Egyptians to abduct the wives of strangers for sexual purposes (*Genesis* 12:12).

The followers of Moses, however, rebelled against both the chains and the moral values of their taskmasters. In reproach of Egypt's immorality, Moses found it necessary to remind his flock, "After the doings of the land of Egypt in which you dwelled, shall you not do" (*Leviticus* 18:3).

George sympathizes with Moses' problem in dealing with the masses. After leaving Egypt, the people began to succumb to their former Egyptian influences and "the constant disposition of accustomed ideas to reassert themselves in the minds of the people" (George 1878:11). The Israelites troubled Moses with their occasional backsliding. They lapsed into a form of Egyptian idolatry with the worship of the golden calf (*Exodus* 32:10).

Moses gains great respect in the eyes of Henry George for rejecting God's offer to replace the existing Israelites with a new nation composed of Moses and his descendants. This is what George means when he speaks of Moses "subordinating to the good of his people the natural disposition to found a dynasty which in his case would have been so easy" (George 1878:23). Moses declines the Divine offer in favor of preserving the present, albeit sinful, people, and receives George's praise for "his unselfish desire to make humanity better, happier, nobler" (George 1878:23). Nor is Moses discouraged by the whining of a mob that complains "who will give us meat? How we remember the fish that we ate in Egypt at no expense" (*Numbers* 11:4–5).

Moses led the Israelites to renounce all the conventional mores of Egypt, the idolatry, the witchcraft, and the sexual promiscuity (*Leviticus* 18:13). Egypt must be rejected as a land identified with disease (*Deuteronomy* 7:15).

Also repugnant to Moses was the Egyptian ideology that chose to enslave live men in order to build temples and pyramids to honor dead men. Here, George is most perceptive in noting that the Pentateuch of Moses shows almost no explicit concern about life after death (George 1878:13).[2]

George is impressed with Moses' interest in the living compared to Egyptian involvement with the dead. George comments that anyone can locate the lavish tombs of the ancient Pharaohs even in this day. In contrast, Moses arranged for his own discreet burial so that "no man knoweth of his sepulcher unto this day" (George 1878:24).[3] George could have also noted that Moses was buried outside the promised land of Canaan; nor were his remains ever transported to, nor any tomb erected in, Canaan. Again, possibly this was intended to encourage reverence for the living teachings of Moses and not merely the deceased personality, Moses.

George sees Moses as the ultimate crusader who will create a new "social state in which deep degrading poverty should be unknown" (George 1878:16). Does not George identify with Moses who expresses his love for humanity even as he scolds them for their bad conduct? *Leviticus* 19 lists an inventory of abominations associated with Egypt, yet concludes on a note of compassion for mankind. Moses declares that a major lesson must be learned from the Egyptian experience. One must love even the stranger, "for you were strangers in the land of Egypt" (*Leviticus* 19:34; also see *Exodus* 22:20 and 23:9).

George and Moses are two revolutionaries with similar goals. To paraphrase George, they both sought to eliminate poverty-driven crime, justice for the rich only, governments made up of politicians who rob the people, hereditary or class distinctions, want in the midst of plenty, and crime that festers even in the shadow of the church (George 1878:17–18).

Moses, the Political Reformer

GEORGE SPEAKS OF the Mosaic state as "a commonwealth of the individual—a commonwealth whose ideal it was that every man should sit under his own vine and fig tree, with none to vex him or make him afraid" (George 1878, 12). While the vine and fig tree illustration is actually post-Moses Scripture (*I Kings* 4:25), George is fundamentally correct with respect to the Biblical emphasis on individual freedom. For George, all government is a threat. "We pin our faith to universal suffrage, yet the control of public affairs is passing into the hands of a class of professional politicians, and our governments are becoming a means for the robbery of the people" (George 1878:17).

Moses, too, envisions only a minimal role for government. A judicial system is required since disputes about law and practice are unavoidable. However, there is hardly any need for a legislature since the Divine code is eternal and all-comprehensive. The executive or enforcement agent would effectively be the threat of Divine punishment, with perhaps a little help from officers of the court system (*Exodus* 18:21). Of course, for George, the smaller the government, the less likely it will indulge in levying inappropriate taxes.

Only with great reluctance does Moses condone the possible introduction of a monarchy in the future. The appointment of a king is viewed as an undesirable accommodation to the pressures of the populace. The masses, if they became anxious over national defenses might demand "a king over me like all the nations that are round about me" (*Deuteronomy* 17:14–20). For George, the monarchy would be a regression to Egyptian practices. He contends, "the monarchical principle shows itself . . . as the far reaching influence of the great leader is somewhat spent" (George 1878:11).

It is certain that both Moses, and much later, the prophet Samuel, thought of the rule of a king as a poor alternative to a nation of free individuals. They preferred to rely on God who, in time of need, would send a "Judge" (not a king). The "judge," with the help of Heaven, would repel Israel's enemies.[4] Surely George would support Samuel's admonition that the king will "take your sons . . . for himself and his chariots," "he will take your fields . . . you shall be his servants," "and you shall cry out in that day because of your king which you shall have chosen; and the Lord will not hear you in that day" (*I Samuel* 8:11–18).

Indeed, warns Moses, if Israel must have a king, his sovereignty should be severely limited. He must completely abide by the same Mosaic code incumbent upon all other citizens. He is required to write, by his own hand, a copy of the Books of Moses. This scroll of the Torah he must carry with him at all times. Furthermore, he must study the Laws of Moses "all the days of his life so that he may fear the Lord his God, to keep all the words of this law and these statutes, to do them" (*Deuteronomy* 17:14–20).

The king is to be chosen by God (a lottery) and not in the fashion of other nations, that simply select the most powerful of their nobility who may have acquired his status by violence. He is also forbidden the self-indulgences of most monarchs including the acquisition of large harems of wives, stocks of silver and gold, or large stables of horses for military adventures (*Deuteronomy* 17:14–20).

It took more than two hundred years after the death of Moses before the prophet Samuel finally succumbed to the insistent demands of the people and agreed to anoint King Saul. Shortly afterwards, the selection was reconfirmed by lottery and Divine oracle (*I Samuel* 10).

Despite all the restrictions imposed upon the monarch to safeguard against tyranny, neither Moses, nor Samuel, nor George, approves any system which makes "the few the masters of the many" (George 1878:19).

Moses, the Economic and Social Reformer

HENRY GEORGE PRAISES Moses for having discovered the root of all economic evil, namely, "possession by a class, of the land upon which and from which the whole people must live." In fact, George blames the Egyptian enslavement on domination by greedy landowners (George 1878:18). It is interesting to speculate that Israel's own ancestor, Joseph, the chief minister of the Pharaoh, may have been the cause of Israel's bondage. Two hundred years before the Exodus, "was it not Joseph who cunningly bought up and monopolized much of the land in behalf of the Pharaoh during the seven years of famine?" (*Genesis* 47:20)

But Moses now intends to prevent exploitation by the voracious landowner. He offers an outline for a highly equitable distribution of the land in the soon to be conquered Canaan. The land would be divided by lottery, which implies that equity would be assured by infallible Divine determination rather than compromised by human error. The acreage would be allocated on the basis of family size (*Numbers* 33:54). Since we find almost no complaints about the fairness of the distribution voiced later in the book of Joshua, it is reasonable to assume that heed was paid to the relative fertility of different parcels of land, with all allotments equal in productive value. In the ideal, the Mosaic distribution would appear as an attempt to avoid the differential and monopoly rents which in George's view are the source of most poverty and the primary impediment of progress.

If, for any reason, land should accumulate temporarily in the hands of the few, there was a remedy. The land would eventually revert to the original small landholders at least once each 50 years, in the Jubilee year (*Leviticus* 25:13). Any tendency towards large and permanent accumulations of land quickly receive Divine rebuke with the words "and the land shall not be sold in perpetuity, for the land is Mine; for ye are but strangers and settlers with Me" (*Leviticus* 25:23).

While Henry George approves of Moses' attempt at equitable distribution, he suggests that the techniques "may not be suitable for every time and people" (George 1887:19). Undoubtedly, George would prefer his own solution of taxing away the exploitable surplus.

Scholars interpret Moses' remonstrations against moving a neighbor's boundary markers to be more than a mere reiteration of the general prohibition against theft (*Deuteronomy* 19:24, and comments of Bachya Abrabanel). The Mosaic code is not given to superfluous repetitions of the Commandments. A scrutiny of the verse against moving the boundary "which they of old time have set, in thine inheritance which thou shalt inherit, in the land which the Lord thy God giveth thee to possess it" indicates stern Divine disapproval of any attempts to upset the original equitable land distribution.

To further protect the many from the few, Moses did not give the Levitical tribes an equal share of the land. The tribe of Levi and the sub-group Kohein constituted the priestly class. They ministered to the religious needs of the people and were able to wield considerable influence. Despite their leadership role, they were given only small parcels of land and could live only in certain assigned towns and houses. George seems to have overlooked that Moses was himself a Levite, who by his own decree had renounced land ownership and economic power for himself and his heirs.

It follows that George's major obstacle to economic progress, namely "unearned" rental income, is unlikely to manifest itself in the ideal community of Moses. Like George, Moses permits nominal ownership of land. But also like George, Moses considers land ownership more like a Divine loan, given equally to all and not intended for monopoly exploitation. However, even Henry George would admit that the problem of poverty is not totally solved by the elimination of unearned rental income alone. Poverty can also arise in an agrarian society from the vicissitudes of nature such as drought and infestation; in an urban society from disease, accident, or any of the multitude of misfortunes that plague human beings.

The Mosaic code is also much concerned with this type of poverty. Deuteronomy anguishes that "the poor shall never cease out of the land" (*Deuteronomy* 15:11). So does Henry George over the New Testament equivalent, "the poor ye have always with ye" (Auchmuty 1980:82, citing George *SP*:78). George severely criticizes those who quote these passages as a means of evading social responsibility. He would have strengthened his argument if he had noted that Moses responded in the same verse with a strong demand for charity: "thou shalt open thy hand unto the poor and needy brother" (*Deuteronomy* 15:11).

Moses, however, does not rely on free-will offerings. He institutes an entire code of compulsory taxes, enforced by Divine wrath and the religious courts (Shapiro 1971).

George notes the Mosaic obligation "for the reaper to leave something for the gleaner" (George 1878:12). But Moses had also demanded annual tithes and other gifts for the landless Levite and other poor. Failure to observe the tithes would invoke not only severe Divine punishment but in most cases would render the grain religiously inedible and consequently unsalable. The Moses anti-poverty program earns George's praise as the program which instructs, "Do your duty in this world that you may be happier and the world better." In contrast, George condemns those who maintain, "Leave the world to itself that you may save your own soul" (George 1878:15).

Would George consider the Mosaic tithes to be undesirable taxes on production? Not likely. In Moses' purely agrarian economy all rent differentials have been eliminated by an ideal land distribution. In theory all families would produce equal output, hence, taxes on output would fall equally upon all inhabitants. Thus tithes should satisfy George's canons of good taxation.

Another institution admired by George (1878:12) includes the remission of all debts every seventh (sabbatical) year (*Deuteronomy* 15). While cancellation of debt may be impractical in a modern society, the idea of abolishing inescapable grinding debt is laudable.

Assuredly, the seventh year abolition of debts demanded of lenders much faith in fellow human beings and in Providence. It is not easy for a lender to subscribe to "beware that there be not a thought in thy wicked heart, saying, 'The seventh year of release is at hand,' and thine eye be evil against thy poor brother, and thou lendest him nought; and he cry unto the Lord against thee, and it be a sin unto thee. Thou shalt surely give him, and thine heart shall not be grieved when thou givest unto him because . . . the Lord shall bless thee in all thy works" (*Deuteronomy* 15:8–9).

Conclusion

AS EXPECTED, HUMAN faith faltered during the post-biblical years. Hardship was created by the reluctance of lenders to issue loans at the approach of the Sabbatical year. An official circumvention of the sabbatical cancellation was finally devised in the first century

B.C. Still, one may remark that our present laws allowing for bankruptcy and a fresh start are not extremely remote from Moses' cancellation rule.

George also congratulates Moses for introducing the Sabbath day. He argues that the day made workers more productive, not less, and "not merely happier but richer" (George 1878:20). It should be stressed that this invention of Judaism was unique. To this writer's knowledge, a weekly day of rest for all (even slaves and animals) has been practiced only by Judaism and its daughter religions of Christianity and Islam. Surcease is granted to unending drudgery, and a revival of the spirit is generated by the day of rest. George calls attention to a similar service provided by Moses' sabbatical year during which all farming ceases (George 1878:20). An entire year is devoted to refreshment of the mind, the soul, the very earth itself (*Leviticus* 25).

Henry George has focused on the implications of the Sabbath day, the Sabbatical year, and the Jubilee Year. These three periods have a common theme, namely, *restitutio ad integrum*, or restoring society to the original wholesome condition that Moses sought to initiate. The Jubilee restored the original equal claim on the land to all persons. George would do this with his single tax on land. The Sabbatical year restored many people's equal claim on wealth. George, of course, ascribed much of the prevailing inequality to landowners' exploitation, which his single tax would eliminate.

The Sabbath day and the Sabbatical year, with their cessation of labor, restored equal dignity to all human beings. George suggested, in lieu of a Sabbatical year, relief from labor in the form of a shorter working day (George 1878:20).

Can we not conclude from this review that the "Moses" essay is much more than an eloquent sermon subordinate to George's more extensive writings? Is it not really essential Henry George? George delivered his "Moses" lecture in 1878 and published his masterwork, *Progress and Poverty*, one year later. In preparation for his speech, George studied and analyzed the ideas of Moses which helped to formulate his later writings. Without doubt, Moses of the Bible helped to make George the political, social, and economic reformer that he became.

In the spirit of appreciation for George the humanitarian, this writer would say that from Moses to "Moses," there is none like Henry George.

Notes

1. See also Geiger 1933:336–80 for more citations on George's views on religion.

2. References to the hereafter in the Five Books of Moses are vague, such as that Enoch "walked with God, and he was not, for God took him" *(Genesis* 5:24); or allusion to Sheol, a place where the soul lived on in an ethereal shadowy existence *(Genesis* 37:35 and *Numbers* 16:33).

3. George quotes from *Deuteronomy* 34:37. Note that the Pentateuch's primary concern with modifying human behavior in this world does not diminish the importance of the concept of the hereafter and immortality in Judaism. See the heading "Afterlife" in the *Encyclopedia Judaica* (New York: Macmillan, 1971).

4. *The Book of Judges* describes the episodes of temporary leaders, called judges, such as Jepthah, Samson, Deborah, Gideon, and others who arose during the two centuries between Moses and Samuel.

References

Ackerman, Bruce. 1980. *Social Justice in the Liberal State*. New Haven: Yale University Press.

Andelson, Robert V. 1979. "Neo-Georgism." In *Critics of Henry George*, Robert V. Andelson, ed. 381–393.

———, ed. 1979. *Critics of Henry George*. Rutherford, Madison, and Teaneck, NJ: Fairleigh Dickinson University Press.

Andelson, Robert V., and James M. Dawsey. 1992. *From Wasteland to Promised Land: Liberation Theology for a Post-Marxist World*. London: Shepheard Walwyn.

Arnott, Richard. 1996. "Neutral Property Taxation." Unpublished paper.

Auchmuty, A. C. 1980. *The Economics and Philosophy of Henry George*. London.

Audretsch, David B. 1998. *Industrial Policy and Competitive Advantage*. Cheltenham, UK: Edward Elgar.

Backhaus, Jürgen G. 1997. "Henry George's Ingenious Tax: A Contemporary Restatement." *The American Journal of Economics and Sociology* 56(4):453–474.

Barker, Charles Albro. 1991, 1974 reprints. *Henry George*. New York: Robert Schalkenbach Foundation (1991 edition). Westport, CT: Greenwood Press (1974 edition). Original edition, New York: Oxford University Press, 1955.

Bastiat, Frederic. 1964. *Economic Harmonies*. Trans. W. Hayden Boyers and ed. George B. de Huszar. Princeton, NJ: Van Nostrand.

Bentick, B. L. 1979. "The Impact of Taxation and Valuation Practices on the Timing and Efficiency of Land Use." *Journal of Political Economy* 87(4):859–868.

Berryman, Phillip. 1987. *Liberation Theology*. New York: Pantheon.

Blaug, Mark. 1986. *Great Economists before Keynes: An Introduction to the Lives and Works of One Hundred Great Economists of the Past*. New York: Cambridge University Press.

Block, Walter. 1976. *Defending the Undefendable*. New York: Fleet Press Corporation.

———. 1998. "A Libertarian Case for Free Immigration." *Journal of Libertarian Studies* 13(Summer):167–186.

Böhm-Bawerk, Eugen von. 1959. *Capital and Interest*. Trans. George D. Huncke and Hans F. Sennholz. 3 vols. South Holland, IL: Libertarian Press. First published in German in 1884.

Breckenfeld, Gurney. 1983. "Higher Taxes that Promote Development." *Fortune* 8(August):68–71.

Brodsky, Harold. 1970. "Residential Land and Improvement Values in a Central City." *Land Economics* 46(3):229–247.

Brown, Harry Gunnison. 1980. "The Challenge of Australian Tax Policy." In *Selected Articles by Harry Gunnison Brown: The Case for Land Value Taxation*. New York: Robert Schalkenbach Foundation.

Buchanan, James. 1989. "Economic Interdependence and the Work Ethic." Fairfax, VA: Center for Study of Public Choice, George Mason University. May. A draft paper at time of the 1990 lecture in this volume.

Case, Karl E. 1978. *Property Taxation: The Need for Reform*. Cambridge, MA: Ballinger.

Chacholiades, M. 1981. *Principles of International Economics*. New York: McGraw-Hill.

Clark, John Bates. 1899. *The Distribution of Wealth*. New York. Macmillan and Company.

Clinton, William. 1998. "State of the Union Address." *New York Times* January 26: A-19.

Collier, Charles 1979. "Rutherford: The Devil Quotes Scripture." In *Critics of Henry George*, Robert V. Andelson, ed. 222–233.

Cord, Steven B. 1965. *Henry George: Dreamer or Realist?* Philadelphia: University of Pennsylvania Press.

———. 1993. "How to Save Brazil's Rain Forest." *Incentive Taxation* June:3.

Deardorff, Alan V. and Robert M. Stern, eds. 1994. *The Stolper-Samuelson Theorem: A Golden Jubilee*. Ann Arbor: University of Michigan Press.

DeMille, Anna George. 1946. "Haymarket and Tariff Reform." *American Journal of Economics and Sociology* 5(4):545–551.

Dolan, Edwin G., ed. 1976. *The Foundations of Modern Austrian Economics*. Mission, KS: Sheed and Ward.

Dworkin, Ronald. 1981. "What is Equality? Part 2: Equality of Resources." *Philosophy and Public Affairs* 10(4):283–345.

Edwards, Mary E. 1984. "Site Value Taxation in Australia: Where Land is Taxed More and Improvements Less, Average Housing Values are Higher." *American Journal of Economics and Sociology* 43(4):485–494.

Ellis, Marc H., and Otto Maduro, eds. 1990. *Expanding the View: Gustavo Gutierrez and the Future of Liberation Theology*. Maryknoll, NY: Orbis Books.

Feldstein, Martin. 1997. "How Big Should Government Be?" *National Tax Journal* 50(2):197–213.

Field, Alexander. 1983. "Land Abundance, Interest/Profit Rates, and Nineteenth-century American and British Technology." *Journal of Economic History* 43(2):405–431.

Fuller, Aaron B. 1979. "Davenport: 'Single Taxer of the Looser Observance.'" In *Critics of Henry George*, Robert V. Andelson, ed. 293–302.

Geiger, George Raymond. 1933. *The Philosophy of Henry George*. New York: Macmillan.

George, Henry. [1878] 1904. "Moses." First delivered in San Francisco in June 1878. In *The Complete Works of Henry George*. New York: Doubleday, Page and Co. Vol. 8.

———. [1879] 1981. *Progress and Poverty, An Inquiry into the Causes of Industrial Depressions and of Increase of Want with Increase in Wealth*. New York: Robert Schalkenbach Foundation. Cited in texts in this volume as *P&P*.

———. [1883] 1966. *Social Problems*. New York: Robert Schalkenbach Foundation. Cited in texts in this volume as *SP*.

———. [1886] 1966. *Protection or Free Trade: An Examination of the Tariff Question, with Especial Regard for the Interests of Labor*. New York: Robert Schalkenbach Foundation. Cited in texts in this volume as *PFT*.

———. 1886–87. "Labor in Pennsylvania." Parts 1–4. *North American Review*, Part I (August 1886, Vol. 143):165–182; Part II (September 1886, Vol. 143): 268–277; Part III (October 1886, Vol. 143): 360–370; Part IV (January 1887, Vol. 144):86–95. Cited in texts in this volume as *LP*.

———. [1887] 1904. "Thou Shalt Not Steal." An address before the Anti-Poverty Society, May 8, 1887. In *The Complete Works of Henry George*. Vol. 8. New York: Doubleday, Page and Co.

———. 1889. "Thy Kingdom Come." Sermon delivered at the city hall in Glasgow, Scotland in 1889, circulated in tract form by the Scottish Land Restoration League.

———. [1892] 1965. *A Perplexed Philosopher*. New York: Robert Schalkenbach Foundation. Cited in texts in this volume as *PPh*.

———. [1897] 1981. *The Science of Political Economy*. New York: Robert Schalkenbach Foundation. Cited in texts in this volume as *SPE*.

George, Henry, ed. 1888–1892. *The Standard*. New York. Cited in texts in this volume as *TS*.

George Jr., Henry. [1900] 1905. *The Life of Henry George*. New York: Doubleday, Page & Company.

George, Susan. 1976. *How the Other Half Dies*. New York: Penguin Books.

Goldhagen, Daniel Jonah. 1996. *Hitler's Willing Executioners: Ordinary Germans and the Holocaust*. New York: Alfred A. Knopf.

Grampp, William D. 1965. *Economic Liberalism*. 2 vols. New York: Random House.

Harriss, C. Lowell. 1979. "Rothbard's Anarcho-capitalist Critique." In *Critics of Henry George*, Robert V. Andelson, ed. 354–370.

Harsanyi, John. 1975. "Can the Maximin Principle Serve as a Basis for Morality? A Critique of John Rawls's Theory." *American Political Science Review* 69(2):594–606.

Harter, Chuck. 1993. "We, the People." Radio show. June 16.

Hayek, Friedrich A. 1944. *The Road to Serfdom*. Chicago: University of Chicago Press.

———. 1945. "The Use of Knowledge in Society." *American Economic Review* 35(4):519–530.

———. 1967. "The Results of Human Action but not of Human Design." In *Studies in Philosophy, Politics, and Economics*. Chicago: University of Chicago Press, 96–105.

———. 1988. "The Fatal Conceit: The Errors of Socialism. In *The Collected Works of F. A. Hayek*, W. W. Bartley, ed. Chicago: University of Chicago.

Hébert, Robert F. 1979. "Marshall: A Professional Economist Guards the Purity of his Discipline." In *Critics of Henry George*, Robert V. Andelson, ed. 56–71.

Hollander, Samuel. 1973. *The Economics of Adam Smith*. Toronto: University of Toronto.

Humphrey, Thomas M. 1996. "The Early History of the Box Diagram." *Economic Quarterly* 82(1): 37–75.

Hutchinson, A. R. 1963. *Public Charges upon Land Values*. Melbourne: Land Values Research Group.

Irwin, Douglas A. 1996. *Against the Tide: An Intellectual History of Free Trade*. Princeton: Princeton University Press.

Krugman, Paul R. 1986. Introduction. In *Strategic Trade Policy and the New International Economics*. Cambridge: MIT Press.

———. 1990. *Rethinking International Trade*. Cambridge: MIT Press.

———. 1996a. *Pop Internationalism*. Cambridge: MIT Press.

———. 1996b. "A Country is not a Company." *Harvard Business Review* January/February:40–51.

Jensen, Jens P. 1931. *Property Taxation in the United States*. Chicago: University of Chicago Press.

Landa, Janet Tai. 1994. *Trust, Ethnicity, and Identity: Beyond the New Institutional Economics of Ethnic Trading Networks, Contract Law, and Gift-Exchange*. Ann Arbor: University of Michigan Press.

Langfur, Hal. 1987. "Brazil's Land Reform Program is Caught in a Violent Crossfire." *Christian Science Monitor*. May 7:11.

Leibenstein, Harvey. 1976. *Beyond Economic Man*. Cambridge: Harvard University Press.

Lerner, Abba P. 1961. *Everybody's Business: A Reexamination of Current Assumptions in Economics and Public Policy*. New York: Harper and Row.

Lissner, Will. 1980. "Preface" to *Protection or Free Trade*, by Henry George. New York: Robert Schalkenbach Foundation.

Lusht, Kenneth M. 1992a. *Site Value Tax and Land Development Patterns: Evidence from Melbourne, Australia*. Working Paper Series in

Real Estate. University Park, MD: College of Business Administration, Pennsylvania State University.

———. 1992b. *The Site Value Tax and Residential Development*. Cambridge, MA: Lincoln Institute of Land Policy.

Maneschi, A. 1998. "The Dynamic Nature of Comparative Advantage and the Gains from Trade in Classical Economics." *Journal of the History of Economic Thought* 20 (June):133–144.

Marshall, Alfred. [1883] 1969. "Three Lectures on Progress and Poverty." *Journal of Law and Economics* 12(1): 184–212. Lectures presented in 1883 in St. Philip's Vestry Hall, Bristol, England, on February 19, February 26, and March 5. Originally published in *Daily Bristol Times and Mirror* and the *Western Daily Press* (Bristol) on February 20, February 27, and March 6, 1883. Two published versions compared and edited by Ronald H. Coase and George J. Stigler. (Cf. Stigler 1969.) Immediately following and also edited by Stigler, *Journal of Law and Economics* 12(1):212–17 contains correspondence between Alfred R. Wallace and Alfred Marshall. Originally published in *Western Daily Press* (Bristol, England) on March 17, March 19, March 23, and March 24, 1883. (Cf. Stigler 1969.)

———. 1920. *Principles of Economics*. 8th ed. New York: Macmillan and Company.

Marshall, Alfred, and Mary P. 1879. *Economics of Industry*. London: Macmillan and Company.

Marshall, Alfred, and Henry George. [1884] 1969. "Appendix: Mr. Henry George at Oxford, Disorderly Meeting." *Journal of Law and Economics* 12(1):217–226. Originally published in *Jackson's Oxford Journal*, March 15, 1884.

Martin, Thomas L. 1989. "Protection or Free Trade: An Analysis of the Ideas of Henry George on International Commerce and Wages." *American Journal of Economics and Sociology* 48(4):489–501. (This essay reproduced in this volume.)

Menger, Carl. [1871] 1959. *Principles of Economics*. Trans. and ed. by James Dingwall and Bert F. Hoselitz. Glencoe, IL: The Free Press.

———. 1883. *Untersuchungen über die Methode der Sozialwissenschaften und der politischen Ökonomie insbesondere*. Leipzig: Duncker und Humblot.

Mikesell, John L. 1997. "The American Retail Sales Tax: Considerations on their Structure, Operations, and Potential as a Foundation for a Federal Sales Tax." *National Tax Journal* 50(1):149–165.

Mises, Ludwig von. [1949] 1963. *Human Action*. Chicago: Henry Regnery Company. Orginal edition, New Haven, CT: Yale University Press.

———. [1912] 1981. *The Theory of Money and Credit*. Trans. H. E. Batson. Indianapolis, IN: Liberty Classics.

Mitchell, George W. 1956. "Is This Where We Came In?" *Proceedings of the Forty-Ninth Annual Conference*. National Tax Association.

Mokyr, Joel. 1990. *The Lever of Riches: Technological Creativity and Economic Progress*. Oxford: Oxford University Press.

Morrow, Lance 1992. "Africa: The Scramble for Survival." *Time* September 7:42.

Moss, Laurence S., ed. 1976. *The Economics of Ludwig von Mises*. Kansas City, Kansas: Sheed and Ward.

Murray, Matthew N. 1997. "Would Tax Evasion and Tax Avoidance Undermine a National Retail Sales Tax?" *National Tax Journal* 50(1):167–182.

Netzer, Dick. 1984. "On Modernizing Local Public Finance: Why Aren't Property Taxes in Urban Areas Being Reformed into Land Value Taxes?" *American Journal of Economics and Sociology* 43(4):497–501.

Nevins, Allan. 1933. *Grover Cleveland, A Study in Courage*. New York: Dodd, Mead & Company.

Newton, Bernard. 1971–72. "The Impact of Henry George on British Economists." Parts 1–3. *American Journal of Economics and Sociology* Part I, April 1971, 30(2):179–186; Part II, July 1971, 30(3):317–327; Part III, January 1972, 31(1):87–102.

North, Douglass. 1990. *Institutions, Institutional Change and Economic Performance*. Cambridge: Cambridge University Press.

Oates, Wallace E., and Robert M. Schwab. 1997. "The Impact of Urban Land Taxation: The Pittsburgh Experience." *National Tax Journal* 50(1):1–21.

O'Driscoll, Gerald P. 1977. *Economics as a Coordination Problem*. Sheed Andrews and McMeel. Kansas City, Kansas.

Organization for Economic Cooperation and Development. 1996. *Revenue Statistics of OECD Countries, 1965–95*. Paris: OECD.

Pigou, Arthur C., ed. 1925. *Memorials of Alfred Marshall*. London: Macmillan.

Pope John Paul II. 1991. "Centesimus Annus." In *Proclaiming Justice & Peace: Papal Documents from Rerum Novarum through Centesimus Annus,* Michael Walsh and Brian Davies, eds. Mystic, CT: Twenty-Third Publications.

Post, Louis. 1930. *The Prophet of San Francisco: Personal Memories and Interpretations of Henry George*. New York: Vanguard Press.

Rawls, John. 1958. "Justice as Fairness." *Philosophical Review*. 67:164–194.

———. 1971. *A Theory of Justice*. Cambridge: Harvard University Press.

———. 1973. "Distributive Justice." In *Economic Justice,* E. S. Phelps, ed. Harmondsworth, UK: Penguin.

Reid, Margaret. 1962. *Housing and Income*. Chicago: University of Chicago Press.

Reitano, Joanne. 1994. *The Tariff Question in the Gilded Age: The Great Debate of 1888*. University Park, MD: Pennsylvania State University Press.

Richardson, James D. 1896–1899, 1909. *A Compilation of the Messages and Papers of the Presidents*. Washington, DC: Government Printing Office.

Roakes, Susan L., Richard Barrows, and Harvey M. Jacobs. 1994. "The Impact of Land Value and Real Property Taxation on the Timing of Central City Redevelopment." *Journal of Planning, Education and Research* 13:174–184.

Rogowski, Ronald. 1989. *Commerce and Coalitions: How Trade Affects Domestic Political Arguments*. Princeton: Princeton University Press.

Romero, Oscar. 1985. *Voice of the Voiceless.* Maryknoll, NY: Orbis Books.

Rose, Edward J. 1968. *Henry George*. New York: Twayne Publishers.

Rothbard, Murray N. 1962. *Man, Economy, and State.* 2 vols. Princeton, NJ: Van Nostrand.

———. 1970. *Power and Market.* Menlo Park, CA: Institute for Humane Studies.

———. 1973. *For a New Liberty*. New York: Macmillan.

———. 1979. *Individualism and the Philosophy of the Social Sciences.* San Francisco: Cato Institute.

———. 1982. *The Ethics of Liberty.* Atlantic Highlands: Humanities Press.

Samuelson, Paul. 1938. "Welfare Economics and International Trade." *American Economic Review* (June). Reprinted in J. E. Stiglitz *The Collected Scientific Papers of Paul A. Samuelson*, Vol. 2, J. E. Stiglitz, ed. Cambridge: MIT Press, 1966.

Sass, Steven A. 1993. "An Uneasy Relationship: The Business Community and Academic Economists at the University." In *Economists & Higher Learning in the Nineteenth Century*, W. J. Barber, ed. New Brunswick, NJ: Transaction Publishers.

Schumpeter, Joseph A. 1954. *History of Economic Analysis.* Edited from manuscript by Elizabeth Boody Schumpeter. New York: Oxford University Press.

Schwab, Robert. 1998. Paper presented at the annual meeting of the National Tax Association, Austin, TX, in October, for publication in *Proceedings*.

Shapiro, Aharon. 1971. "The Poverty Program of Judaism." *Review of Social Economy.* September.

Shoumatoff, Alex. 1990. *The World is Burning: Murder in the Rain Forest.* Boston: Little, Brown, and Company.

Shoup, Donald C. 1969. "Advance Land Acquisition by Local Governments: A Cost-benefit Analysis." *Yale Economic Essays* 9(2):147–207.

———. 1970. "The Optimal Timing of Urban Development." *Papers of the Regional Science Association* 25:33–44.

Simon, Julian L. 1981. *The Ultimate Resource*. Princeton, NJ.

Skouras, Thanos. 1978. "The Non-neutrality of Land Taxation." *Public Finance* 33:113–134.

Smith, Adam. [1776] 1976. *An Inquiry into the Nature and Causes of the Wealth of Nations*. 2 vols. Oxford: Oxford University Press.

Smith, Mike. 1993. "Child Hunger is Greatest in the South." *The Atlanta Constitution* June 16:A-3.

Solow, Robert M., and William S. Vickrey. 1971. "Land Use in a Long Narrow City." *Journal of Economic Theory* 3(4):430–447.

Sowell, Thomas. 1998. *Conquests and Cultures*. New York: Basic Books.

Spadaro, Louis M., ed. 1978. *New Directions in Austrian Economics*. Kansas City, MO: Sheed Andrews and McMeel.

Stanwood, Edward. [1903] 1967. *American Tariff Controversies of the Nineteenth Century*. New York: Russell and Russell.

Steckel, Richard H., and Roderick Floud. 1997. *Health and Welfare during Industrialization*. Chicago: University of Chicago Press.

Stigler, George. 1969. "Alfred Marshall's Lectures on *Progress and Poverty*." *Journal of Law and Economics* 12(1):181–183.

———. 1982. *The Economist as Preacher and Other Essays*. Chicago: University of Chicago Press.

Stolper, Wolfgang F., and Paul A. Samuelson. 1941. "Protection and Real Wages." *The Review of Economic Studies* 9 (November): 58–73.

Taussig, Frank. [1885] 1893. *The Tariff History of the United States*. New York: G. P. Putnam's Sons.

Thompson, Robert E. 1875. *Social Science and National Economy*. Philadelphia, PA: Porter and Coates.

Thurow, Lester. 1993. *Head to Head: The Coming Economic Battle among Japan, Europe, and America*. New York: Warner Books.

Tideman, Nicolaus. 1982. "A Tax on Land is Neutral." *National Tax Journal* 35:109–111.

———. 1995. *Taxing Land is Better than Neutral: Land Taxes, Land Speculation, and the Timing of Development*. Cambridge, MA: Lincoln Institute of Land Policy.

———. 1997. *The Relationship between the Average Cost and the Marginal Cost of Public Funds*. Unpublished paper available from Prof. Tideman <ntideman@vt.edu> or from the Robert Schalkenbach Foundation website <www.schalkenbach.org>.

United States Bureau of the Census. 1997. *Statistical Abstract of the United States, 1996*.

Vickrey, William S. 1970a. "Some Thoughts on External Economies in Urban Growth." *Proceedings of the AREUEA, 1969* (American Real Estate and Urban Economics Association) IV:3–20.

———. 1970b. "Defining Land Value for Taxation Purposes." In *The Assessment of Land Value*, Daniel M. Holland, ed. 25–36. Madison: University of Wisconsin Press.

Viner, Jacob. [1937] 1964. *Studies in the Theory of International Trade*. London: George Allen & Unwin.

Wasserman, Louis. 1979. "The Essential Henry George." In *Critics of Henry George*, Robert V. Andelson, ed. 29–43.

Weir, Robert E. 1997. "A Fragile Alliance: Henry George and the Knights of Labor." *The American Journal of Economics and Sociology* 56(4):421–440.

Whitaker, John K. 1997. "Enemies or Allies? Henry George and Francis Amasa Walker One Century Later." *Journal of Economic Literature* 35 (December):1891–1915.

Wicksteed, Philip H. [1894] 1932. *An Essay on the Co-ordination of the Laws of Distribution*. London: London School of Economics and Political Science. (Original published by Macmillan.)

———. [1910] 1933. *The Common Sense of Political Economy*. Rev. ed. London: G. Routledge and Sons.

Woodruff, A. M., and L. L. Ecker-Racz. 1969. "Property Taxes and Land Use Patterns in Australia and New Zealand." In *Land and Building Taxes: Their Effect on Economic Development*, Arthur P. Becker, ed. Madison: University of Wisconsin Press.

World Bank. *World Indicators*. http://www.worldbank.org/data/databytopic/databytopic.html

Yeager, Leland B. 1954. "The Methodology of Henry George and Carl Menger." *American Journal of Economics and Sociology* 13(2): 233–238.

Yinger, John, Axel Borsch-Supan, Howard S. Bloom, and Helen F. Ladd. 1988. *Property Taxes and House Values: The Theory and Estimation of Intrajurisdictional Property Tax Capitalization*. Boston, MA: Academic Press.

Youngman, Joan M., and Jane H. Malme. 1994. *An International Survey of Taxes on Land and Buildings*. Boston, MA: Kluwer Law and Taxation Publishers.

Index

A

B

C

D

E

F

G

H

I

J

K

L

M

N

O

P

R

S

T

U

V

W

Y